# Religion, Death and the Senses

## Religion and the Senses

Series Editor: Graham Harvey, The Open University, UK

Everyday and/or vernacular religions are now at the cutting edge of the study of religions. The agenda of Religious Studies as well as that of other disciplines which overlap in some aspects with the study of religion (e.g. Classics, History, Sociology, Anthropology and [in some places] Philosophy) has been revitalised by this focus on lived reality. This resonates with the growing interest in materiality and embodiment which have both pro-voked 'turns' in academic debate and teaching. Criticisms, however, have been levelled against the ways in which 'materiality' does not always engage with materials (stuff) and 'embodiment' sometimes suggests the priority of some interiority (mind, agency, etc.).

The proposed series aims to push further the project of placing lived, material and bodily religion at the definitive centre of studies of religion(s). It will do this by foregrounding bodily sensation and material practice as religion (rather than expressions, experiences or representations of some-thing prior to bodies, acts and things). It develops the interdisciplinary conversation encouraged by Paul Stoller's *Sensuous Scholarship* (1997) and, especially, presents and promotes research about real life religion approached through performative and materialist methods, as illustrated by, e.g., Manuel Vasquez's *More than Belief* (2011) and Graham Harvey's *Food, Sex and Strangers* (2013).

Published:

*Religion and Senses of Place*
Edited by Graham Harvey and Opinderjit Kaur Takhar

*Religion and Sight*
Edited by Louise Child and Aaron Rosen

*Religion and Touch*
Edited by Christina Welch and Amy Whitehead

*Sensual Religion: Religion and the Five Senses*
Edited by Graham Harvey and Jessica Hughes

Forthcoming:

*Religion and Senses of Humour*
Edited by Stephen E. Gregg and Nicole Graham

*Tasting Religion*
Edited by Aldea Mulhern and Graham Harvey

# Religion, Death and
the Senses

Edited by
Christina Welch and Jasmine Hazel Shadrack

SHEFFIELD UK   BRISTOL CT

Published by Equinox Publishing Ltd.

UK:     Office 415, The Workstation, 15 Paternoster Row, Sheffield, South Yorkshire S1 2BX
USA:    ISD, 70 Enterprise Drive, Bristol, CT 06010

www.equinoxpub.com

First published 2024

British Library Cataloguing-in-Publication Data
A catalogue record for this book is available from the British Library.
ISBN-13    978 1 80050 493 6  (hardback)
           978 1 80050 494 3  (paperback)
           978 1 80050 495 0  (ePDF)
           978 1 80050 586 5  (ePub)

Library of Congress Cataloging-in-Publication Data

Names: Welch, Christina, editor. | Shadrack, Jasmine Hazel, editor.
Title: Religion, death and the senses / edited by Christina Welch and
   Jasmine Hazel Shadrack.
Description: Sheffield, South  Yorkshire ; Bristol, CT : Equinox
   Publishing, Ltd, 2024. | Series: Religion and the senses | Includes
   bibliographical references and index. | Summary: "The uniqueness of this
   collection lies in two areas, firstly its deep engagement with a range
   of physical and socio-cultural sensual responses to death and dying, and
   secondly, through its contributors who are drawn from a wide spectrum of
   professional, practical, and theoretical expertise and scholarship in
   fields which continue to redefine our understanding of mortality"--
   Provided by publisher.
Identifiers: LCCN 2024013189 (print) | LCCN 2024013190 (ebook) | ISBN
   9781800504936 (hardback) | ISBN 9781800504943 (paperback) | ISBN
   9781800504950 (epdf) | ISBN 9781800505865 (epub)
Subjects: LCSH: Death--Religious aspects--Christianity.
Classification: LCC BT825 .R45 2024  (print) | LCC BT825  (ebook) | DDC
   236/.1--dc23/eng/20240402
LC record available at https://lccn.loc.gov/2024013189
LC ebook record available at https://lccn.loc.gov/2024013190

Typeset by S.J.I. Services, New Delhi, India

We dedicate this book to all who have experienced grief
through bereavement,
and we want to honour those who work with the dead,
the dying and the bereaved in any capacity.

# Contents

# List of Figures

# Acknowledgements

The editors would like to thank all of the contributors for sparing the time to write their chapters, especially as it was during and just after the global Covid-19 pandemic.

# Series Foreword

## GRAHAM HARVEY

Religion is sensual because it is corporeal and earthy. Religion is something that people (always bodies) do in the world (always physical). It is seen, heard, tasted, smelled and touched and can also involve other senses such as those of place, decency, awe, humour, value and honour. These senses work together (although not always successfully), and they are integral to corporeality. Some of our experiences privilege particular senses – as when we close our eyes to better appreciate music. The sensual impact of religious activities can be staged to employ or heighten one sense at a time, perhaps allowing incense or singing to take a lead. Or they can work together as when the burning of incense coincides with the ringing of bells to direct attention. There are myriad ramifications.

It is true that some religions make the physical senses a battleground: encouraging the suppression of bodily senses and desires in favour of 'more spiritual' leanings. In doing so, they do not contradict the assertion that religion is sensual but, rather, they evidence it. Progress in seeking putatively non-material gains or experiences, or of seeking mystical and transcendent states, may be recognised by degrees of success in restraining the more everyday senses. If these senses are not restrained, they may be trained to serve 'more elevated' purposes. Paying attention to the feeling of inward and outward breathing to initiate mindfulness does not negate sensuality but employs it. The banning of music creates alternative sonic environments (e.g. of silence or of spoken words) that are deemed suitable to the feel of agreeable ways of being religious. Similarly, quasi-cyborg interactions in online and virtual religion do not challenge the sensuality of religious activities but are conducted through the touch of keyboards, the sight of screens and the hearing of digital sounds. Examples could be multiplied.

This series has deep foundations in approaches to religion which emphasise the everyday, practice or performance, materiality, embodiment and affect. It owes much to the scholarship of religion and gender which brings into sharp focus the importance of attending to lived realities and refuses to waft away the stench of patriarchal power dynamics. *Religion and the Senses* begins with the assumption that religion is something people do. For some people, this 'doing of religion' is especially about cognition: the encouragement of correct believing or correct understanding. These activities have been emphasised by scholars as well as religious practitioners in most publications about religion. However, religion is just as much about the preparation, eating and waste-management of the foods people eat or avoid as it is about the putative meanings of food-rules. Communities are made by eating together, sharing appropriate foods at appropriate times, and equally by avoiding inappropriate foods and those who eat them. Groups may be riven by the wearing of the wrong costume or by visual attention to inappropriate media. Religious conflicts can be less about differences of belief than about the censorial setting apart of sensory worlds.

*Religion and the Senses* builds on these relatively familiar perspectives on lived religion. However, the series is more than summative of existing knowledge. It seeks to advance the cutting edge of debates. It is provocative because it engages with the sensuality of religion on the understanding that religion is *fully* sensual, corporeal and earthy. It pushes further an existing project in which religious senses largely serve to enhance appreciation of the lived reality of religions. Great advances in understanding and analysing religion have been made. However, just as debates about 'materiality' have not always engaged with materials (stuff) and those about 'embodiment' have sometimes suggested the priority of some interiority (mind, agency, ideologies, etc.), so those about religion and the senses have sometimes suggested that 'religion' exists before and apart from senses. In the books which comprise *Religion and the Senses*, religion will be pursued as something that is not merely represented by or expressed in sensual data (e.g. arts and acts), but is a matter of bodies moving through the world. Attending to sensuality does not (merely) add colour and drama to our views of religion(s). It is not only about the vignettes that introduce our debates or the colourful descriptions that enliven our analysis of ideas. Religion is the smelling, tasting, touching, hearing and seeing of the world in particular ways. We need to attend to everything from bodily affects to trained enculturation (not to evoke a nature/culture dualism but to indicate a rich diversity of topics) in order to understand how sensual religion propels people in their daily and ritual negotiations with life.

This foreword has made use of the conventional idea that there are five senses, albeit with some recognition that these can or must work together (sometimes conflictually). However, the series is not restricted to discussion of those five senses or their synaesthetic interactions. These are our entry points, our 'starting from where we are' places. The journey towards a richer and fuller sense of religion will entail a much wider notion of senses. It will require us to explore senses of place, decorum, decency, value, health/well-being, the uncanny, humour, honour and others. These 'extra' senses provide even greater possibilities for considering movement, relationships, interactions, locations and other matters.

Some of these 'senses' might make more immediate sense than others – e.g. sense of place is a relatively familiar theme in discussing religious locations and commitments. Sense of value encourages consideration of religion and economic systems (e.g. capitalist, gift and sacrificial economies), charity or philanthropy, and of ultimate versus putatively lesser 'needs' or concerns. Sense of decorum might bring discussions of religion and costume into dialogue with discussions of religious discipline and deportment (e.g. stipulations that elders should not run, children should be silent, women should be humble). The sense of honour can generate acts of violence against perceived wrong-doers as well as celebration of specific practices. The sense of the uncanny brings us face-to-face with the worlds of possession and ghosts, with feelings of unease or dread that may require the employment of religious specialists. In contrast with the sense of place, perhaps the sense of the uncanny is about dislocation and un-ease in the presence of the unknown, unexpected or unwelcome. As these presences are sometimes faced with edgy trickster tales, they provide an additional reason (if we needed it) to immerse ourselves in the sense of humour. If nothing else, jokes told within a religion (about that religion or about others) are revelatory of what is truly at the heart of that lifeway. Reiterating the synaesthetic and corporeal nature of all the senses, perhaps these religious jokes sometimes provoke throaty chortles or 'belly laughs'. Engaging with these many and varied, but usually interacting senses will require authors and readers to confront a broad spectrum of religious acts and ideas, some more edgy or contested than others.

There are, in short, many good reasons for studying religion and the senses, including the assertion made by this foreword (and contested both by some religionists and by perhaps within some of the following chapters) that religion is fully and definitively sensual, corporeal and worldly.

This series takes up the project of the 'turns' to lived religion, everyday religion, materiality, gender, embodiment and performance. By sustained focus on the senses – perhaps mediating mechanisms between our bodies and our world – we will gain a greatly improved sense of what religion is and what religious people do.

**Graham Harvey** is emeritus professor of religious studies at The Open University, UK, and the series editor for *Religion and the Senses*. He has researched with Jews, Pagans and Indigenous peoples. Most of his recent work has engaged with 'the new animism'. He lives in Northumberland and has recently taken on an allotment in an effort to discover what 'retirement' means.

# Introduction: Death and the Senses

CHRISTINA WELCH AND JASMINE HAZEL SHADRACK

Nearing the end of his life, in November 1789, the American statesman Benjamin Franklin (d. 1790) wrote to the French scientist Jean-Baptiste Le Roy about the ratification of the United States Constitution and famously noted that 'in this world nothing can be said to be certain, except death and taxes' (Franklin 2022). As fascinating as taxes might be to some, it is the universal topic of death that interests us, and interests us greatly. Christina has long been a scholar in the study of religions and of death, and for over 15 years has led a master's degree on the intersections of death, religion and culture; for many years by Distance Learning allowing students to access the course from any part of the world. Most of the students on this course were, and continue to be, in some ways 'death professionals', that is, they work in areas intimately connected with death, dying and bereavement: nurses, funeral directors, cemetery and crematoria workers, embalmers, clergy, counsellors and therapists, teachers ... all people who have to deal with the dead and/or with those they have left behind who are in the midst of grief and/or trauma. As the scholar of death John Troyer notes, such individuals are 'part of Death World' (Troyer 2023). Christina has learnt a lot from Death World folk and continues to exchange knowledge with her students, unpacking theory and providing subject content and context, whilst they open the 'insider' world of working closely with death. Several chapters in this book are authored or co-authored by former students from the course, and their professionally grounded knowledge of death, dying and bereavement lends a perspective to the subject different from the views offered by those of us who are scholars in Death World, rather than experiencing death almost daily on the frontline.

Christina met Jasmine when conceiving this project, which fits in the *Religion and the Senses* series because death is in many ways inherently sacred; it is Other and, to draw on Luhmannian theory, it has connotations with transcendence and is intimately related to the social world of the living (Sariyar 2022: 213, 216). Jasmine is a musician and as such her work around the topic of death has a deeply embodied approach; for Jasmine, the discipline of death studies is predominantly auditory and visual, with the soundscape of music and words combined with the graphic of musical notation – although as a scholar these are also theorised and critiqued especially when it comes to her main area of expertise, extreme metal music. For Christina though, death studies is largely academic with her focus on how religions and cultures deal with death and the dead; although as her publications largely explore death and artworks she too has an embodied and sensory approach to the subject – the senses of visuality and tactility pepper her work. Both Christina and Jasmine therefore recognise that when it comes to death, dying and grief, as humans we are fully holistic creatures; there is none of the alleged mind/body divide when it comes to death – grief is experienced physically and one can't just think one's way out of it. Additionally, although a dead body might have no physical sensations according to science, in some religious traditions it is treated as if still sentient. Of course, treating the dead with respect is normative for those who work with them even in secular settings, but for many religious people, it goes deeper than respect – the dead can hear, be active agents in the world of the living, and/or provide guidance to help the living live better. For the vast majority of people disrespecting the dead is an anathema, but as the concept of respect is culturally contextual, there are many forms that this may take, and some are explored here. This book is, if nothing else, a work that seeks to uncover many of the ways that the dead are treated.

The bulk of this book, however, explores the dead and the living; from those still alive but in the dying process to those the dead leave behind who, through ritual, find ways to connect with/to, and honour, their dearly departed. It also explores, through the academic study of death, the myths and rituals connected with death and grief, and the material and visual culture that remind the living of the finality of death as a concept and/or remind them of the individuals who have died. You will note that on the whole the language used throughout this book is rarely softened – the dead, die; unlike the Monty Python 'Dead Parrot' sketch (1969) we avoid the multiple euphemisms of 'passed over', 'passed on', 'pushing up the daisies', 'at rest', 'sleeping', 'gone to see their maker', 'resting in peace' and 'late'. There are many good reasons for straightforward language when it comes to human mortality, as whilst euphemisms can be gentle and comforting at tough times, they tend to deny the reality that a person is no longer physically alive, and that has socio-cultural and individual effects and affects. In a hospital setting, it can mean that relatives may not be properly prepared for their forthcoming grief (although anticipatory grief is a known emotion); for young children, using terms like 'at rest' or 'sleeping' can induce fear (maybe they too won't wake up from their nap); and for people with mild cognitive impairments, indirect language can be incomprehensible, or at least perplexing.

The use of the term 'dead' is also important as a learning experience because grief over death can be first experienced when non-humans die. Children, at least in the industrial urban West, often get their first 'taste' of death not when a relative dies, but when a pet (animal companion) dies, and this grief can be deep and immense, as many a teacher will testify to. But it must be noted that many animal deaths are un-mourned, notably those that die at human hands for food or on our busy roads, and some shot for sport. And beyond this there are animals that are dying due to the effects of global climate change. Although animal deaths do not form part of this book (we couldn't include everything, sadly), we felt it important to note deaths in the wider-than-human world, and indeed, studies suggest that some animals experience grief (King 2013; Finton 2022), and that plants can in certain conditions, using mycorrhizal networks, keep other plants from dying (Yin 2017).

In this book we have tried to get a relatively broad spread of cultural and religious contexts, despite the academic study of death tending to focus on the Western world. Although to nuance this, it must be noted when we say Western world, what we mean is that the academic study of death has historically focused on a specific portion of the Western world, usually those wealthy enough to have a grave memorial, studies of death and grief traditions in urban or semi-urban locations, and the death of non-marginalised individuals and/or groups. We have tried to open the subject up a little, but we recognise that there is only so much we can do in a single volume of this size. Still, we hope that by exploring death, dying and bereavement through the senses, some of the oft-marginalised voices may get heard, and that perhaps the baton can get passed to other scholars who can explore those Other/Othered voices.

The academic study of the senses is a relatively new field but one that has long quietly contributed to both the study of death, and the study of religion. Religion is a complex term and there are many works that deal with the trickiness of imposing the category 'religion' onto peoples and their lifeways. In this book the term is a problematic catch-all, and whilst this work is part of the *Religion and the Senses* series, the focus is on the sensory side of death rather than the religious or spiritual aspects of death, dying and/or bereavement. In many ways though, for many people death, dying and bereavement are experienced as religious (as in set-aside or Other from the everyday) and/or spiritual (as in relating to something inherently ineffable yet also personal). Experiencing the death of another is a liminal time, when we are betwixt and between this experience, and the norms of our daily life; although to be frank, our everyday norms before-the-death will never be the same as they are after-the-death. We gradually get accustomed to life with grief (to varying degrees), but a death of someone we know ruptures our life forever, and typically the more connected we were to them, the larger the tear in our own world. For those living in Death World, death is experienced regularly and coping mechanisms have evolved to help them deal with the constant first-hand exposure; but we all, in some way and at some time, confront second-hand death, that is, death mediated through mass media; from books and films where characters die (the beach where the *Harry Potter* elf Dobby died now has a shrine; BBC 2022) through the deaths of real-life celebrities, to social media snaps of graves and television footage of distant (and not-so distant) conflicts and disasters. The Covid-19 pandemic (2020) brought this mediated death into the fore though, with many countries announcing death figures on a daily basis.

In order to deal with the changes that come to us with the death of another, myths about an afterlife and/or a figure representing death itself, and rituals develop; here myth is not understood as a pretend story, but an explanation. Artworks in all their forms give visuality to these myths whilst the music and spoken words of a ritual lend them voice. Sometimes, these are sounds and pictures 'against death' as Douglas Davies would term them; as a sociologist of death, he has noted how ritualised words and actions can help soften the blow of grief and the finality of death (Davies 2002: 1), but imagery of an imagined idyllic afterlife can do the same. Deeply connected to – indeed inseparable from – these myths and rituals are other sensory ways we deal with death and the dead, and in the chapters of this book we touch on the five physical senses of sight, smell, sound, taste and touch, and add (indeed start with) the sense of proprioception in the form of self-movement or kinaesthesia. In many ways, how these physical senses play out is culturally contextualised. Although we all have bodies that sense and thus we should in essence be able to pretty much sense similarly (barring of course impairments from birth, through accident or disease, and gradual decline in the natural aging process), it would be incorrect to assume that we all experience the world around us in the same way – colour blindness (colour vision deficiency) is a case in point, and Covid-19 in some cases caused anosmia and ageusia (loss of smell and taste respectively; Tanasa et al. 2020). We wanted to unpack the cultural aspect of the sense of death a little further with this book, thinking through some of the evidently cultural ways that death is dealt with, choosing the sense of decency, the sense of humour and the sense of loss. There are of course many other cultural senses we could have chosen, but we felt these were the most common yet also the most marginalised in academic discourse.

Of course, no sense operates alone; we are multisensory creatures and whilst some of us may have some senses more attuned than others, it is rare that we move without also sensing the smells and sights of our environment. When we taste we also smell – these senses are intimately combined – and often how we react to (feel about) what we see, smell and/or taste, is culturally conditioned. However, we needed to provide a structure to this book and as such went for two chapters on each of the nine senses we chose to focus on, and we provide here a brief summary of them, arranged in order of the contents. Some of these chapters readers may find confronting, but the topic of death is one that challenges and a human's response to challenges is rarely just cerebral. We therefore acknowledge that some readers may have a visceral reaction to what we present. We did not want to sugar-coat such an important topic by glossing over realities, but chapters where readers may find the content a little too visceral are marked with a content warning.

## DEATH AND THE PHYSICAL SENSES

*Death and the Sense of Proprioception/Movement*

In Chapter 1 on kinetic death, Dr Candi K. Cann details the history of the Japanese dance, the O'bon, and the ways in which it has established its tradition in the island of O'ahu, Hawai'i. Through ethnographic fieldwork and interviews, she provides an in-depth examination of specific aspects of certain dances performed at the Shinshu Kyokai Buddhist Mission. Cann begins with the Story of Mokuren and the release of his mother's spirit from the realm of the Hungry Ghosts. This myth is the pivotal moment in the origin of the O'bon dance. She details the O'bon festival in Japan and then its placement in Hawai'i, unpacking the ways in which the unique music and dance movements demonstrate cultural hybridisation and diaspora.

Dr Olu Taiwo's Chapter 2, 'Egungun – Moving the Masks of Our Ancestors', investigates a new self-confidence among cultures whose ancestry has an ancient past, whose 'stories have been altered by the explicit agenda of white-supremacists' who had ultimate control over printed narratives. The unearthing of these stories free from a racist yoke, has revealed patterns of behaviours, embedded in ritual and theatre, such as one associated with the Yoruba called the Dance of Egungun. Taiwo examines this dance as praxis, from ancestral worship to the expression of symbolic power, existing as a cyclical coexistent relationship; and notes that death in this context shows transition, not finality. This movement is emancipation, reclamation and celebration, the Egungun dancer performing at a place where different phases of reality coexist.

### Death and the Sense of Sight

Chapter 3 deals with how Western art confronts the subject of mortality, with Dr Celia Grace Kenny focusing on the vanitas genre and its contribution to the ways we represent death visually. She takes us through a description of this visual art form in the sixteenth and seventeenth centuries, in order to situate the continuity/discontinuity of twenty-first century vanitas art, finishing with a case study focused on the work of Philip Braham. Braham is a contemporary Scottish artist and philosopher and Kenny was able to gain an interview with him to dive deep into his collection entitled *Suicide Notes*. Kenny's chapter brings into focus the relationship between seeing and death.

In Chapter 4 Dr Kate Kingsbury takes us through the material culture of death and its varied visual representations from the Grim Reaper to Santa Muerte. It is through these diverse images and ideologies, Kingsbury states, that humans not only make sense of death, but also seek to master their own mortality. Taking the reader through the semiotics of death, she explores the fascinating images and representations of the Old World Grim Reaper, and its New World depictions La Parca, Ah Puch, Iyadzehe Qcuañe, Quetzalcoatl, Rey Pascual and Santa Muerte. Kingsbury notes that these diverse contexts and images can offer various understandings, not only those relating to death.

### Death and the Sense of Smell

In Chapter 5 Dr Helen Frisby documents the significance of the sense of smell, noting that historically it has been largely overlooked as part of the funerary ritual. In her chapter, she seeks to address this scholarly gap by investigating some of the meanings and functions of olfaction in folk funerals in Britain between c. 1850 and 1920. Frisby's main source material for this is examining antiquarian accounts of that time that reference funerary smellscapes. She states that 'smell performs important emotional and social functions within the funerary context', particularly through personal association. Frisby's research helps make room for olfaction and its value as part of the bereavement process. We come across folklore again in Chapter 9 with Beverley Roger's exploration of death and the sense of taste.

Chapter 6 by Dr Wendy Birch, 'The Sense of Smell and the Odour of Death', examines the 'undeniably disagreeable' smell of death. She explores the necrophilic and necrophobic responses to what happens to the human body after death, the effect on the living and how this is used by the police and recovery personnel in cases involving dead human bodies. Birch also investigates how this smell of the dead can aid in returning the deceased human body to its 'volatile organic compounds'. By detailing the four distinct stages of human body decomposition, Birch is able to elucidate upon this often difficult to describe process.

### Death and the Sense of Sound

Chapter 7 explores death and the sense of sound. Here Suzi Garrod and Dr Christina Welch examine how sound connects with death, dying, grief and bereavement. This co-written chapter is separated into two sections; practitioner-led and theory-led. Garrod inhabits Death World as a practising death doula who integrates sound therapy with psycho-educational and practical interventions. Welch is a death studies scholar so takes a more theory-led approach to the topic. Together, the authors offer two sides to the sound of death, showcasing not only the academic and the professional practice of sounding out death, but what this means for death education, end-of-life care and grief support.

In Chapter 8, Dr Jasmine Hazel Shadrack takes an autoethnographic approach to examining the impact of two pieces of music that were played at her mother's funeral. One piece is considered popular music, whilst the other is an operatic duet; the two combined provide the musicological frame she uses to investigate the reasons why these pieces affect such different emotional responses. The autoethnography provides the methodological structure to disentangle the grief from the music itself and the funerary context, analysing the ways in which these songs continue to have such a lasting impact for her. Her personal perspective has much in common with that of Chapter 11 where Enya Healey-Rawlings explores death and the sense of touch.

### Death and the Sense of Taste

Chapter 9 explores the sense of death through food, both food for the dead and food for the living. In examining the role of food in death rituals Beverley Rogers notes that 'edible responses to the act of processing the spiritual and sacred nature of death' are vital in supporting the bereaved. Rogers also explores the role that food plays in mourning, drawing on different cultures across different time periods to demonstrate how the bereaved come together in a shared ritual space for support and to envision what life can look like after the death event.

Taste and death in Chapter 10 picks up on the topic of funeral foods but then takes a slightly different turn into the concept of cannibalism, where Dr Christina Welch explores the taste of the dead, plunging into death and the sense of taste as a holistic and 'fully somatic' experience. She focuses on three areas: food traditionally eaten at funerals, the deliberate ingestion of dry human remains and, lastly, the purposeful ingestion of wet human remains. Welch navigates her way through this varied funeral fare to offer the reader a clear and stark perspective on different death rituals of food, from wake foods to cannibalism.

### Death and the Sense of Touch

Chapter 11 is by Enya Healey-Rawlings who through a personal narrative on crafting explores how handicrafts can help continue bonds between the living and the loved ones they have lost. Enya focuses on knitting, embroidery and sewing as activities rooted in social history that have forged bonds along her maternal familial line. However, she begins her chapter by examining continuing bonds as theory, following this with a discussion of how crafting is tied to the concept of continuing bonds. The ritualistic and meditative nature of crafting is explored in relation to the grieving process and the necessity of ensuring these crafts' longevity as continuing tradition.

In Chapter 12, Dr Heidi Dawson-Hobbis's contribution to death and the sense of touch again takes a personal perspective but places the sense in the realm of bio-anthropology. Dawson-Hobbis, who regularly works with human skeletal remains in her research and teaching, discusses the importance of touch in analysing dry bones. When excavating and/or examining exhumed human skeletal remains, the person could have died thousands of years ago or over one hundred years ago; the touch of the bones can help determine the time frame. In this chapter she explores the look and the feel of bones and how this can help contextualise the burial environment, and estimate the age-at-death of the deceased. She also reflects on how these remains are understood by the students and professionals that work with them through primary research, unearthing the rarely considered sense of touch in the discipline of biological anthropology.

## DEATH AND THE CULTURAL SENSES

### Death and the Sense of Decency

Chapter 13 is co authored by Lucy Jacklin and Dr Christina Welch who compare and contrast the private viewing of fleshy embalmed bodies in funeral homes with the public display of de-fleshed, plastinated corpses at BODY WORLDS – the travelling museum of polymer-preserved dead bodies. This chapter draws on both practice-based and academic analysis; Jacklin having been employed in the funeral service since 2016 and Welch having focused on teaching death theory and the socio-cultural and religious approaches to death and dying since 2008. This dual approach offers a rich position from which to explore the sense of decency when displaying the dead.

Chapter 14 explores death and the sense of decency from the perspective of what is termed 'dark tourism'. Dr Alasdair Richardson and Dr Christina Welch's co-authored chapter navigates the difficult path between education and objectification of memorial sites. Richardson examines English school trips to concentration camps such as Auschwitz-Birkenau and the difficulties in recognising the magnitude of events whilst engaging with objects and effects left behind. The human remains, whether as ashes or hair, occupy dual spaces as remembrance and objects, raising questions about preserved individuality versus tourist attractions. Welch briefly compares Auschwitz-Birkenau with a lesser-known site of the *Shoah/Holocaust* of Paneriai before moving on to a second case study, that of the burial places of enslaved Africans trafficked to Brazil. The differentiation in tourist numbers and the ways in which dark tourism has impacted these memorial places and burial types, serve to foreground how this kind of tourism may not always function in the ways it was intended, and raises questions around what might or might not be considered decent when it comes to places and spaces connected to the death of humans.

*Death and the Sense of Humour*

Chapter 15 is by Dr Laura Hubner who focuses on satire in the time of the Covid-19 pandemic, having been granted an 'in conversation' interview with British satirist and digital collagist, Christopher 'Cold War Steve' Spencer. This chapter recalls the globally traumatic event of the 2020 Coronavirus pandemic in the context of Britain, and the British government's response to the crisis. Hubner foregrounds the use of humour through Spencer's reaction to Covid-19, and his use of humour as a coping mechanism that buttressed the media and government spin. Cold War Steve's range of artistic and satirical public events and outputs during this time 'kept him "sane"' which centres the need for humour during traumatic events.

Chapter 16 by Angie McLachlan also deals with the need for humour as a coping mechanism when dealing with death. As an embalmer and Death World educator, she takes a practitioner's perspective on why funeral workers might need to cope with death in a way that other people may find unusual. In doing so, she offers valuable insights into her more than thirty-year experience of death care, positing humour as an important coping strategy. McLachlan writes that 'humour can be the difference between coping and not coping with one's work'. This chapter demonstrates the importance of funerary workers' self-care whilst navigating compassionate listening, communication skills and the event management requirements of the profession.

*Death and the Sense of Loss*

Chapter 17 provides an analysis of the sense of loss when a glacier dies. In exploring human grief at the death of an important natural feature, Jonatan Spejlborg Juelsbo examines the memorial event surrounding a glacier so far in decline, that it was declared dead. In his close reading of the memorial service for Okjökull in Iceland, he places ecological devastation at the heart of the research, asking us to consider the sense of loss and mourning that accompanies such drastic changes in the environment. Focusing on 'Glacier OK', in the western part of Iceland, Juelsbo argues that these memorial practices for the glaciers which are so much a part of Iceland's identity are 'complex assemblages of mourning, ontological positioning, political statements, and activist practice' in direct relation to humans and non-humans alike.

In Chapter 18, Kym Swan explores grave goods as a form of continuing bonds, noting two core themes. The first looks at the relationships between people and how these develop during the grieving process. The second examines the use and representation of objects gifted to the dead that give material expression to the enduring bond between the deceased and the bereaved. The ritualistic marking of personal connections that survive post-mortem, Swan notes, has a long history that suggests a deep connection to 'religious, spiritual and social practices'. Her chapter details that understanding the cultural and ancestral impact in respect of these rituals has great meaning in the social act of dying.

Finally, in the Afterword, Professor Graham Harvey, series editor for *Religion and the Senses*, provides his thoughts which tie this book into the series, and provide the reader with a focus around which to ponder the chapters herein.

## BIBLIOGRAPHY

BBC. 2022. 'Harry Potter: Dobby's Grave on Welsh Beach Saved for Now', *BBC* 31 October 2022. https://www.bbc.com/news/uk-wales-63462109

Davies, Douglas J. 2002. *Death, Ritual and Belief: The Rhetoric of Funerary Rites*, 2nd edition. London and New York: Continuum.

Finton, Caitlyn. 2022. 'Animals Respond to Death in Many Ways. Mourning Might Be One of Them', *Discover* 21 January 2022. https://www.discovermagazine.com/planet-earth/animals-respond-to-death-in-many-ways-mourning-might-be-one-of-them

Franklin. 2022. 'Benjamin Franklin's Last Great Quote and the Constitution', Constitution Center 13 November 2022. https://constitutioncenter.org/blog/benjamin-franklins-last-great-quote-and-the-constitution

King, Barbara J. 2013. *How Animals Grieve*. Chicago: University of Chicago Press.

Monty Python. 1969. 'Monty Python Dead Parrot'. https://www.youtube.com/watch?v=vZw35VUBdzo

Sariyar, Mural. 2022. 'Death from the Perspective of Luhmann's System Theory', *Open Theology* 8: 205–220. https://doi.org/10.1515/opth-2022-0196

Tanasa, Ingrid A., Manciuc, Carmen, Carauleanu, Alexandru, Navloan, Dan B., Bohiltea, Roxana E. and Nemescu, Dragos. 2020. 'Anosmia and Ageusia Associated with Coronavirus Infections (COVID-19) – What is Known?', *Experimental and Therapeutic Medicine* 20(3): 2344–2347. https://www.ncbi.nlm.nih.gov/pmc/articles/PMC7401831/ https://doi.org/10.3892/etm.2020.8808

Troyer, John. 2023. 'Even though I Grew up in Death World, and Still Live there, It Couldn't Prepare Me for Being My Family's Sole Survivor', *Psyche* 16 May 2023. https://psyche.co/ideas/i-thought-i-knew-everything-about-death-then-grief-struck-me?fbclid=IwAR1W2bgeDfYmYBOyBJb13Q_bV-5eSZowjfTqv0pqYpCpMdsDMf2Ggn0K3ws

Yin, David. 2017. 'Food, Poison, and Espionage: Mycorrhizal Networks in Action', *Arnoldia* 75(2): 2–11. https://arboretum.harvard.edu/stories/food-poison-and-espionage-mycorrhizal-networks-in-action/

**Christina Welch** is an interdisciplinary Religious Studies scholar. She led the master's degree in Death, Religion and Culture (formerly MA in Religion: The Rituals and Rhetoric of Death) at the University of Winchester from 2007 until 2021, and continues to teach on the programme. She has research interests around visual and material culture, particularly in relation to religion and/or death. She also works on issues around heritage, especially as they relate to religion and/or death in the Caribbean.

**Jasmine Hazel Shadrack** is a musician, composer, psychoanalyst and feminist autoethnographer with over twenty years of teaching, lecturing and research experience. She is adjunct professor at the Don Wright Faculty for Music Research and Composition, Western University, Canada, and a member of the National Coalition for Independent Scholars. She sits on the editorial boards for the International Society for Metal and Music Studies and Intellect's new series entitled *Advances in Metal Music and Culture*. Her monograph *Black Metal, Trauma, Subjectivity and Sound: Screaming the Abyss* was published by Emerald in 2021.

Part One

# PHYSICAL SENSES

Chapter 1

# Kinetic Death: O'Bon – Hawai'i's Japanese Dance for the Dead

## CANDI K. CANN

The Japanese O'bon dance festival dates back over five hundred years to the Buddhist sutra of Mokuren (Mulian in Chinese), named after the son who made sacrifices to the Buddhist bodhisattva, Avalokiteshvara (Chinese: Guanyin), in thanksgiving for his mother's release from hell. In celebration of her release, Mokuren supposedly danced for joy, beginning the history of the Dance for the Dead festival in Japan.[1] When Japanese immigrants arrived in Hawai'i, they brought the custom of dancing O'bon, and as Japanese Buddhism became established in Hawai'i, each Buddhist temple became known for its local traditions, dances, dress and food. Now, in the summer months, Hawai'ian residents eagerly look forward to the various O'bon dances celebrated across the islands, visiting various temples and purchasing the local treats while dancing in commemoration of the dead. This chapter offers a brief history of the O'bon tradition on the island of O'ahu, Hawai'i, and then examines more specific aspects of these dances at the Shinshu Kyokai Buddhist Mission through ethnographic fieldwork and interviews.[2]

---

1   See Grant and Idema (2011) and Parać (2016) for more on the tale of Mokuren/ Mulian and its importance to Japanese folk Buddhism.
2   See http://www.shinshukyokai.org/index-2.html for more on the Shinshu Kyokai Mission.

The story of Mokuren/Mulian is an important one in Buddhist lore, since the sutra also marks the transition from traditional Theravada Buddhism, generally found in Southeast Asia, to Mahayana Buddhism, found in China, Japan and Korea, melding traditional Buddhist values with the Confucian concern for family and society. The sutra of Mokuren highlights the transition from a Buddhism in which the only way to reach enlightenment is through the self, to a Buddhism that heralds the bodhisattva ideal. With this ideal, the bodhisattva operates as a Buddhist adept who intercedes on behalf of Buddhist believers in order to aid them in their path to enlightenment. In a culture dominated by the Confucian values of family and filial piety, the more traditional path of self-enlightenment was viewed as inappropriate and unfilial because of its traditional emphasis on monasticism and self-enlightenment. The Mokuren sutra emphasised the importance of filial piety alongside the Buddhist worldview, allowing for families to honour the traditional Confucian system in which they operated, while also offering a new theological approach to Buddhism that provided a pathway for intercessory enlightenment. Thus, the story of Mokuren is an important one in Japan, as it offers a narrative affirmation of Buddhist enlightenment accompanied by, and even accomplished through, traditional Confucian filial piety.

## THE STORY OF MOKUREN

In the sutra, Mokuren, a disciple of the Buddha, used his supernatural powers to look upon his deceased mother, and discovered she had fallen into the Realm of Hungry Ghosts and was suffering. In Buddhism, Hungry Ghosts are beings who have large stomachs but throats as small as a pinhole, so they are always suffering from hunger and thirst that can never be satiated. Greatly disturbed, Mokuren went to the Buddha and asked how he could secure his mother's release from this realm of suffering. The Buddha instructed him to make offerings to the monks who had just completed their summer retreat, on the fifteenth day of the seventh month. The offerings included food and drink given to the monastic community, who would then give prayers of intercession on behalf of Mokuren's mother. Additionally, the Buddha instructed Mokuren to prepare a wine offering, symbolising the blood from childbirth that his mother shed when he was born. Mokuren did all these things and, as a result, his mother was released from the realm of the Hungry Ghosts.[3] In acknowledgement of his mother's love for him, and her release from hell, Mokuren performed a dance of joy, which has since become the Bon Odori, or O'bon dance.[4] This dance is meant to both honour dead ancestors and invite them to return to the earth to receive gifts of prayers and appreciation.

## THE O'BON FESTIVAL IN JAPAN

In Japan, the festival of O'bon lasts for three days, with the dates of those three days varying today across different regions of the country. When the lunar calendar was changed to the Gregorian calendar in 1873 under the Meiji era in Japan, the exact dates for the celebration of O'bon shifted in various localities. But no matter when it is celebrated in each prefecture, it is almost always a three-day celebration. Because the O'bon festival was originally based on the lunar calendar, it is celebrated sometime from around the middle of July to the middle of August and coincides with the ghost festival which is celebrated in other parts of Asia. The ghost festival celebrates the annual opening of the gates of hell and is believed to be the day that spirits come to earth to roam the streets and eat and drink. It is celebrated throughout China and Southeast Asia, and during this time, families visit and clean the tombs, offer prayers on behalf of, and to, the dead, and offer food and drink to the dead. Similarly, the purpose of O'bon is to honour and remember the dead, to feed and nourish the dead, and to strengthen one's lineage ties with one's ancestors, remembering one's place in the family and the world. Honouring the dead also functions as a way to recognise the reciprocal relationship between the realms of the living and the dead, in which the living are expected to care for the dead, but in return the dead are expected to watch over and protect the living. In this way, the bon dance not only serves as a reminder of one's ancestors, but also reinforces one's place in the world, both living and dead. By the late nineteenth century, O'bon travelled to Hawai'i along with the first

3  It is important to note here that the offerings recognise the interdependence of not just Mokuren and his mother, but of the Buddhist layperson and sangha of monks as well. The exchanges of hospitality for prayers cement this relationship, affirming the reliance of the sangha on the larger lay community, and of the lay community on the sangha.

4  In Japanese, the 'O' is an honorific term placed before nouns to give respect or honour. 'Odori' means dance. Frequently, bon dance is referred to as either O'bon, or Bon Odori.

Japanese immigrants to the islands, thus taking the Japanese dance for the dead to foreign shores.

## THE O'BON FESTIVAL IN HAWAI'I

The first Japanese arrived in the islands of Hawai'i on 8 February 1885. Those first 900 immigrants came to the islands to work on the sugarcane plantations, and would plant the seeds for Hawai'i's thriving Japanese American community today – nearly 14% of the total island population. When Japanese immigrants arrived in Hawai'i, they brought the custom of dancing O'bon. Judy Van Zile writes on the popularity of bon dance among the early settlers from Japan: 'it is believed that the first bon dances were performed in the fields where the immigrants labored, and in between houses on the plantation. Later dances were held in temple courtyards. As work schedules began to conform to the Western five-day week, bon dances began to be scheduled for weekends' (Van Zile 1982). At the turn of the twentieth century, many Japanese immigrants could only celebrate O'bon on the weekends because of their jobs. Because the festival requires a professional music troupe and dance troupe who travel from temple to temple to lead the communities in the festivities and teach them how to conduct the dances, the three-day festivities gradually turned into an entire season so that each temple could have its turn without disrupting work schedules.

Each neighbourhood temple usually has its own cemetery or columbarium, so it is important for each temple to have its own dance to honour its local dead. The local newspapers print a special section listing all the O'bon dances taking place on each island, because it is common for people to visit other temples in addition to their own. Attendance at various temples during the season may be to show solidarity and support, while some go to honour family members whose remains are at these temples, and others go to help out with the festivities. This is partly why temples take turns celebrating O'bon, and why in Hawai'i, the bon dance festival lasts about a month, rather than three days as in Japan. Many go, however, because the dances are also fun summer festivals that offer food and treats that people come from far and wide to sample. In the summer months, Hawai'ian residents eagerly look forward to the various O'bon dances celebrated across the islands, visiting various temples and purchasing the local treats while dancing in commemoration of the dead. The Library of Congress Local Legacies Project writes on their website:

> Although the dance nearly died out with the onslaught of anti-Japanese fervor that swept Hawaii during the 1940s, a post WW II event spurred its revival in 1951 when four Japanese-American veterans' groups sponsored a bon dance to honor the war dead from Hawaii. That revival was also powered by tourism and the convergence of several island traditions: interfaith services, interracial marriages, racial harmony, and bon dance clubs. Today the bon dancers are not only Japanese Buddhists, but Filipino, Chinese, Korean, Portuguese and native Hawaiian, Protestant and Catholic .... Each bon dance club specializes in the music and dance of one of the prefectures of Hawaii's immigrants. (LOC Local Legacies Project 2000)

Currently, there are about ninety Japanese Buddhist temples throughout Hawai'i, and each temple holds its own O'bon dance for the community, with professional island dance troupes and musicians moving from one temple to another as they hold their O'bon celebrations. Because each temple has its own graveyard, the troupes must visit each one and the temple then honours its dead with food, festivities and dancing.

I first encountered bon dancing when I was nineteen years old and my friend, whose Buddhist father had died, invited me to accompany her and her mother, both Christians, to the local temple bon dance, where they were celebrating and volunteering with the food booths. I learned various dances, ate the mochi (Japanese rice cake) that the temple was known for, and participated in the festival-like atmosphere. That night we returned to my friend's home, where her mother made offerings of oranges and incense to the ancestral tablet placed at the centre of their living room, and we all went to sleep, stuffed with food, and tired. To me, bon dancing was simply something people did in Hawai'i, and it wouldn't be until I saw how different it was in Japan that I began to think about Hawai'i's bon dance season as something unique.

## MUSIC AND DANCE

Bon dance music is unique to the bon dance festivities and is often a hybrid of local music and Japanese culture, reflecting Japanese identity within a larger American diaspora. As Minako Waseda writes:

> In Hawai'i, where Japanese Americans form a tightly-knit ethnic community, it was possible to both keep the homeland bon dance and create variants with newly-composed lyrics .... These aspects of home culture maintenance coexist with cultural hybridization. In Hawai'i, American popular songs

> were incorporated into bon dance, reflecting the Americanization of the younger generation .... (Waseda 2008: 1)

The music functions simultaneously to affirm broader pan-Japanese identity while emphasising Japanese American identity. Through Japanese traditional songs, and the local hybridisation meant to appeal to a broader audience, the music played at the bon dance creates cultural bonds not only between the living and the dead, but between the temple and the broader community as well, with people from a wide variety of ethnic identities invited to stop by and partake in the bon dance festival. Because the dead being honoured are usually the local dead buried or kept at the temple, the kinship ties honoured in the bon dance festivities move beyond those who practice at each particular temple.

The music is usually live – with drums and flute interspersed with traditional instruments such as the shamisen, and a singer who stands at the centre of the dancers singing the bon dance lyrics. The singing has an important function, as it is often utilised as a way to affirm and assert collective identity, whether it be of a school, a company or, in this case, a temple. As Waseda writes:

> Japanese culture seems to place particular value on the function of collective singing as a means of solidifying group identity. It is common for a Japanese school to have its own 'school song' (kōka). Such a song advocates the ideals of the school and is sung by the teachers and students at various assemblies and ceremonies to constantly foster a sense of group identity. Similarly, many Japanese companies have their own 'company songs' (shaka). This custom of creating and singing a so-to-speak 'identity song' has much to do with the Japanese ideology of group solidarity. (Waseda 2005: 208 n 83)

Collective singing serves an important function in helping to create a collective Japanese identity, and the music of O'bon is no different. While the lyrics of various O'bon songs may shift, each song will have a chorus that will be sung collectively by the audience or the backup singers at various times throughout the song. This call and response allows even those not familiar with all the lyrics to participate in the singing. Bon dance music changes with each generation, often revealing influences from cultural hybridisation, accompanied by shifts in dance moves as well. The art form thus is not static, and both the lyrics and the choreography reveal the influence of geography and culture, reflecting local identity and occupation. In Japan, for example, there are 'coal mining' dances that illustrate the miners' movements, while in Hawai'i dances evoke plantation life and some even include traditional hula steps. Bon dances often incorporate props from the local culture or local industry – with examples ranging from fans (for plantation workers) to towels (for the fisherfolk).

In most O'bon dances, the dance is performed around a central wooden stage called a yagura (a scaffolded wooden tower built specially for the event), and dancers move clockwise or counter-clockwise around the yagura, depending on the dance. Generally, the singers and the drummers of the taiko percussion instruments perform on the yagura in order to be seen by the dancers. The troupe usually divides into singers and dancers, with members choosing to specialise in either the singing – usually performed standing on the yagura which is placed in the centre of the dance area – or the dancing, with the professional troupe dancers circumambulating the tower in prescribed steps in time to the songs. The first ring around the tower comprises the professional dancers and the Sensei, or the official dance teacher. The next rings are reserved for community members and people just learning the dances. Temples on different islands incorporate musical variations into their songs, and the professional dance troupe creates and choreographs a signature dance for each temple. This maintains the unity between temples, while simultaneously distinguishing each temple with unique dance moves that become their kinetic dance signature.

## KINETIC GRIEF

Bon dance can be viewed as an expression of kinetic grief – it is a way of moving that represents one's mourning for the dead, and is a highly ritualised and communal expression of celebrating one's loved ones who have died. Bon dances are formal communal dances that have a set number of steps, and a ritualised style that a dancer is expected to learn and follow. But the dance also allows the physical response of moving one's body, and 'doing something' with one's grief. At the most basic level, the gentle exercise of dancing allows for a dopamine release that can help manage grief. In this way, Bon dance is a physical expression of grief that draws on a communally learned and shared set of ritual expressions to help bridge the divide between the worlds of the living and the dead. Simpkins and Myers-Coffman discuss the importance of body memory and grief in dance therapy after a death: 'Kinesthetic awareness is constant even if another sense is disengaged. The concept of body memory, which utilizes kinesthetic awareness, is not only complex, but also holistic: it requires an integrated view of systems of the mind and the body' (2017: 191). Bodily memory is experiential, developed through repeated movement, and links the individual to their external sensory world – whether local or imaginary.

O'bon, through its annually observed ritual re-enactment of Mokuren achieving his mother's release from the world of Hungry Ghosts, allows the participant to utilise bodily memory to continue a relationship with the dead. Additionally, the dance can be learnt and the dancer gradually perfects their ability to dance the steps of each dance, allowing them to feel a sense of accomplishment as they gradually learn how to participate fully in the dancing group. The mourning dancers remember they are not alone in their grief, and as they move around the yagura tower, they are reminded that death and grief are a universal experience. The community dances beside them as they learn how to 'do' grief. The structured nature of bon dance allows one to be in community with others, without being forced to interact in ways that may feel uncomfortable or unnatural. Additionally, having professional bon dance troupe members whose job is to perform the dance in a ritually correct way takes the pressure off dancers who may be newer or unfamiliar with the dance steps. As the dance is being performed correctly by the professionals, the audience knows that the dead will be able to mingle with the living, even if the others don't perform well. The dance can also be viewed as a form of moving meditation. The music tends to be formulaic, with lyrics centred around an often-repeated chorus that is echoed by dancers and participants. The music thus allows the dancer to concentrate on predictable steps while centring on a repeated and anticipated rhythm. Bon dance music is purposely accessible and meant to be easy to follow along so that all can participate. The spiritual purpose of the music and the festivities is to reassure the dead that all is well with the living.

## SHINSHU KYOKAI BUDDHIST MISSION'S BON DANCE

The annual bon dance at the Shinshu Kyokai Buddhist Mission follows O'bon services for the dead, usually held the week before and after the dances themselves. The services honour the deceased ancestors of the mission, while the dances themselves serve as an extension into the broader community, serving food, offering entertainment, and helping to forge a network extending to the neighbourhood surrounding the temple. The preparations are extensive for the dance, and volunteer dance troupes travel from temple to temple throughout the islands, teaching the traditional dances for the dead as a way to safeguard the temple's relationship to the community and to strengthen its local Buddhist and Japanese identity. All people in the community – old, young, everyone in between, Japanese, non-Japanese – are invited to attend and participate.

In Hawai'i the troupes of professional singers and dancers all wear similar clothing to distinguish them as the experts. This helps the lay people identify whom they should be watching if they need guidance on how to perform the dance. Traditionally, it is customary for a dancer to wear a yukata, or a Japanese kimono made of unlined cotton, usually worn in the warm summer months in Japan. Sometimes, people will wear a blue 'happi' coat, a special tube-sleeved coat worn during festivals, though I have also seen some people in full kimono, and others in their regular everyday clothes. The Shinshu Kyokai Mission leaders told me that the 'old school people' didn't like people dancing unless they were wearing the yukata or happi, but now they are just glad when people show up. The martial arts clubs also help with the dance, since several martial arts clubs practise on temple grounds, and assisting with the bon dance allows them to give back to the community where they learn. The week before the bon dance, the various clubs come to each temple and practise the dances they know they will be performing. Since each temple generally has its own special dances, the elders at the Shinshu Kyokai Mission told me proudly that they have a special choreographed dance that they perform just for their community.

The bon dance is not simply a religious dance, but also a festival, in which many foods, souvenirs and treats are sold and enjoyed. Each temple usually has a specialty food that it is known for, and many people will go to a particular temple for the food they can only purchase from that temple during the bon dance season. In this way, the Hawai'ian O'bon dances are similar to those in Japan, where particular temples on different islands are known for special treats – a particular type of mochi or rice cake, or a certain kind of noodles. For example, Maui temples are known for their chao fan, or fried rice; on Kaua'i, people love the 'flying saucer' – two pieces of bread with stuffing inside and sealed at the edges, like a pasty pie. On O'ahu, people like saimin (a noodle soup) and mochi. The Shinshu Kyokai Mission is known for its lilikoi mochi – or passion fruit rice cake – and the temple leader proudly told me that six pans sell out in an hour and a half. There are only two occasions in a year when lilikoi mochi is available – New Year's and O'bon – and people come from all over the island to enjoy it during these two festivals. But the mission's funnel cake corn dog is also quite popular – a mixture of dinner and desert all wrapped in one – and the line for this is always long.

While the Shinshu Kyokai Mission tries to make money beyond the costs of putting on the festival, the mission leaders said that as long as the mission breaks even, they are happy. In addition to the selling of food, Shinshu Kyokai also takes donations, though the donations are generally reciprocal, whether between the living and the dead, or the temple and the community. One such example is the memorial papers given to bon dance participants who donate a small amount of money. In exchange for the donation, bon dance attendees are given a small folded white paper, on which they will write the name of a deceased person and tie it onto one of the various strings hanging over the courtyard. These memorial papers offer a way for the dead to participate in the festival, while intercessory prayers are offered on behalf of the dead by the living. As Robert John Smith writes in his book *Ancestor Worship in Contemporary Japan*, 'the periodic merging of the two worlds (living and dead) strengthens the sense of continuity of the house and reassures the dead of the living's continuing concern for their well being' (1974: 104). Dennis Klass utilises Smith's examination of Japanese religion for his work on Continuing Bonds Theory, and the bon dance helps to illustrate Klass's assertion that in Japanese religion, the regular insertion of the dead into the world of the living through the ritualistic and communally performed bon dance helps the living maintain continuing bonds with the dead (Klass et al. 2014). In Hawai'i though, because the dance lasts a season rather than the three days found in Japan, O'bon also serves to reinforce a feeling local and cultural belonging – both for those in Hawai'i, and for the larger Japanese diaspora.

The souvenir towels (tenugui in Japanese) sold by the Shinshu Kyokai mission are another way that the temple reinforces its identity in the community. Each temple in the islands sells a souvenir towel, and many people visit various temples and collect the towels sold by each of them. The practice of selling souvenir towels is quite popular throughout all of the Japanese temples in Hawai'i, as well as in Japan. The temple leaders told me that the practice is based on the idea of reciprocity – when you give a donation, you receive a towel in return. The Shinshu Kyokai Mission leaders pointed out that they have their towels silk-screened in Japan, and in this way, too, the temples reinforce their Japanese origins. Each year almost every temple will design a new towel with special artwork and with that festival's year printed on the towel to commemorate the annual dance. The towels are used in martial arts as headbands, in the kitchen as dish towels, or even just to tie up gifts. There are also several popular bon dances where towels feature as a prop in the dance, which is how they originally became a popular souvenir item in the first place. Even during the Covid-19 pandemic of 2020–21, when most temple bon dances were forced to move online, the towels remained a popular feature and souvenir, with online shops touting the towels' design choice, colour, and the fact that they had been made in Japan.

## CONCLUSION: MAPPING PLACE AND IDENTITY THROUGH DANCE

All of the features of the bon dance are meant to reinscribe the dead onto the world of the living. O'bon usually begins with the lighting of fire lanterns (now often supplemented with electric lanterns and lights) meant to welcome and guide the spirits of the dead back home. Lanterns are lit and hung near the temple and at home during the O'bon season, and at the conclusion of the season, floating lanterns are lit and released, along with prayers, incense and flowers, to guide the dead back into their world. The graves and columbarium niches are cleaned, and services for the dead are usually held the day before, during and/or after the bon dance season of a particular temple. The living both invite the dead, and send them off. But more importantly, the sense of identity and place of both living and dead is reinscribed through these annual ritual dances. The souvenir towels, lanterns and clothes come from Japan, the music is sung in Japanese using Japanese instruments, and the foods served at the temples are a mix of both Japanese and local favourites. The festival is an opportunity to demonstrate Japanese identity – one's ties to the Japanese community both in Japan and in Hawai'i – and an opportunity to reaffirm one's place to one's ancestors, and to one's descendants. O'bon dance in Hawai'i is an opportunity to remember one's history, and to honour one's future, all through dancing in the present.

## BIBLIOGRAPHY

Bell Vila, Marlon. 2021. *Family, Ancestor Worship and Young Adults: The Obon Festival in Contemporary Japan.* MA dissertation, University of Ottawa. https://ruor.uottawa.ca/bitstream/10393/41705/3/Bell_Vila_Marlon_2021_Thesis.pdf

Grant, Beata and Idema, Wilt L. 2011. *Escape from Blood Pond Hell: The Tales of Mulian and Woman Huang.* Seattle: University of Washington Press.

Klass, Dennis, Silverman, Phyllis R. and Nickman, Steven. 2014. *Continuing Bonds: New Understandings of Grief.* Abingdon: Taylor & Francis.

Kurashige, Lon. 2002. *Japanese American Celebration and Conflict: A History of Ethnic Identity and Festival, 1934–1990*. No. 8. Berkeley: University of California Press.

Library of Congress Local Legacies Project. 2000. 'The Obon in Hawai'i'. https://memory.loc.gov/diglib/legacies/loc.afc.afc-legacies.200002880/ last accessed 17 August 2022.

Osa, Susan. 2006. 'Gathering of Joy: A History of Japanese American Obon Festivals and Bon Odori', *Discover Nikkei* 8 July 2006. http://www.discovernikkei.org/en/journal/2006/7/8/obon/ last accessed 14 July 2022.

Parać, Iva Lakić. 2016. 'Bodhisattva Jizō and Folk Religious Influences: Elements of Folk Religion in Jizō's Understanding in Japan', *Asian Studies* 4(1): 115–129. http://doi.org/10.4312/as.2016.4.1.115-129

Shinhu Kyokai Mission. n.d. 'Shinshu Kyokai Mission'. http://www.shinshukyokai.org/ last accessed 17 August 2022.

Simpkins, Sara Anne and Myers-Coffman, Katherine. 2017. 'Continuing Bonds in the Body: Body Memory and Experiencing the Loss of a Caregiver during Adolescence', *American Journal of Dance Therapy* 39(2): 189–208. https://doi.org/10.1007/s10465-017-9260-6

Smith, Robert John. 1974. *Ancestor Worship in Contemporary Japan*. Stanford, CA: Stanford University Press.

Tatsuguchi, Yoshiko and Lois A. Suzuki. 1985. *Shinshu Kyokai Mission of Hawaii 1914–1984: A Legacy of Seventy Years*. Honolulu: University of Hawai'i Press.

Van Zile, Judy. 1982. *Japanese Bon Dance in Hawaii*. Kalilua, Hawaii: Press Pacifica.

Wada, Julia Y., Pogosian, Barbara, Sato, Yumi and Grivetti, Louis E. 1999. 'Japanese Festival Foods', *Ecology of Food and Nutrition* 38(4): 307–350. https://doi.org/10.1080/03670244.1999.9991584

Waseda, Minako. 2005. 'Extraordinary Circumstances, Exceptional Practices: Music in Japanese American Concentration Camps', *Journal of Asian American Studies* 8(2): 171–209. https://history.msu.edu/files/2010/04/Minako-Waseda1.pdf last accessed 14 July 2022.

Waseda, Minako. 2008. 'The Formation of Bon Dance Repertoire in Japanese Diasporas: A Comparative Study of Hawai'i and Southern California'. https://www.musicology-japan.org/publish/v56/Waseda_e.pdf

Wong, Yutian (ed.). 2016. *Contemporary Directions in Asian American Dance*. Madison: University of Wisconsin Press.

**Candi K. Cann** received her PhD and AM degrees from Harvard University following an MA from the University of Hawai'i. She currently works in the Baylor Interdisciplinary Core at Baylor University, Texas. Her research focuses on death and dying, and the impact of remembering (and forgetting) in shaping how lives are recalled, remembered and celebrated. She is author of four books and is a 2023 Fulbright Scholar in South Korea.

## Chapter 2

# Egungun – Moving the Masks of Our Ancestors

OLU TAIWO

There is an African proverb that states – and I paraphrase here – when you are young and you fall down, at the moment you get up, look to the future and remain positive. On the contrary, when you are older and you rise from your fall, you should look to the past and reflect on what you have learnt.

There is profound wisdom in this proverb at many levels of human operation. At a personal level, one such operation can be seen when we are learning something new: the moment we fall and fail, it is important to continue looking to the future. However, as soon as we start to get accomplished and our skill level increases, when we fail, progress is best served by reflecting on what we can learn from our mistakes.

At the level of our current transcultural experience, where contemporary culture is being reshaped by the expression and dissemination of untold stories, we can draw an analogy between this proverb and the wider culture, examples being

1. The renewed self-confidence that is now exuding from cultures whose ancestry has an ancient past, whilst still being active in the present; whose stories were altered by the explicit agendas of white-supremacists who controlled authorship.
2. Also, cultures whose past has been truncated by:
    - alien abduction – their people being stolen or sold into slavery by another culture and stripped of their identity;

- cultural diaspora and the appropriation as well as the reinterpretation of a parent culture;
- futurists and post-humanists who wish to separate from the past and start anew.

The outpouring of human consciousness via the internet has moved at an astonishing rate. It has revealed previously untold stories from suppressed cultures who once needed the permission of their neo-colonial overlords for validation. Using social media platforms, they are able to publish and author a counter-narrative and share it with the world, on their own terms, with their own agenda, perspective and set of existential assumptions.

From an African perspective, and from my perspective as a man of African heritage, we consider the age and experience of humanity through a long lens, spanning the millennia. Ancient African, Sumerian and Sanskrit based cultures are the elders of humanity. Their patterns of behaviour are encoded in their cultural practices such as ritual or theatre. On the other hand we have cultures truncated by alien abduction, via the slave trade – people who have been torn from their roots and gas-lighted to believe that they are inferior and that their history started at being enslaved; and through ethnic diasporas, with appropriation and reinterpretation of culture as a way to anchor oneself, to root one's sense of identity in the past (despite its inherent dangers of becoming rigid and dogmatic). The last of the three examples included in point 2 of the transcultural experience noted above, are the futurists and post-humanists who seek to redesign the nature of human interaction through digital technology and embodied knowledge. The first part of the proverb may apply to them as they are young and new to the game of pattern recognition that has developed over aeons of time. It is in their nature to always look forward after getting up from a fall.

As I mentioned earlier, we can see patterns of behaviour that are encoded in ritual/theatre. These serve as poetic shortcuts to layers of understanding accomplished by deep contemplation. One such ritual practice associated with the Yoruba culture is the dance of Egungun; which, in praxis, has multiple functions and meanings, from ancestor worship to providing routes to the expression of great symbolic power. According to Henry John Drewal, Egungun refers 'to any masquerade or masked figure. At the basis of this definition is the belief in the presence of some supernatural force. As the Yoruba art historian Rowland Abiodun has suggested, the term Egungun in its essence, refers to "power concealed"' (Drewal 2023: 1).

'Power concealed' is an interesting concept with regard to the Yoruba's traditional ancient relationship to temporal existence, which includes the world of the living (present moment), ancestors (past) and the unborn (future). This apparent sequential arrangement from a Western point of view is conceived as teleological, requiring a beginning, middle and end point. However, when we consider the concept of 'power concealed' from a Yoruba position, we see a cyclical coexistent relationship. As Wole Soyinka explains, 'continuity for the Yoruba operates both through the cyclic concept of time and the animist interfusion of all matter and consciousness' (Soyinka 1993: 30).

This then is the presumption of existence that contextualises the position the Egungun performer will perform in. Death in this context is not the end resulting at a point of finality, but a place of transition, a place where different phases of reality cross and coexist. Before I expand on the traditional Yoruba worldview, I will recount an experience of a performance at the Edinburgh Festival.

## THE COVENANT

Anyone who has performed at the Edinburgh Fringe Festival in Scotland, would know that each company is in a race to compete for the attention of the festival's public. The Imule Theatre Company, which I was part of, took two plays to the 1991 festival: a ritualised version of *Romeo and Juliet*, and our newly devised play *The Covenant*, based on the Yoruba creation myth. The play was conceived by the company members with the final script written by Dr David Evans. I served as a principal performer and choreographer, as well as contributing to the development of the mythical, poetic and physical content. As part of our play, we built our own Egungun (Image 2.1).

The performance provided a comprehensive account of a version of the Yoruba creation myth. However, the part of the play that I want to focus on, for the purpose of this chapter, concerns the myth that poetically explains how death came to be, the importance of which was made evident in the structure of our performance.

Our play started and ended with the Egungun, interacting with the audience as is traditional. This was a continuation of the street theatre performance which we had used as publicity the previous day in Princes Street, Edinburgh, one of the city's main thoroughfares where tourists and locals alike would see us. It was fortuitous that another group from

Oxford brought Wole Soyinka's 1975 play *Death and the King's Horseman* to Edinburgh; this play is based on an actual event that took place in Nigeria in 1946, when colonial authorities prevented the Yoruba king's horseman, Elesin Oba, from committing dutiful ritual suicide following the death of his king. In Yoruba myth, the world can only continue on if each newly deceased king is joined by his men in the afterlife, and to prevent this from happening has major consequences for the continuation of the Yoruba nation.

**Image 2.1** Egungun. © Miguel Lacerd, Adeyinka 2022.

So, before playing at the festival, the Oxford group also went to Princes Street where they had two Egungun costumes worn by characters from Soyinka's play – Jane and Simon Pilkings. In the play's context, Simon Pilkings , a district officer in Nigeria, confiscates ritual outfits from a traditional performance group who are dancing in celebration of the death of the king. The Pilkings use the costumes to attend a fancy dress event in their district in honour of a visiting English prince.

With both groups in that part of the city, there was a moment of seren-dipity when all three Egunguns terrorised car drivers and pedestrians up and down Princes Street, with yours truly playing a talking drum and oth-ers handing out leaflets. This was also a moment of irony, with the chaos of a simulated Yoruba ritual in the heart of modern-day Edinburgh, which mirrored Soyinka's exploration in his play, where Elesin, rather than being prevented from doing his duty by colonial authorities, himself gets dis-tracted. Thus the blame is placed on the king's horseman and the focus is not on colonialism but on the notion of duty. The mirrored juxtaposition in Princes Street highlighted the mythic and historic clash of cultures, and the consequences of being distracted by worldly desires.

We wanted our play to start and end within the liminal space of ritual celebration, observing the dance of the ancestor beyond death. The play was in two parts with the first performed with Orunmila (Orisha/divin-ity of the oracle) narrating the mythopoetic story of creation, along with Ogun (Orisha of war and creativity), Oya (Orisha of tornadoes and cemeter-ies; who is the mother of Egungun) and Orisha-nla (Orisha for the creation of the sky and humanity). They each contributed to the chorus movement, metaphorically representing the creative force in movement form. This culminated in a harmonious balance between the Orishas and humanity – between the created and the creations of the created.

The second part was based on the myth of how death came to be. This section had a *commedia dell'arte* feel in the way we presented the narrative of the downfall of mankind. Ultimately the Creator stopped direct access between the created and the creations of the created. I will explain below.

## MYTHOLOGICAL STRUCTURE OF THE YORUBA PANTHEON

Before we start, we need to consider the mythological structure of the Yoruba pantheon as a metaphor for spiritual wholeness. Contrary to the 'Pagan' label given to us by the British colonial overlords, we Yoruba believe in one supreme deity called Olodumare (the Creator). It is said that it is impossible to approach the supreme deity with our limited per-ception; which is already a precis, a summary of reality concerning the out-there-ness of the external world. However, if Olodumare is equated metaphorically to a palace whose presence and boundaries are ubiquitous and undetermined, then the different rooms in the palace equate to many divinities aka Orishas (the created) that are responsible for the smooth run-ning of this ubiquitous palace. Within *The Covenant*, as mentioned above, we used four of these rooms: Orunmila, Ogun, Oya and Orisha-nla. In this mythopoetic landscape, the various stories, parables and proverbs serve as a metaphorical map providing formulas for understanding how our ancient Yoruba psyche operates. One such story conceives of how death came to be, resulting from a similar hubris in humanity as that exemplified in Soyinka's play *Death and the King's Horseman*.

## HEAVEN AND EARTH SEPARATED BY DEATH

After the creations of the created were complete, the newly created humans could freely enter heaven and the Orishas could come down and commune with their human creations. There was however an incident, which angered Olodumare so much that the Creator separated heaven and earth. Humans (aka the creations of the created), revealed to Olodumare that they had developed a careless disregard for the sacred order and cleanliness of heaven. The Supreme being therefore split heaven and earth. Human beings experienced for the first time the pain and loss that comes with this existential separation, resulting from the isolation created by restriction of their direct contact with heaven. Olodumare created a chthonic gap between heaven and earth, regulated by death; all due to the fact that humans had disrespected their easy access into heaven.

In the transmission of the narrative, the myth is careful not to stipulate the specific offensive action, so that each generation can fill in the act, contextualised by their values. Some say that a human who went up to heaven drank too much of the sacred palm wine and threw up there; some say that a human being went up to heaven and stole something important disturbing the sacred order. Whatever it was, humans as a whole lost the right to casually visit heaven whilst they were alive, leaving them forever doomed to seek out the meaning of existence without unnecessary distraction. The only way that humans could gain direct access to heaven would be through death and passing through the veil of forgetfulness – which would disinfect the person of offending behaviour and prevent this passing into heaven. However, notwithstanding these restrictions, faint shadows lingered in our memories, of an innocence that was lost, haunting our imaginative world in our mythopoetic landscapes and giving us feelings of bliss and completeness.

The performance of the Egungun is one such gateway reminder, drawing our attention to the fact that linear time is a model and not a reality. We are reminded that the world of the living coexists with the worlds of both the ancestors and the unborn. We are reminded that we can gain fleeting glimpses of the divine through dancing in resonance with specific rhythms played on the drums.

On their part, the Orishas, through no fault of their own, lost the right to cavort with humans and visit earth directly. Heaven was now blocked from earth by a thick blanket of primordial swamp, full of unformed life-forms and labyrinthine pathways. The Orishas thus lost the direct nourishment that came from the pure worship given to them by their human creations. Desperate, the Orishas plotted to go behind the Supreme being's back and cut a pathway in secret, from heaven to earth through this primordial swamp. With Orish-nla's leadership and Ogun's power and technical know-how, they succeeded in creating their own path to return to earth. The metaphorical implication of this myth is that if we submit to the moment when dancing to the rhythms of the divine (the divine who has been knocking on our internal door constantly, even though the Orishas may seem distant), they will cross the primordial swamp to us. Impartial improvisation, then, not only permits the performer a living dialogue with the other performers in the event, but also serves as a hot line to the divine. Entrance to the chthonic realms must be randomly generated, either through the use of a chance procedure (a random generator, or binary system where there are only two possible outcomes) or trance-induced improvision. Ritual expression through the Golden Triangle of song/story, rhythm/music and dance/movement – underpinned by a sense of the theatrical – can bridge the dimensions of our ancestors (the past), the living (the present) and the unborn (the future).

> The work of improvisation is often immediate and spontaneous because of the multilogics of performance and the interrelationships between performers and between the various performative genres – drumming, singing, dancing. (Drewal 1992: 7)

This expression is achieved by inviting individuals to partake in the improvisational play around a language of performative forms. This is cultural co-creation taking place in temporal space and contextualised within the context of the living community.

## IFA DIVINATION: THE DIVINE GUIDE

In 2017, after attending the winter solstice at Stonehenge, I contemplated on the forgotten memories of our monuments that marked our passage around the Sun, from the perspective of my Yoruba ancestors. Nabta Playa in Africa, the world's first astronomical site in the Nubian Desert, pre-dates the building of Stonehenge, being a 7,000-year-old stone circle that tracks the summer solstice amongst other things. While these megalithic structures are UNESCO World Heritage Sites, the UNESCO listing also includes instances of intangible culture.

In 2008, the Ifa divination system of the Yoruba, which employs a body of poetic texts and mathematical algorithms as part of its structure, was inscribed by UNESCO on the list of Intangible Cultural Heritage of Humanity. This significant global acknowledgement of the value of this particular African knowledge heritage has sparked considerable interest. Ifa refers to the mystical oracle called Orunmila, regarded by the Yoruba as an avatar or divinity of wisdom. He is widely regarded as the originator of the Ifa divination system. With his system of divination, he is able to provide a way to communicate with the Creator's unified matrix.

With the relatively recent international recognition of the Ifa divination system, there have been debates surrounding the creative legacies and collaborative practices resulting from the cultural heritage of the Yoruba people and their connection to the divine through the divination practice of Ifa. In this age of virtual reality and artificial intelligence, the Yoruba's mythopoeic cultural landscape is in danger of being obscured by the fog of Hollywood's mythic reconstruction of African historical origins. The first *Black Panther* movie (2018) both reveals and submerges African-American history; it is as though after abducting and snatching the Africans from their roots, their ancestral past is wrapped in a fantasy. In addition, the film repurposes the political potency of the Black Panther movement from reality to fantasy; a movement that was vilified by the US government and some of its people. Interestingly, after the tragic death of the movie's actor Chadwick Boseman, the fantasy sequel titled *Black Panther: Wakanda Forever* (2022), confronted the transitory concept of death as a gateway to the world of the ancestors. We, the audience, experience both the sense of loss and grief that comes with the sudden death of someone, and the sense of renewal and continuity for those who remain anchored in the world of the living.

Representations of strong black African role models are important, whether real or virtual; however, this should not be at the expense of our actual ancestral heritage. Via current archaeological research, we are witnessing our reinstallation in our rightful historical place in the global story, while we are also being digitally edited back into history. It is crucial that this heritage be reclaimed and retold, as a counterpoint to the digitised hegemony of Westernised narratives, which have intentionally marginalised our stories, while still propagating false information and assumptions about Sub-Saharan histories, cultures and origins.

## PLAY AND IMPROVISATION

When the Egungun performs, it is spontaneous. It responds to the environment as a series of relatives: brothers, sisters, aunties, uncles. The performing Egungun responds to the Ashé (Chi) inherent in all things, in all spaces. In performing this duet, it interacts with temporal space and the ancestors; it plays and responds to internal feelings as well as to things and beings in the immediate environment.

> The agency of performers is implicit in the Yoruba concept of power known as Ashe .... Ashe has no moral connotations; it is neither good nor bad. Rather, it is a generative force or potential present in all things – rocks, hills, streams, mountains, plants, animals, ancestors, deities – and in utterances – prayers, songs, curses, and even everyday speech. Ashe is the power of transformation. Humans possess this generative force and through education, initiation, and experience learn to manipulate it to enhance their own lives and the lives of those around them. (Drewal 1992: 27)

The power of improvisation here, then, is more than just the ability to generate movement phrases and ideas; it is the ability to dialogue with the live moment. It involves

> [m]oment-to-moment manoeuvring based on acquired in-body techniques to achieve a particular effect and/or style of performance. In improvisation, each move is contingent on a previous move and in some measure influences the one that follows. Improvisation requires a mastery of the logic of action and in-body ... together with the skill to intervene in them and transform them .... Each performance each time, is generated anew. (Drewal 1992: 7)

## CONCLUDING WORDS

The Egungun represents the ever-present phenomenon of ancestors in our lives. The nature of the ritual is performative and improvisational around a set of movement phrases and forms. The Egungun embodies the spirit of play and improvisation as it interacts with a participant audience. There are usually a number of masquerade protectors with sticks that they use to clear a path for the moving ancestor. Death is not the final act in this cultural practice, but denotes the end of one phase and the beginning of another.

## BIBLIOGRAPHY

Drewal, Henry John. 2023. 'The Arts of Egungun among Yoruba Peoples', *African Arts* 11(3): 18–98. https://doi.org/10.2307/3335409

Drewal, Margaret Thompson. 1992. *Yoruba Ritual*. Indianapolis: Indiana University Press.

Gilroy, Paul. 1993. *The Black Atlantic*. London: Verso.

Soyinka, Wole. 1993. *Art Dialogue and Outrage*. London: Methuen.

Wenger, Susanne and Chesi, Gert. 1983. *A Life with the Gods in Their Yoruba Homeland*. Woergl: Perlinger.

**Olu Taiwo** is Senior Lecturer in Physical Theatre, Acting and Movement at the University of Winchester. He has a background in fine art, street performance art, African percussion and various martial arts. He has performed nationally and internationally and given lecture demonstrations promoting concepts surrounding practice as research, including how practice explores relationships between 'effort' and 'performative action'.

Chapter 3

# Death in Sight: Confronting Mortality in Contemporary Art

## CELIA GRACE KENNY

*The eye is not satisfied with seeing*
*nor the ear filled with hearing*
Ecclesiastes 1:8b

*Endless invention, endless experiment,*
*Brings knowledge of speech, but not of silence*
T.S. Eliot

In the broadest sense, the topic of this chapter is the contribution of visual art to the way we *see* human mortality. More specifically, my focus is on vanitas art, in which the content is imbued with a symbolic vocabulary intended as a reminder of the transience of all material things, and the brevity of life itself. The chapter will be developed through three sections. In the first, I offer a description – rather than a definition – of vanitas. If a definition offers closure, then a description leaves open the possibility that we might continue to add to our understanding of the genre in question. This will become important as I introduce contemporary paintings and photographs which, while they do not necessarily share the historic symbols used by early vanitas painters, nevertheless have the capacity to expand our awareness of human mortality.

With reference to paintings from the sixteenth and seventeenth centuries, I look closely at some of the symbolic elements, interpreting them in terms of the political, social and religious tensions of the time. I will show that vanitas art of that period was both constructed and received as a vehicle for the dissemination of religious and moral messages in relation to the brevity of life, the fleeting quality of material and sensual pleasure, and the inevitability of death.

In the second section, my concern is with the idea of continuity/discontinuity in the vanitas art of the twenty-first century. I will argue that the waning of ecclesiastical authority and loss of widespread belief in a three-tiered cosmology of Heaven, Hell and Earth, have ushered in a new landscape of the imagination. The contours of Earth have taken on compelling significance in what I will go on to describe as the intensification of immanence. As a result, the contemporary artist, like the theologian and the philosopher, is inclined to confront human mortality absent of metaphysical props or notions of transcendence in the religious sense.

Moving from vanitas in broad brush stroke, through the discontinuities brought about by the new cosmology, I conclude, in the third part of the chapter, with a close look at the work of Philip Braham, a contemporary Scottish artist and philosopher. I have chosen Braham's work because of its eloquence, but also because of the explicit nature of one of his collections, which he has called *Suicide Notes*. These are photographic images of the places where a number of individuals chose to end their lives.

## VANITAS ART IN HISTORICAL CONTEXT

I begin by analysing a painting executed in the context of seventeenth century Netherlands, a time and a place riven by complex social and political change. In terms of religion, there was tension brought on by the splintering of church unity in the wake of the Reformation. Politically, the Dutch had fought for their freedom from Spanish rule, establishing the Dutch Republic as a Protestant state. Culturally, increasing urbanisation in northern Europe and the expansion of trade centres resulted in the creation of wealth and a desire to amass personal wealth. In the world of the artist, a turn to the secular – in the sense of the pull of the material world – had resulted in a move away from traditional religious art. Iconoclasm and the loss of church patronage forced painters to turn their eye and their hand to a new style of representation.

In that period of transition and uncertainty, it was natural for people from all backgrounds to reflect at many levels on the transience of material things and the fleeting quality of human life. Vanitas art emerged as an expression of existential doubts coupled by the fear induced by church-led belief in Heaven, Purgatory and Hell. It was a form of art which transformed the familiar genre of still-life painting through the introduction of a symbolic vocabulary that was explicit in its allusions to death, the dangers of materialism, and a re-awakened belief in the pre-Socratic dictum that man is the measure of all things (Protagoras of Abdera, fifth century).

The elements of a vanitas painting typically include: fruit, flowers, books, wine, things of aesthetic beauty such as richly embroidered tapestry, gilded bowls and elaborate candlesticks. The arrangements of these objects in typical vanitas art appears at first sight to be indicative of the still-life genre from a number of eras and cultures. The vanitas artist, however, worked with a religious/moral message in mind, intending the paintings to function as a warning of the ultimate futility of material wealth in the context of human mortality.

Even as the hand of the painter draws the eye to objects of beauty, cultural richness and scientific interest, there is a simultaneous jolt to the moral sensibility of the viewer through the deliberate inclusion of symbols of death and decay. A bowl heavily laden with sumptuous fruit is seen, on closer inspection, to be worm-infested; an hourglass is placed close to a young face in a wordless reminder that youth and beauty pass. Less subtle, perhaps, is the inclusion of the representation of a human skull stripped of all flesh, intended as a visual rendering of the biblical message from which vanitas art takes its name: 'vanity, vanity, all is vanity' (Ecclesiastes 1:2). Death lies in wait for rich and poor, earthly power is short-lived, and the pleasures of the flesh are fleeting attempts to deny the finality of human mortality. Examples will illustrate these points.

From 1550 to 1650, centred on the Dutch city of Leiden – a Protestant stronghold – there arose developments in the genre of still-life painting that came to be known as vanitas art. For our purpose here, two characteristics of vanitas painting are worth noting. The first concerns the intention of the artists; that is, the message that they set out to convey through the medium of paint. The second concerns the fact that the range of symbolic artefacts employed by the artists was understood to carry theological and political meaning in the context of the rapidly changing social and religious environment of Europe. Vanitas art was received, by both the ecclesiastical hierarchy and their 'flocks', as visual warnings of the dangers that ensue from church disunity, the waning of ecclesiastical authority, and secularisation.

Hans Holbein the younger worked in sixteenth century Basle and later in London. In the wake of the Reformation throughout Europe, church commissions began to dry up and waves of iconoclasm oversaw the destruction of much religious art. Like many others, Holbein turned to portrait painting in what seemed to be a less overtly religious option. Holbein was Roman Catholic, but he accepted commissions from Humanists and Protestants. *The Ambassadors* was painted in 1533 (Image 3.1) and it offers a wealth of symbolism and a visual record of the religious and political context from which vanitas art emerged. The figures have been identified as Jean de Dinteville, a diplomat and George de Selve, bishop of Lavour. De Dinteville (left) is clothed in sumptuous robes trimmed with lynx, and De Selve (right) is in cleric's vestments. A close-up of De Selve's robe, however, reveals an elaborately woven cloth with a lining of fur. Was this Holbein's observation that the desire for material wealth was shared by the ambassadors of both church and state?

**Image 3.1** Hans Holbein the Younger, *The Ambassadors* (1533). National Gallery of London. https://commons.wikimedia.org/wiki/Category:The_Ambassadors_ (Holbein)#/media/File:Hans_Holbein_the_Younger_-_The_Ambassadors_-_Google_ Art_Project.jpg

If we move our gaze from the men to their immediate surroundings, what we see is a selection of typical vanitas symbolic objects: a type of sundial, indicating the measurement of time; two globes, one astrological and one planetary, signifying the increasing ability of science to measure both sacred and secular space. Note the lute with a broken string, which might well be indicative of the discord in the church, as it continued to be riven by the split between traditionalists and reformers. An arithmetic textbook, opened at a lesson on division might also be put there to suggest political and social fractures. And then, in the top left of the painting, the merest glimpse of a crucifix, as if to proclaim that the central message of Christianity has been almost obscured by these powerful male individuals, by their power, their wealth, and the instruments through which they felt assured that man was becoming god-like in his understanding and control of the natural world.

Finally, and most important for our purpose, is the presence of two skulls. One tiny one on de Dinteville's hatband and, in the foreground, an anamorphic representation of a skull: an image which only becomes recognisable when looked at from an oblique angle; it is a *memento mori*, remember you are going to die. So, here, in Holbein's painting, *The Ambassadors*, is a classic example of traditional vanitas art. The message is that it is not fine robes, political power or church authority that marks us out as being distinctly human. It is, ultimately, the awareness that to be human is to be mortal.

I turn to another example of seventeenth century vanitas art, a painting by Georges de la Tour, a French artist who was much influenced by the Italian painter, Caravaggio. The painting in question is called *The Penitent Magdalen*, probably finished in 1640 (Image 3.2). Given what has been said already about the typical content of vanitas paintings, the eye will no doubt be drawn to the mirror, the lit candle and, of course, the skull. Let's look more closely at the choice of subject, the arrangement of objects and the technique which the artist employed.

The subject is a biblical figure: Mary of Magdala, prominent in the story of the life and death of Jesus of Nazareth. According to the biblical narrative, Mary was one of the first disciples to encounter the risen Christ. The posture of the Magdalen is reflective, hence the symbol of the mirror. She appears penitent, which may be why she is seen to have removed her pearls (they are lying on the table): the translucence of a pearl is associated with vanity when it adorns a female neck. Reflective and penitent, Mary is also depicted as grieving, as she rests her folded, prayerful hands on a skull.

**Image 3.2** Georges de la Tour, *The Penitent Magdalen* (1640). Metropolitan Museum of New York. https://commons.wikimedia.org/wiki/File:The_Penitent_Magdalen_MET_DT7252.jpg

I would suggest that, given Mary's significance in religious history, the skull in this painting is more than a symbol of mortality in general. Placed on the lap of Mary the disciple, the skull would resonate with the Christian viewer as a signal of resurrection hope; the belief that Jesus, although man, was not confined by mortality. Even in these splintered church times, this was a tenet shared by both traditionalists and reformers. If seeing is believing, then de la Tour managed to combine the wistfulness of regret, an acknowledgment of the futility of pretty decoration, and an awful reminder that the skull is but a temporary holding place for the mind's experience of hope and longing.

### Vanity and Meaninglessness

At this point, let me go more deeply into the etymology of the term *vanitas*, so as to disrupt the most common translation of the word in relation to its roots. The various phrases associated with the folly and hubris of vanitas can be traced back to the biblical book of Ecclesiastes, found in what Christians call the Old Testament, written in Hebrew as opposed to the Greek of the New Testament. During the fourth and fifth centuries BCE, a Latin version of the bible, said to be overseen by St Jerome, came into circulation through the Latin-speaking Western church, becoming known and widely used as the Vulgate (common version) of the bible. It is through the Latin language, therefore, that the translation of the phrases involving *vanitas* have come to be understood in the English language as 'vanity of vanities'.

Behind the Latin translation, however, stands a Hebrew word transliterated as *hebel*. My contention is that the Hebrew metaphor of *hebel*, as it was used in the book of Ecclesiastes, offers a vital clue in understanding the distinction between the aims and objectives of seventeenth century vanitas art and the role of contemporary artists who set out to heighten our sensitivity and awareness of the conjunction of mortality and desire.

## Hebel in the Preaching of Qoheleth

The biblical book of Ecclesiastes is bound up with the name of Qoheleth the preacher. It is a point of contention as to whether Qoheleth was a character dreamed up by the compilers of Ecclesiastes, the author of the work itself, or a schema used to rework cultural material found elsewhere. I may safely leave the fine points of these deliberations to biblical scholars, since my concern, in the context of this chapter, is with the fact that the term *hebel* was put into the mouth of Qoheleth, who returned again and again to the significance of this metaphor in his deliberations about human nature, the limitations of knowledge, and the place of death within the purpose of a human life.

*Hebel*, in wider usage in the time that Ecclesiastes was written, was suggestive of the lightness of air. Stuart Weeks points out that, in post-biblical usage, 'the word, or its Aramaic cognate, is used of breath, vapour … [or] hot air' (2014: 105). Weeks points out that *hebel* has no equivalent established metaphor in English. He claims, however, that 'the idea of an illusion … and of corresponding human delusion, comes close to catching the sense of *hebel* in Ecclesiastes …' (Weeks 2014: 119). Staying with the idea of illusion/delusion, let me expand on the way that Qoheleth contextualises this objective/subjective dualism within the notion of time.

Arguably the best-known section of Ecclesiastes is chapter three. Used frequently in funeral services, this poetic interlude draws attention to what the Greeks understood as *chronos* and *kairos*. That is, the idea that, within the chronology of the passing of human lives, there are specific *kairos* moments, which do not lend themselves to measurement by sundial or clock. In the words of Qoheleth, 'for everything there is a season and a time for every matter under the sun ... a time to be born, and a time to die ... [God] has put a sense of past and future ... yet [humans] cannot find out what God has done from the beginning to the end' (Ecc 3:11).

This brief consideration of the concept of *hebel* allows me to return to my earlier claim that sixteenth and seventeenth century vanitas art was both constructed and received as a vehicle for the dissemination of religious and moral messages in relation to the brevity of life, the fleeting quality of material and sensual pleasure, and the inevitability of death. In Holbein, and de la Tour, we see clear examples of the symbols commonly employed to convey the attraction of wealth, the pride of grandeur and the stark fact that death is, indeed, the leveller.

## AFTER METAPHYSICS

It is important to remember that seventeenth century vanitas paintings were created, disseminated and interpreted against the three-tiered cosmology – Heaven, Purgatory and Hell – which informed church debates of the time. At the most obvious level, vanitas artists set out to convey a moral message: a warning that it is not fine robes, political power or church authority that mark us out as being distinctive in our creaturehood. More fundamentally, the subject matter of these artists, expressed through a recognisable symbolic vocabulary, invites us to confront the underlying fear which gives rise to *all* forms of materialism: that is, the stark reality that we are mortal. It is the comprehension – and apprehension – of our own death that provokes the desire for union with (or power over) others while we are alive, and the equally compelling wish to leave a mark that will remain when we are gone.

Vanitas art was certainly driven, in particular epochs, by a church-led moral agenda. I would contend, however, that the fundamental question which gave rise to this type of art concerns the relationship between the transience of the human and the permanence of the universe. If this is accepted, then the task of the contemporary vanitas artist will be shaped by these things at least: (1) an acceptance that metaphysical props used by theologians of the past have largely lost their persuasion; (2) an acknowledgment that the generations who have been influenced by deep ecology experience their relationship to the earth with a new immediacy, a conviction that our bodies and the body of the earth are inextricably linked and interdependent. In sum, traditional notions of transcendence are giving way to a type of radical immanence, in which human flourishing is re-envisaged as an end in itself, not simply the means by which we placate a figurehead external to the planet, or secure for ourselves a seat in an imagined a-historical time and place. The reality frame has tilted on its axis.

## Shifting the Reality Frame

Writing about the use of metaphors in science, Sally McFague quotes Max Planck, whose name is synonymous with quantum theory: 'new ideas [in science] are not generated by deduction, but by *artistically* creative imagination' (in McFague 1982: 75). This reflects the twentieth century waning of a positivistic view of science (scientism), and the rise of an acceptance that scientists, like artists, envisage the world through the exercise of their analogical imagination. Put differently, art and science, in order to influence the way we *see* things, expand our imagination through the constant reinvention of the models and symbols which represent so-called reality. A model of the universe, a depiction of the landscape, or a photograph of a human face; these images have the capacity to recalibrate the way we understand our place in the scheme of things.

It is noteworthy that our symbolic worlds rest, not only on scientific observation, but on prevailing theological convictions within any given context. Thus, it was that the cosmological theories of Copernicus proved to be revolutionary for both scientists and churchmen; and it might be significant that Copernicus, physician and astronomer, was also a paid canon of the church. In *The Reality Frame*, Brian Clegg reminds us that Copernicus and Galileo, in order to move towards the modern astronomical view, had to detach themselves from the frame of reference of the Earth (2017: 246). Clegg goes on to point out that Copernicus introduced a double shift, both from the limitations of the physical earth, and also a conceptual shift in terms of how we understand the place of humans in the cosmos (2017: 246). It is significant that scholars of many disciplines have recorded their belief that shifts in the reality frame implied in contemporary physics pose challenges for existing theories within their fields (O'Murchu 2017: 29). Crucially, for the artist, the ideas expounded in quantum theory '... describe a new and more profound way of understanding reality, in fact, one known to mystics for thousands of years' (O'Murchu 2017: 29).

Therefore it is that the waning of ecclesiastical authority and loss of widespread belief in a three-tiered cosmology have ushered in a new landscape of the imagination. The contours of Earth have taken on compelling significance in what I have described as the intensification of immanence. As a result, the contemporary artist, like the theologian and the scientist, is inclined to confront human mortality absent of metaphysical props or notions of transcendence in the traditionally religious sense.

## TRANSIENCE AND PERMANENCE IN THE WORK OF PHILIP BRAHAM

Philip Braham is a Scottish artist and philosopher, a graduate of Duncan of Jordanstone College of Art and Design, and recipient of numerous awards including the Royal Scottish Academy Guthrie Award for painting, and the Royal Scottish Academy Morton Award for lens-based work. In 2021, Braham was elected to the Royal Scottish Academy.

Braham's aesthetic sensibility is deeply influenced by a contemplative approach to the effects of light and time on the landscape. Employing both the painter's brush and the photographic lens, his work evokes the contrast between the transience of the human condition and the seeming durability of the earth. Braham's paintings and photographs do not share the historic symbols used by early vanitas painters, nor are they tied to a church-borne moral message. If it is accepted, however, that the concept of vanitas is bound up with the clash of transience and permanence in the experience of the mortal human, it is reasonable to interpret Braham's work as a mode of contemporary vanitas art.

My aim, in this last section of the chapter, is to focus closely on Braham's development of a unique symbolic vocabulary and to describe the way that he employs a range of images to evoke the contrast between transience and permanence; the ephemeral life of the human in relation to the enduring quality of the cosmos. The point has been made that, unlike historical vanitas art, Braham does not include overtly metaphysical or religious symbols in his works. Rather, he relies on the landscape and the power of light to convey the view that the most fundamental characteristic of our experience of reality is the changeability of all things. Nothing abides forever. In Braham's paintings and photographs, we are granted the insight that light and time conceal as much as they reveal. It is, therefore, in the contemplation of the constant flow of things that we might begin to understand mortality. In order to deepen these points – and after many conversations with the artist – I have chosen to focus in depth on two works from Braham's collection, *Suicide Notes*.

In 2010, during the Edinburgh festival, the Royal Scottish Academy exhibited a set of photographs by Braham in which he had documented twenty-one particular sites in Scotland where people had chosen to end their life by suicide. He brought to these images a non-religious spirituality and a sense of the sacrality of the human person. To the uninitiated eye, the series of photographs which make up *Suicide Notes* comes across as a collection of aesthetically pleasing landscape art. For the subjects behind the images, however, the photographs re-present the point at which light became dark and time became eternity. It is my contention that Philip Braham's collection, *Suicide Notes,* brings uniquely into focus the relationship between seeing and death.

In the artist's own words:

The circumstance of our death is rarely chosen. Life drives us on until death inadvertently overtakes us along the way. By exception, those intent on taking their own lives choose where, when and how death will come. The conscious decision to take one's life in the open, before nature, represents a private farewell to the world and an acknowledgement that one is utterly alone in death if not in life. The landscapes here stand as modest monuments to the subjects absent in this series of photographs. (Braham 2015)

**Image 3.3** Philip Braham, *Copse on Gallow Hill, Tealing* (2009). Chromogenic Inkjet on Museo Silver Photo Rag. Reproduced by permission given by the artist, 2023

*Copse on Gallow Hill, Tealing* (2009) (Image 3.3) is a photograph from Braham's 2010 collection, *Suicide Notes*. The artist added, simply, 'A man's body was discovered by the roadside on the outskirts of Tealing in Angus on 15th February 2009. He had shot himself in the head.'

Suicide, and the personal decisions which lead to the act, pose some of the deepest philosophical questions for ethicists, theologians, physicians, lawyers, and those of us who have been personally involved in the anguish that follows this particular type of death. However, it is important to note that, following the logic of this chapter, my intention is to focus on *Suicide Notes* inasmuch as the photographs, themselves, can be interpreted as belonging to the genre of vanitas art, and as they evoke a mindfulness of mortality and the fleeting nature of human life. Accordingly, I will focus on some key elements in Braham's symbolic vocabulary through which he invites us to contemplate the relationship between death and the landscape.

Taken as a whole, the most striking feature of *Copse on Gallow Hill, Tealing* is the snowy barrenness of the land. There is a sense of a cold stillness that is a familiar feature of northern landscapes. The seeming absence of movement almost involves the ear as well as the eye in its powerful suggestion of silence. We are called back to the words of Qoheleth, 'For everything there is a season', for while there appears to be, on the surface, an absence of vitality, we – and the farmer – know that what remains hidden is the seed. The Romanian poet, Lucian Blaga (1968) wrote:

> Glory to seeds, past, present and future
> A thought of strong summer, a great heaven of light
> is hidden in all of them as they sleep.
> Throbbing in the dreams of seeds
> there are fields sighing and gardens at noon,
> wild woods of centuries' nations of leaves
> and the murmur of a people of singers.

Braham, here depicting the paused narrative in the flux of seasonal change, has given us the idea of *dormancy*: the productive sleep of the seed that comes before the restoration of life in a wholly new form. The Christian reader will be struck by the analogy with Christ's death and resurrection. The ecologist will be reminded by an apparently virginal winter field that nature's cycle must be protected if we are to nurture all the lives that are yet to come. The historian might also ponder the inclusion of another powerful symbol which Braham has opted to feature in the frame of this photograph. In the back left, we can see a mound, a small hill which remains as evidence of the activity that gave *Gallow Hill* its name. Here was the scene from which prisoners looked out to catch their last glimpse of the Scottish landscape before they ascended to a death that they, doubtless, did not choose.

**Image 3.4** Philip Braham, *Fallen Tree, Ashkirk* (2009). Chromogenic Inkjet on Museo Silver Photo Rag. Reproduced by permission given by the artist, 2023

Like *Copse on Gallow Hill* (Image 3.3), *Fallen Tree, Ashkirk* (Image 3.4) was photographed at the scene where a suicide took place. Once again, Braham directs our attention to the effect of light and shadow on the materiality of the landscape and here the focus is on trees, those that stand and those that fall. The tree comes with a rich history of symbolic meaning, associated with gatherings both sacred and profane. Tales of forests speak of mystery, danger and the enchantment and be-wilderment of the traveller. Herman Hesse connected the forest with the idea of restless longing:

> A fierce desire to wander and roam tears my heart when I hear trees rustling in the wind in the evening wind ... this longing to travel reveals its seed, its meaning .... It is a longing for home, for the memory of your mother, for new images and parables for life ... every step is a birth, every step is death, every grave is the mother. (2022)

Braham's forest leaves us with a tantalising question: what is more important; the group which remains upright, or the one fallen and already dying back into the ground from which it came? If we recall that Germanic literature often used the idea of the forest to symbolise the ideal society, then the contrast between the majority of the upright and the loneliness of the fallen is bound to evoke in us a sense of compassion.

## CONCLUDING WORDS

So it is that a comparative study of vanitas art past and present reveals, not only the transience of human life, but also the lack of durability of a text in relation to its meaning(s). The work of the artist belongs in the chain of signifiers which inform and express the relationship between death and human desire at any given time.

In the context of this volume as a whole, my focus has been on the sense of vision and the way that our seeing contributes to how we understand human mortality. In the English language, the verb 'to see' conveys both the literal sense of using our eyes, and the metaphorical idea of knowing, comprehending and enlightenment. It is crucial, therefore, that we habitually juxtapose the literal and the metaphoric when we speak of knowledge in relation to death. In other words, the empirical world which unfolds before our eyes is only the forerunner to the continuous work of interpretation, disputation and the flow of human consciousness. Further, it is at the threshold of the rational and the intuitive, where the pull of life meets the certainty of death, that sight might become *insight*.

## BIBLIOGRAPHY

Blaga, Lucian. 1968. *Poemele Luminii Mirabila Samânta*. Trans. R. MacGregor-Hastie. Sibiu, Romania: Pentru Literatura Universala.

Braham, Philip. 2015. *After Absence – Shadows, Echoes and Traces in the Work of Philip Braham*. Beirut: MTA Collection.

Clegg, Brian. 2017. *The Reality Frame: Relativity and Our Place in the Universe*. London: Icon Books Ltd.

Hesse, Hermann. 2022. *Trees: An Anthology of Writings and Paintings*. Trans. Damion Searls. San Diego, CA: Kales Press.

McFague, Sally. 1982. *Metaphorical Theology: Models of God in Religious Language*. London: SCM Fortress Press.

O'Murchu, Diarmuid. 2017. *Incarnation: A New Evolutionary Threshold*. Maryland: Orbis Books.

Weeks, Stuart. 2014. *Ecclesiastes and Scepticism*. London: Bloomsbury.

**Celia Grace Kenny** is a freelance researcher, writer and lecturer in the field of contemporary religion working particularly at the intersection of theology, religion and ethics. She is regularly published in edited collections and academic journals notably in regard to religion, politics and the law, and was appointed honorary lecturer at Queens University Belfast in 2017. Since 2012, she has been visiting lecturer at Trinity College Dublin, Cardiff University and Leuven KU. In 2023, Celia was granted a European Excellence Award by Trinity College Dublin.

Chapter 4

# Images of Death and Their Metamorphosis: From the Grim Reaper to Santa Muerte

KATE KINGSBURY

Death is neither formless nor faceless in material culture or in our minds. Humans, as a way of understanding and dealing with their inevitable mortality and to give a shape to death (life's greatest mystery of all), have long sought to depict death using rich visual representations. This iconography is inextricable from the thanatologies, and the cultures the latter stem from. Via these visual representations of death, humans transmit eschatologies and their ideas around the 'metaphysics of death' (Simmel 2007: 76). Through these images and ideologies, humans not only seek to make sense of death, but they also pursue the quest of mastering their own mortality, and that of others. Moreover, images of death often embody cultural and religious understandings of life.

While all human beings die, understandings of life and death in different cultures are often dissimilar, and even the gender of death varies (see Kingsbury 2020; Welch 2015, 2020). In fact, the same iconography and imagery of death often takes on a new life, meaning different things in different contexts across time and space. In this chapter I explore this phenomenon, through an analysis of how Christian medieval iconography of death morphed in the so-called 'New World' when Spanish clergy took imagery of their grim reaper, a female figure known as 'La Parca', to convert Indigenous peoples to Christianity in Mexico. This resulted in many iterations and new understandings of this iconography. It also impelled spiritual reworkings of death, eventually culminating, in Mexico, in one of the most popular images and folk saints of death in our post-modern era, Santa Muerte (see Image 4.1). She is the female folk saint of death who, as Chesnut details, has about 10–12 million followers (Chesnut 2017: 33). As I describe, the result of this transportation of a visual representation of death was not only new images and icons of death but new understandings of life and death.

**Image 4.1** Santa Muerte statue with scythe. © Kingsbury 2022.

## OF SKULLS AND SKELETONS: A SEMIOTICS OF DEATH

In Christian traditions, since the medieval ages, symbols such as skulls and reapers have rendered palpable and transmittable thanatologies across Europe. These signifiers of death in their depictions of defleshed heads and bodies, do not merely illustrate by association with the deceased corpse, but also seek to relate 'an ontology and a cosmology to an aesthetics and a morality' (Geertz 1973: 127). It is through rituals and ceremonies of various kinds that symbols pertaining to death and the meanings and worldviews they represent have long been disseminated, not just in Christian traditions, but in all cultures.

Humankind has long had a universal desire to understand death, for it comes to us all no matter our race, sexuality, class or creed (or age), yet the semiotics of death are dissimilar across cultures even when the visual representations are similar. Indeed, interestingly when it comes to icons of death, cultures frequently 'recycle symbols used by others and give them a different, possibly opposite meaning' (Henshilwood and d'Errico 2011: 7). From the 'new images [that] are constructed' come the 'new understandings they make possible' (Greenfield and Droogers 2003: 33); in other words these catalyse new representations of death not only epistemologically but also visually. As this chapter will explore, the refashioning of Spanish Catholic death iconography gave rise to syncretic, new visual representations and understandings of death when the image of the Grim Reaper was brought to the so-called New World.

## DEATH IN THE OLD WORLD: THE GRIM REAPER

The Grim Reaper is one of the most well-known European images of death. This image originated during a pandemic not entirely dissimilar to that of Covid-19, that of the Black Death. Yet while during the coronavirus pandemic 6.4 million people died as of 2022, the Black Death killed 25 million in Europe alone (Benedictow 2004). The Black Death, also known as the Pestilence and the bubonic plague, was a deadly disease caused by the bacterium *Yersinia pestis* which decimated European populations from 1346 to 1353 (and beyond). It affected the lymphatic system resulting in swollen lymph nodes, known as buboes (Cohn and Cohn 2003). Upon reaching the lungs, it killed those who had contracted it. It spread from Central Asia to Europe via, akin to Covid-19, people travelling abroad from infected places (Spyrou et al. 2022).

In Europe, at least one-third of the total populace died, hence death and the dying became a familiar presence. This is when, as Guthke notes, death first became represented visually in Europe as the skeletal figure of the Grim Reaper (Guthke 1999: 48; see also Van Marle 1971: 361–363). During this time of mass death, it is said that 'terrifying figures' with scythes were seen lurking around the doors of people's homes, the occupants of which died thereafter from the plague (Bramley 1990: 210). Such reports admixed with the imagination of medieval European painters and sculptors created the Grim Reaper, a personified image of death, where the mysteries of the end of life take on an anthropomorphic appearance that is mapped to certain social, cultural and religious beliefs and practices (Marin-Arrese 1996: 45).

Obviously, the skeletal figure directly portrays the fleshless cadavers that littered *en masse* the streets and graves of Europe at the time of the plague. But many elements of the Grim Reaper derive from cultural and religious European elements. For example, the cowl portrays the vestments that clergy donned when conducting funerals and mortuary rites. The scythe, unlike the direct representations of skeletal bodies and clergy in their robes, is a symbolic aspect of the reaper's familiar figure. In the mythological traditions of Ancient Greece, life was imagined akin to a thread that can be snipped at any moment. In Greek eschatology, it was imagined that three elderly sisters, the Moirai, also known as the Fates, apportioned life and death. Clotho was the Spinner who, holding a distaff, spun the thread of life, entwining light and dark strands. Lachesis, the Apportioner, measured out the cord. Atropos, the oldest, also known as the 'inflexible', or 'she who cannot be turned', wielded a large pair of shears with which she cut the thread of life (Dietrich 1965).

This representation of Atropos merged with the Grim Reaper when the shears became replaced with the scythe. The instrument is also referred to in Revelation 14:14–20 as both a weapon and an instrument of renewal (Canovas 2011: 562). It played a key role in daily life in the Middle Ages. Peasants in fourteenth century Europe used scythes and sickles to reap their harvests. Since the farmers lopped the heads of their crops during harvest, death was imagined as a skeletal person performing a similar action in cutting the thread of life short and collecting the souls of the living. The scythe thus came to comprise an eschatological instrument in Christian theology and iconography.

Churches and graveyards began to be decorated with representations of the Grim Reaper. Indeed, such art even extended to theatrical performances sometimes set in cemeteries, where Catholic clerics had thespians enact a 'danse macabre', a dance of death. One actor would dress as the Grim Reaper while the others, representing people from all walks of society, swayed their bodies. The Grim Reaper approached them one by one, scythe in hand, reaping their soul (Knoll and Oosterwijk 2011).

The genre of the danse macabre became popular, featuring in a range of art and literature during the time. Such imagery also spawned a new style of art, often seen in paintings. Known as *memento mori*, as Kenny notes in the previous chapter, it featured skulls, withering flowers and other symbols associated with death. These depictions were not merely artistic renditions, they served to remind people of the brevity of life, of how death, seen as the negation of life, loomed large. They also represented and spread Christian eschatological ideas. Images of the Grim Reaper not only exemplified the moment one's soul was reaped but embodied Christian notions about death and morality. These ascetic ideas included the notion that the pleasures of life are but vapid and fleeting, as alluded to in Ecclesiastes 1:2, *Vanitas vanitatum, omnia vanitas* – Vanity of vanities, all is vanity, and the phrase once used in the coronation of Popes, *sic transit gloria mundi* – thus pass worldly glories (Knoll and Oosterwijck 2011: 24).

As everything was but fleeting and mere vanitas, images of death such as the Grim Reaper reminded people of the importance of engaging in Christian behaviours for a 'good death' – in Spanish a 'buena muerte' or a 'santa muerte', a holy death. During the time of the plague the Church began to define and collate their beliefs and practices concerning death, dying and the afterlife, into what was known as the *ars moriendi*. This comprised a corpus of Christian writings that provided guidance for the dying and those attending them, including prescribed prayers and recommended behaviours such as confession to ensure this 'good death' and salvation.

In the *ars moriendi* and in general in Christian eschatology, death was seen as the opposite of life, it was an end, a moment of departure and finality wherein one's behaviour in life, as either a sinner, or a good, repentant Christian would determine whether one went to the fiery pits of hell where the devil awaited with other sinners, or one was greeted by God at the pearly gates of heaven.

## REPRESENTATIONS OF DEATH IN THE NEW WORLD

For the Spanish, while death was sometimes depicted as male – as King Death, as I will describe – it was most often a female figure. For example, the Grim Reaper was a feminine figure known as La Parca. The name etymologically derives from the Roman version of the Moirai, the Parcae (Guthke 1999: 20). Spanish representations of death may also largely be female as, unlike in Germanic derived languages where death is masculine, in Latin languages death is a feminine-gender word (Card and Wilson 2006: 87). Whyte suggests that death was depicted as female in Spain because death as the gate to eternal life is always represented together with the Virgin Mary (1977: 79) who served as heavenly advocate or intercessor for sinners on earth, earning her the title 'Queen of Heaven' (McMichael and Wrisley Shelby 2019: 366).

La Parca, as well as other deathly imagery was utilised in the so-called 'New World' by Spanish clergy in a 'similar didactic fashion among the Indigenous peoples of the Americas' as in Europe, to instil catechism (Kingsbury and Chesnut 2020: 199). Both Spanish colonisers and missionaries justified their physical and epistemic acts of genocidal violence by imagining the Indigenous people they met as barbaric savages, whose souls could only be saved by religious conversion to Christianity (Barabas 2000).

Religious representations of Jesus, Mary and various saints, as well as La Parca and other deathly imagery served as pedagogic tools to proselytise Indigenous people and, much as in Europe, to teach them Christian eschatology and the importance of prayer – to Jesus, Mary and the many saints. They were symbols wielded to encourage people to confess and engage in what was considered proper Christian behaviour for *una santa muerte* (a holy death) – that is to say one that led to heaven, not hellfire. The Spanish were not aware of the context within which their images and deathly representations would be re-interpreted and re-envisioned both visually and epistemologically by Indigenous people and how *una santa muerte* would literally become reconfigured as a saint of death.

## IMAGES OF DEATH AS LIFE

Across pre-Hispanic Mexico and its neighbour Guatemala (which were not defined by the boundaries of today), Indigenous peoples including but not limited to the Aztec, the Zapotec, the Maya, the Mixtec and the Tarascans had complex relationships and spiritual praxes related to death deities (Jansen and Pérez Jiménez 2017).

Visually represented in ways not dissimilar to La Parca and other Christian icons of death, myriad skeletal deities featured in pre-Columbian spirituality. They were also anthropomorphic, like the Grim Reaper. For example, Ah Puch, a Mayan death deity, was depicted as a cadaverous person with a skull for a head and protruding skeletal ribs. He presided over Xibalba, the underworld (Rivard 2012). Thus, the Spanish clergy introduced La Parca and other visual cues and anthropomorphic images of death into cultures where somewhat similar anthropomorphic images of death also existed. However, for the Spanish their iconography of death represented finality, the Christian concept of a good sin-free death after a life rich with prayer and free of sin. For Indigenous people, their figures of death represented deities, from Mictecahihuatl to Xonaxi Quecuya, who not only acted as psychopomps taking the dead to the afterlife/next-world but also had the power to gift and 'foment life' (Luján and Sessions 2001: 319); see Image 4.2 for the meshing of Santa Muerte with pre-Columbian imagery.

**Image 4.2** Santa Muerte with Aztec imagery. © Kingsbury 2022.

Unlike the Grim Reaper, some Indigenous female figures of death depicted semi-skeletal goddesses in late pregnancy portraying the fecundity of death as a 'source of life' (Bloch and Parry 1982: 6–7). Death, rather than spelling departure and finality as in Christian theology, was linked across Indigenous mythologies with the regeneration of life, as exemplified in the Mayan ball game, 'an analogy in action of death and rebirth' (Kingsbury and Chesnut 2021: 224). Furst argues that perhaps we should not refer to these figures as 'death gods' since despite appearing similar to the Christian reaper and other Catholic representations of death they were often 'the antithesis of death gods' since they had 'generative and life-sustaining functions' (1982: 207). While some did indeed act as psychopomps, many were associated with fertility, health and well-being.

For example, Lady 9 Grass, known in Mixtec as Iyadzehe Qcuañe, was a Mixtec goddess who was portrayed by Indigenous peoples in the Codex Vienna as a woman with a skull for a face, wearing the colours associated with death, black and white, and a *quechquimitl*, a diamond-shaped woman's garment. Atop her skull sat an elaborate feathered headdress that featured a coronet of skulls at its base. Iyadzehe Qcuañe was the Matron of the Temple of Death. As inherent in her name, she is understood as the 'Power of Death' and keeper of its secrets (Jansen and Pérez Jiménez 2017: 194). She was often depicted with offerings that were given to her by supplicants, such as bundles of plants that included hallucinogen mushrooms, pulque (a fermented-cactus alcohol) as well as offerings of blood which she was portrayed as drinking. In return for these, she ensured fertility and the proper growth of the primary crop, maize.

Many skeletal figures and death deities across pre-Hispanic traditions had life-generative properties deriving from local ontologies wherein bones are like seeds, and generate new life (Jansen and Pérez Jiménez 2017: 220). Life and death were viewed not as polar opposites as in Christian eschatology, but part of a constant flowing cycle of transformation and regeneration. For the Mixtec, and many other pre-Hispanic people in Mexico, life was not the negation of death; rather, their epistemology held that 'life contains within itself the seed of death; death, the fertile, energizing seed of life' (Maffie 1999: X–16). This is evident in the Aztec myth of the journey of Quetzalcoatl into the world of the dead when he robs the bones from which human beings are created.

## NEW VISIONS OF DEATH IN THE NEW WORLD

Humans do not all see the same imagery in the same way. Culture, religion, epoch and context, to name but a few of the many factors, alter our views of the same visual representation. Indigenous peoples saw the newly imported Christian depictions of death in an entirely different manner from Catholic Europeans, from within the framework of their own spiritual and cultural contexts. This included spiritual praxes wherein deathly supernatural figures were appeased for gifts of life, healing and even success in war and politics. This is why some Indigenous groups in Mexico and Guatemala, and even in Argentina and Paraguay, took Christian images of death for supernatural figures and began worshipping them (Perdigón Castañeda 2008: 31–34; see also Chesnut 2017: 48).

For Catholics, death entailed departure, the end, for all except Jesus who triumphed over death on the crucifix salvifically, thus permitting the possibility of redemption for Christians. In the New World, La Parca was seen quite differently by some Indigenous people, who re-envisioned her and saw not Jesus as triumphant, but death. The Spanish introduced a plethora of saints and even saint relics, such as skeletons, that Indigenous peoples observed Spaniards praying to. Some Indigenous people began to venerate the Spanish death icons such as the Grim Reaper, perceiving them as saints and deities, desirous to access death's awesome power of life in accordance with their Indigenous ontologies. This created new visual images and mental perceptions of death.

In Guatemala, a novel depiction of death emerged in the 1650s. It consisted of a male skeleton with a crown atop his skull, holding a scythe like the reaper and wearing a cape. Known as Rey (King) Pascual, he is a syncretic visual and ideological bricolage. He melds the seventeenth century Spanish Franciscan saint Pascual Bailón, introduced to the region by the Spanish, with Maya religion, as well as a popular Spanish depiction of death known as 'King Death'. The latter was a skeletal figure as a monarch replete with crown, and alluded to the idea of death as the ultimate equaliser that ends life for all, in keeping with Christian understandings. We find this figure described in the famous book *Don Quixote* by Cervantes where, in *Las Cortes de la Muerte*, King Death holds court to an audience from all walks of life (Cervantes 1605: part 2, ch 11).

The Spanish friar never went to Guatemala in his lifetime. But in the 1650s, a prominent Maya villager had a vision of him as a skeleton with a crown atop his skull while his village was being wracked by plague, and the deathly apparition is credited with ending this pandemic. The vision reveals the vestiges of Indigenous thanatology in imagining death as life-giving. Since that time, local Maya began to venerate the figure for miracles, especially of healing, despite the Church's insistence that devotees apostatise. Visual representations and altars to the folk saint of death may be found across the region to this day.

In 1754, again there are records of Christian images of death being reworked in keeping with local epistemologies. Curanderos are castigated for turning to paintings of death for healing rituals (Perdigón Castañeda 2008: 31). Indubitably, skeletal imagery was not being seen nor utilised in the ways the Church intended but was being worshipped and used for divination by certain groups of Indigenous people, for which they received cruel punishments. Visual representations of death were asked to intervene in earthly causes, in keeping with pre-Conquest ideals whereby death deities were 'involved in the daily routine of life, birth and death' (Harrington 1988: 32).

In 1797, a colonial document within the archives of the Inquisition entitled 'Concerning the Superstitions of Various Indians from the Town of San Luis de la Paz' mentions Santa Muerte but not in the Christian sense of a holy death. The Chichimec people of the present-day state of Guanajuato were using the name to refer to a figure of death derived from Church representations. Instead of viewing the image as a depiction of finality, at night they would '[assemble] in their chapel to drink peyote until they lose their minds; they light upside-down candles, some of which are black' and '[dance before] a figure of death that they call Santa Muerte ... threatening to whip and burn it if it does not perform a miracle' (Perdigón Castañeda 2008: 21). The clergy punished the 'heretics' and destroyed both the representation of death and the chapel where it was housed.

If one scouts the colonial records and inquisition archives one will find other such references. Veneration of these deathly figures often led to severe punishment from whipping to *auto da fe* (heretic burning). In response to such torture by the Church, devotees of such figures of death went underground. But still records detail, once again in the 1860s, a group of Mestizos Penitentes turning to deathly imagery; this time an image of death in a cart filled with stones, which in Spain was pulled in a re-enactment of Christ's suffering on the procession to Calvary, became a supernatural personification of death referred to as Santa Muerte, and Comadre Sebastiana (Steele 2005).

Centuries passed and it may be that death was being supplicated clandestinely in the privacy of people's homes following years of persecution by the Spanish for such activities, but we can only assume this, as there is no evidence until the 1940s. This is when two Americans and a Mexican anthropologist note a new version of the Grim Reaper being turned to by women in Mexico City, and on the border of Oaxaca and Guerrero. They prayed to this figure known as Santa Muerte, or in English Holy Death, to castigate and return errant husbands (Aguirre Beltran 1958; Lewis 1961; Toor 1947). The earliest image of this new iteration of the Grim Reaper as Santa Muerte features the skeleton dressed in the usual cowl, with the scales of justice in one hand and the globe in the other. She features on a prayer card. Once again, this new syncretic image of death is not a representation of the finality and mysteries of death anthropomorphised, but is seen as having powers, namely of love, in keeping with the Indigenous idea of death being able to breathe new life into things and bring fertility – in this case, to amorous relationships.

## THE IMAGE OF DEATH AS GIVER AND TAKER OF LIFE

By the 1990s, this image of death, known as Santa Muerte, had developed into a multifaceted miracle worker (Kingsbury and Chesnut 2020). At this time, not only prayer cards circulated but small and large-scale effigies of the saint as well as candles with her image on them began to be sold across Mexico, including in Mercado Sonora, the 'witchcraft market' located in the Mexican capital. Resembling the Grim Reaper, these images could be turned to use for any number of favours and miracles. The son of a woman known as Enriqueta Romero, affectionately dubbed Doña Queta, bought one of these statues. Doña Queta and her statue are now legendary among Santa Muerte devotees.

Devotion to death was previously a covert religious folk faith hidden in the shadows. On Day of the Dead 2001, Doña Queta brought the veneration of Holy Death into public light when she decided to place her statue outside and established a street altar in front of her home in Tepito, Mexico City (see Image 4.3). Her public gesture not only encouraged hidden devotees to bring their skeleton saints out of the closet but also led to popularising the faith. The altar quickly became a pilgrimage site for thousands of 'chilangos' (slang for residents of Mexico City) who came to pray to the large statue of death which Doña Queta garbs in wigs of luscious locks and sumptuous dresses, changed every month. Since that time devotion to Santa Muerte has exploded not only across Mexico but across the Americas, even spreading globally as Mexican migrants took their faith with them across borders.

The figure of the Grim Reaper morphed into the folk saint of death through its encounter with Indigenous peoples and their spirituality in the New World. In this context death was perceived as having the power to breathe life into many kinds of ventures, but also to wither life away (Kingsbury 2022) and this catalysed a new image and saint of death. Santa Muerte and her iconography have further morphed with the influence of Santeria, and New Age ideologies (Kingsbury and Chesnut 2021). Statues and candles now feature in myriad hues that are said to correspond to her miraculous powers. White effigies and statues are for help with peace and cleansing, red for petitions of love and passion, black for hexes of vengeance and prayers of protection, blue for aid with academic studies and jobs requiring focus, gold for resolving money issues, yellow for miracles of abundance, green for prayers relating to justice and much more.

**Image 4.3** Doña Queta's altar to Santa Muerte in Tepito. © Kingsbury 2022.

The folk saint still features in her more traditional images and effigies with a scythe in her right hand, just like the Grim Reaper. Sometimes in her left hand she holds the scales of justice, the globe or a translucent orb. However, her iconography is syncretic, and in keeping with Indigenous traditions of the owl as a messenger of death, and death's association with night, the figure is featured with the vespertinal bird. Mictecacihuatl and Mictantecuhtli, the Aztec death deities, are often accompanied by the owl. The K'iche' Maya sacred narrative, the Popol Vuh, states 'and now for the messengers of One and Seven Death' (death deities) 'these messengers of theirs are owls' (in Tedlock 1985: 109). In the Colombino, a Mixtec pictorial, Lady 9 Grass, the death deity already alluded to, is often associated with owls and represented in one image with an arrow decorated with an owl head (Pohl 1994: 79). Moreover, in keeping with the syncretic reconfiguration of the Grim Reaper of death as both saint and psycho-pomp, some effigies of Santa Muerte even feature her wearing an Aztec-style feather headdress. Thus, the image of the Grim Reaper has taken on unexpected significance and new features in the post-colony of Mexico as devotees reconfigure death in novel ways.

## CONCLUDING THOUGHTS

Santa Muerte, a syncretic image of death that comes from the interplay of two cultures, can now be seen on statues, candles, t-shirts, pendants, caps, car stickers or painted on walls across Latin America and even the rest of the globe. The female folk saint is at the centre of the fastest growing new religious movement in the Americas with devotees across the globe. The skeleton saint demonstrates how visual representations of death are never merely direct, static depictions of the end of life but are in perpetuum mobile. They can only be understood from within cultural and religious frameworks, morphing over time and space. When transported into new contexts, images of death may mutate in entirely unexpected ways, generating new understandings not only of death, but also of life.

## BIBLIOGRAPHY

Aguirre Beltrán, Gonzalo. 1958. *Cuijla, esbozo etnográfico de un pueblo negro*. Fondo de Cultura Económica.

Barabas, Alicia M. 2000. 'La construcción del indio como bárbaro: de la etnografía al indigenismo', *Alteridades* 19: 9–20.

Benedictow, Ole Jørgen. 2004. *The Black Death, 1346-1353: The Complete History*. Woodbridge: Boydell & Brewer.

Bloch, Maurice and Parry, Jonathan (eds.). 1982. *Death and the Regeneration of Life*. Combridge: Cambridge University Press.

Bramley, William. 1990. *The Gods of Eden*. New York: Avon Books.

Cánovas, Cristóbal Pagán. 2011. 'The Genesis of the Arrows of Love: Diachronic Conceptual Integration in Greek Mythology', *American Journal of Philology* 132(4): 553–579. https://doi.org/10.1353/ajp.2011.0044

Card, Lorin and Wilson, Freeda. 2006. 'Death-defining Personifications: The Grim Reaper vs. la Grande Faucheuse', *LACUS Forum* 33: 83–93. Linguistic Association of Canada and the United States.

Cervantes, Miguel. 1605 [2018]. *Don Quixote*. Trans. Thomas A. Lathrop. Richmond, Surrey: Alma Classics.

Chesnut, R. Andrew. 2017. *Devoted to Death: Santa Muerte, the Skeleton Saint*. Oxford: Oxford University Press.

Cohn, Samuel K. and Cohn, Samuel K. Jr. 2003. *The Black Death Transformed: Disease and Culture in Early Renaissance Europe*. New York: Pantheon.

Dietrich, Bernard C. 1965. *Death, Fate and the Gods: The Development of a Religious Idea in Greek Popular Belief and in Homer*. London: Athlone Press.

Furst, Jill Leslie. 1982. 'Skeletonization in Mixtec Art: A Re-evaluation'. In Elizabeth H. Boone (ed.), *The Art and Iconography of Late Post-Classic Central Mexico*, pp. 207–225. Washington, DC: Dumbarton Hills.

Geertz, Clifford. 1973. *The Interpretation of Cultures*, Vol. 5019. New York: Basic Books.

Greenfield, Sidney M. and Droogers, Andre. 2003. 'Syncretic Processes and the Definition of New Religions', *Journal of Contemporary Religion* 18(1): 25–36. https://doi.org/10.1080/13537900305495

Guthke, Karl S. 1999. *The Gender of Death: A Cultural History in Art and Literature*. Cambridge: Cambridge University Press.

Harrington, P. 1988. 'Mother of Death, Mother of Rebirth: The Mexican Virgin of Guadalupe', *J Am Acad Relig* 56(1): 25–50. http://doi.org/10.1093/jaarel/LVI.1.25

Henshilwood, Christopher S. and d'Errico, Francesco. 2011. 'Middle Stone Age Engravings and their Significance to the Debate on the Emergence of Symbolic Material Culture', *Homo symbolicus: The Dawn of Language, Imagination and Spirituality*: 75–96. http://doi.org/10.1075/z.168.04hen

Kingsbury, Kate. 2020. 'Death is Women's Work: Santa Muerte, a Folk Saint and Her Female Followers', *International Journal of Latin American Religions* 5: 43–63. https://doi.org/10.1007/s41603-020-00106-2

Kingsbury, Kate. 2022. 'Autoethnography of Holy Death: Belief, Dividuality, and Family in the Study of Santa Muerte', *Journal of Contemporary Ethnography* 51(6): 784–815. https://doi.org/10.1177/08912416221075374

Kingsbury, Kate and Chesnut, R. Andrew. 2020. 'Not just a Narcosaint: Santa Muerte as Matron Saint of the Mexican Drug War', *International Journal of Latin American Religions* 4: 25–47. https://doi.org/10.1007/s41603-020-00095-2

Kingsbury, Kate and Chesnut, R. Andrew. 2021. 'Syncretic Santa Muerte: Holy Death and Religious Bricolage', *Religions* 12(3): 220. https://doi.org/10.3390/rel12030220

Knoll, Stephanie A. and Oosterwijk, Sophie (eds.). 2011. *Mixed Metaphors: The Danse Macabre in Medieval and Early Modern Europe*. Newcastle-upon-Tyne: Cambridge Scholars Publishing.

Jansen, Maarten and Pérez Jiménez, Gabina Aurora. 2017. *Time and the Ancestors: Aztec and Mixtec Ritual Art*. Leiden: Brill.

Lewis, Oscar. 1961. *The Children of Sanchez: Autobiography of a Mexican Family*. New York: Random House.

Luján, L. and Sessions, S. (2001). 'Death Deities'. In David Carrasco (ed.), *The Oxford Encyclopedia of Mesoamerican Cultures: The Civilizations of Mexico and Central America*, pp. 318–320. New York: Oxford University Press.

Maffie, James. 1999. '"The Region of the Fleeting Moment": An Interpretation of Nahuatl Metaphysics in the Era of the Conquest', *Paideusis* 2. http://smu-facweb.smu.ca/~paideusis/volume2/e1n2jm.pdf

Marín-Arrese, Juana I. 1996. 'To Die, to Sleep: A Contrastive Study of Metaphors for Death and Dying in English and Spanish', *Language Sciences* 18(1–2): 37–52. https://doi.org/10.1016/0388-0001(96)00006-X

McMichael, Steven and Wrisley Shelby, Katie. 2019. *Medieval Franciscan Approaches to the Virgin Mary: Mater Misericordiae Sanctissima et Dolorosa.* Leiden: Brill.

Perdigón Castañeda, Katia. 2008. *La Santa Muerte, Protectora de los Hombres.* Conaculta, Mexico: Instituto Nacional de Antropología e Historia.

Pohl, John M.D. 1994. *The Politics of Symbolism in the Mixtec Codices.* Nashville, TN: Vanderbilt University.

Rivard, Jean-Jacques. 2012. 'Cascabeles y ojos del dios maya de la muerte, Ah Puch', *Estudios de Cultura Maya* 5. https://doi.org/10.19130/iifl.ecm.1965.5.663

Simmel, Georg. 2007. 'The Metaphysics of Death', *Theory, Culture & Society* 24(7–8): 72–77. http://doi.org/10.117/0263276407084474

Spyrou, Maria A., Musralina, Lyazzat, Gnecchi Ruscone, Guido A., Kocher, Arthur, Borbone, Pier-Giorgio, Khartanovich, Valeri I., Buzhilova, Alexandra, Djansugurova, Leyla, Bos, Kisten I., Kühnert, Denise, Haak, Wolfgang, Slavin, Philip and Krause, Johanned. 2022. 'The Source of the Black Death in Fourteenth-Century Central Eurasia', *Nature* 606 (7915): 718–724. https://doi.org/10.1038/s41586-022-04800-3

Steele, Thomas J. (ed.). 2005. *The Alabados of New Mexico.* Albuquerque: University of New Mexico Press.

Tedlock, Dennis (trans.). 1985. *Popol Vuh: The Mayan Book of the Dawn of Life.* New York: Simon and Schuster.

Toor, Frances. 1947. *A Treasury of Mexican Folkways; The Customs, Myths, Folklore, Traditions, Beliefs, Fiestas, Dances, and Songs of the Mexican People.* New York: Bonanza Books.

Van Marle, Raimond. 1971. *Iconographie de l'art profane au Moyen-Age et à la Renaissance: et la décoration des demeures*, Vol. 1. New York: Hacker Art Books.

Welch, Christina. 2015. 'Death and the Erotic Woman: The European Gendering of Mortality in Time of Religious Change', *Journal of Gender Studies* 24(4): 399–418. https://doi.org/10.1080/09589236.2014.950557

Welch, Christina. 2020. 'Death in Art and Literature'. In P. Booth and E. Tingle (eds.), *A Companion to Death, Burial and Remembrance in Late Medieval and Early Modern Europe 1300-1700*, pp. 272–299. Leiden: Brill.

Whyte, Florence. 1977. *The Dance of Death in Spain and Catalonia.* New York: Arno Press.

**Kate Kingsbury** obtained her doctorate in anthropology at the University of Oxford. Kingsbury has conducted extensive fieldwork in both Africa and Latin America, specialising in the two titans of religion, Christianity and Islam, in their vernacular forms. Kingsbury is a leading authority on Santa Muerte, being cited in the press, consulted by the media and writing many peer-reviewed papers on the topic. Her current research examines gender, healing, power and death, as she is doing fieldwork with the female followers of the folk saint of death. She is currently Lecturer and Research Associate at the University of British Columbia.

Chapter 5

# Smelling Death: An Olfactory Account of Popular English Funeral Customs, c. 1850–1920

## HELEN FRISBY

'Death is an event of such magnitude in human experience that there is probably no culture on earth that does not ritualise to some degree the deaths of its members' (Classen et al. 1994: 150). Smell is a critical, but hitherto neglected aspect of these funerary rituals both historically and in the present day, working across multiple levels and dimensions of human experiences of death, dying and bereavement. This chapter addresses that scholarly gap, by exploring some of the functions and meanings of olfaction within paraliturgical ('folk') funerary customs in England during the period c. 1850–1920. The main source material for this case study is contemporary antiquarian accounts which either explicitly describe, or at least infer, the elements which would have comprised contemporary funerary smellscapes.

### OLFACTION

Even in terms of its basic physiological operation, olfaction remains the least well understood of all the human senses. What is known, is that molecules of the substance being smelled are drawn into the nasal cavity. Protein receptors located at the top of the nasal cavity pick these molecules up and transmit them to the olfactory bulb (Stoddart 1990: 31).

The olfactory bulb in turn links directly into the oldest parts of the brain (Stoddart 1990: 34) which play a key role in the generation of emotion and memory; hence the ability of smell to 'take one back' instantly and vividly to a place and time. Research into this aspect of smell demonstrates that smells can elicit a person's early memories far more effectively than verbal or visual prompting alone (Willander and Larsson 2006).

To some extent, emotional responses to smell therefore appear to be innate; however, they are also to some degree learned, and therefore subject to cultural conditioning (Stoddart 1990: 138–141). Thus, for this study, the cultural context of Christianity is pertinent. Within the Christian para/liturgical tradition, pleasant and unpleasant smells respectively are believed to embody the presence of otherwise imperceptible benign and/ or malign forces. Moreover, in both their biological and magico-religious respects, smells possess the capacity to *actively* participate in the effects they symbolise; thus, they invite human agency in ritually choreographing traffic between the material world of the living and the intangible realm of the dead (Harvey 2015: 1–2; Jenner 2011: 341; Baum 2013: 325– 326; Reinarz 2014: 26ff; Cuffel et al. 2019). This perceived ability of smell is especially pertinent to the task of restoring order and control at times of bereavement, when the normal spiritual, emotional and social boundaries between the world of the living and that of the dead have broken down.

Three particular mechanisms, operating at once biochemically and magically, for managing the dead may be discerned at work within the funerary rituals discussed here. The first of these are rituals involving olfactory catharsis, in which (in the magico-religious discourse) malign spirits hovering ready to capture the vulnerable newly released soul, and embodied by the foul smell of bodily decomposition, were purged by the counter-application of more agreeable aromas (Corbin 1996: 17–18, 64–65; Stoddart 1990: 121; Reinarz 2014: 25ff; Baum 2013: 328). Alternatively, the foul-smelling spirit of the deceased might itself be felt to require catharsis lest it turn to harm the living. The second olfactory mechanism at work within the funerary rituals discussed below is that of fumigation, in which bad smells – and the spirits embodied therein – were driven away with currents of moving air (Corbin 1996: 94–95; Parkin 2007). A third type of olfactory ritual mechanism discussed below is that of resemblance, in which the malign spirits signified by disagreeable smells were confused and distracted by means of mimicry with similar odours (Baum 2013: 328).

## SMELLSCAPES WITHIN A FUNERARY CONTEXT

Smells also perform important emotional and social functions within a funerary context. Firstly, and most fundamentally, through powerful loops of association – often formed in childhood when these mechanisms are strongest (Willander and Larsson 2006) – they help mark the rites of death as extraordinary occasions set apart from normal life (Classen et al. 1994: 150). Olfaction thus enables the bereaved to confront, repeatedly test, and eventually accept, the reality and finality of events. It is also, as will be seen below, a facilitator for the social bonding necessary in order to navigate and (re)negotiate changed statuses and relationships.

Given the profound nature of these spiritual, social and emotional tasks it performs within a funerary context, smell's relative absence from the history of death, dying and bereavement – indeed from social and cultural history generally (Jenner 2011: 335) – is all the more curious. A partial exception to this is Strange's study, *Death, Grief and Poverty in Britain, 1870-1914*, in which she discusses how the smell of a decaying corpse when washing, dressing and interacting with it prior to the funeral would have emphasised the reality and finality of events to the working-class Victorian bereaved. Strange notes how this encounter would have prompted subjects to engage in the process of negotiating new identities and altered relationships amongst the living and with the deceased (2005: 67, 70ff, 97).

While the smell of the decaying body was indeed a key component of the Victorian and slightly later funerary smellscape, other distinctive smells would also have permeated the funerary experience and some of these are also explored here. I will also intensify Strange's sniffings by engaging with insights to be found in the wider, albeit fragmented academic literature concerning smell from disciplines including micro- and neurobiology – a scientific discourse itself rooted in the historical period under discussion (Corbin 1996: 16ff; Reinarz 2014: 12ff; Jenner 2011: 338ff) – religious studies, social history and social anthropology. This approach does raise certain imaginative and methodological challenges which should be acknowledged. Most obviously, the transitory nature of olfaction necessitates a heavy reliance upon reading between the lines of written sources in order to infer the smells particular ritual practices might have evoked – and doing so, furthermore, within one's own later-modern, relatively deodorised world. To then convey these smells effectively via the visual medium of the written word constitutes another challenge; one hopefully ameliorated by the multidisciplinary approach adopted here to provide as rich a description as possible.

In addition to antiquarian observations of popular funeral customs, the writings of contemporary public health campaigners are another useful source of evidence for the Victorian funerary smellscape. These include notably Edwin Chadwick, whose *Supplementary Report into the Practice of Interment in Towns* (1834) refers copiously, and with barely concealed moral judgement, to the 'stink' and 'stench' of (working class) corpses as they lay for days and often weeks, awaiting burial in small, often poorly ventilated urban dwellings with family life continuing around them (Chadwick 1834: 19ff; Strange 2005: 67–70). And 'stink' these corpses would indeed have done, with more than 80 malodourous volatile organic compounds (VOCs) having been identified as products of this decomposition process. Most prominent within this distinctive olfactory cocktail are dimethyl disulphide (smells like cooking cabbage), toluene (smells like paint thinner), hexene (smells sharp/sweet), benzene (sweet smell), propanone (floral, cucumber smell), pentanone and trimethylene (Statheropoulos et al. 2005).

Trimethylene is also naturally emitted in detectable quantity by *Crataegus monogyna*, a sub-species of the hawthorn blossom plant. A conscious association between the smell of this particular plant and that of decaying bodies was made as far back as 1627, when Bacon's *Sylva Sylvarum* noted that, in places where plague was found, 'it hath a Sent, of the Smell of a Mellow Apple; And (as some say) of May Flowers' (Opie and Tatem 1989: 243). In light of this olfactory resemblance, the prohibition, found in most parts of the British Isles and into present times, against allowing this particular plant indoors because to do so is 'to bring death in' (Britten 1878: 158; Latham 1878: 52; Dyer 1884: 8; Taylor 1929: 125; Vickery 1985: 16–26) becomes understandable as a means of magically exercising agency against the forces of sickness and mortality.

Meanwhile an example of olfactory management of the dead through fumigation is the custom of opening the doors and/or windows. This was done either in a dying person's final moments ('Viator' 1846: 1068) or – more usually – as soon as death occurred, so 'that the spirit may escape' (Eyre 1902: 173) or 'to let the soul go free' (Hayward 1938: 225). In some cases, this logic extended to opening drawers, cupboards, and even locks and bolts (Latham 1878: 60; see also Krebs 1907: 215–216). In scientific terms, the current of dynamic air thus produced would have disrupted and diluted the concentration of unpleasant VOCs produced by decomposition; in the magico-religious discourse, the air current ushered out any malign spirits which might otherwise waylay and harm the vulnerable, newly released soul of the deceased. Alternatively, it may have been the odiferous spirits of the dead themselves which required encouragement to move on; hence also perhaps the popular belief 'that the front door of a house through which a corpse has been carried must be kept wide open till the burial service is concluded, or else another death will follow very soon' (Latham 1878: 57). This interpretation would suggest an ambivalent relationship between the newly dead and still-living; the latter assisting the former out of affection and respect, while also encouraging the potentially confused, jealous or even angry spirit to move on to its proper new place and reasserting boundaries by actively removing the final vestiges of its perceptible presence from the house.

Shortly after death the body would be washed, and its orifices (which typically attract insect activity, contributing significantly to tissue breakdown and therefore the release of odiferous VOCs, within just ten minutes post-mortem [Goff 2009: 28–29]) plugged with absorbent cotton and pleasant-smelling herbs. 'Such tasks', Strange (2005: 71) asserts, 'were usually performed with compassion, and perceived as displays of love and respect for the dead'. Arterial embalming, a chemical intervention which more comprehensively arrests the process of decomposition and its attendant smells (Goff 2009: 29), would not attain mainstream status as a preservation technique until well into the twentieth century (Parsons 2018: 53–64; see chapter by Jacklin and Welch in this book for a detailed account of arterial embalming). Barrier methods (Goff 2009: 29) including the use of laying-out sheets (these having been stored in 'the bottom drawer', thus contributing their own distinctive smell of musty linen) and shrouds were therefore the primary available strategies for delaying and obscuring the olfactory as well as visual evidence of decomposition during the days – sometimes weeks – of laying out at home.

According to Tarlow (2011: 138; see also Strange 2005: 79) the post-medieval period saw the increasing use of individual (as opposed to previously communal parish) coffins, specifically as a means of shielding both the noses and eyes of the bereaved from the gross materiality of decay, 'allow[ing] the body to retain its integrity in the memories and imaginations of those left behind.' Victorian coffins typically consisted of an outer case of fragrant wood such as oak, elm or pine. Meanwhile a secondary inner shell coated with pitch or paraffin wax, and its joints sealed with putty, provided an additional barrier against odiferous leakages (Parsons 2018: 78–79).

It was customary for friends, neighbours and relatives to visit the bereaved household, in order variously to bid goodbye to the deceased, to offer and receive emotional and practical support, and more cynically to perhaps take advantage of the opportunity to assess the bereaved household's domestic and material circumstances (Strange 2005: 80–83). 'This task of admiring the tranquillity of the corpse', remarks Bertram Puckle tartly, was 'a treat which no one from the lower orders of society would miss' (1926: 171–172). Children were expected to participate in these visits, and the smells they encountered in doing so may have contributed toward the strength of some of their memories – both positive and negative – of these experiences as expressed later in life (Emslie 1899: 477; Strange 2005: 83–85; Willander and Larsson 2006).

As they arrived at the door, and sometimes in exchange for a financial contribution, it was customary for visitors to be given a specially baked funeral cake or biscuit (Frisby 2019: 222–223). A popular ingredient in these confections was caraway seed (Coote Lake 1956: 110), and the Denham Tracts make particular note of the olfactory congruence between the sweet, woody aroma of the caraway, and that of a corpse laid out in its wooden coffin: 'Those who have [tasted the cakes] inform me that ... owing to some peculiar spice which is commixt with the flour, fruit, & c., they always, both in smell and taste, remind them of a clay-cold corpse and an oaken coffin' (Hardy 1895: 55). Was this perhaps then a (more or less) subconscious instance of olfactory resemblance, a loop of biochemical associations prompting those who consumed the biscuits to confront the reality of death – or, in the magico-religious discourse, an apotropaic device to baffle any lurking forces and encourage the dead to move on?

Another olfactory resemblance to the decaying corpse was provided by the tobacco customarily smoked at viewings and wakes (the latter referring to an overnight vigil customarily held prior to the funeral, rather than to the post-funeral meal as it does nowadays) and at the burying itself (Blakeborough 1911: 115; Carrick 1929: 282; Fairfax-Blakeborough 1935: 177). In particular, tobacco smoke derives its characteristic earthy odour from some of the same VOCs produced by a decaying corpse, including notably 2-pentanone. A sample of this tobacco was also sometimes provided to the bees as part of the 'telling' ritual (see below).

Additionally, visitors would have contributed their own body odours, comprised of smaller quantities of the same VOCs produced by the decaying corpse, to the olfactory admixture as they pressed into small rooms and filled the landings in order to view the deceased (Watts et al. 1899: 254). Interestingly in this connection, trace amounts of these same sulphides as are found in body odour are nowadays often added to perfumes to elicit a sense of rootedness in place and time (Kjellmer 2021: 79).

Those visiting the bereaved household, then in due course attending the funeral, would also have smelled of musty fabric, as thrifty housewives retrieved years-old mourning costumes from drawers and cupboards for reuse. Writing during the 1920s, Bertram Puckle remarks on how:

> [i]n the more remote English country villages, we may often see special mourning and wedding garments – a weird assortment of past fashions, which are only brought to light on the occasions of special family ceremony from the press where they lay embalmed for generations in lavender and camphor. (1926: 95; see also Fairfax-Blakeborough 1935: 176–177; Moody 1959: 32)

Add then to the smellscape the pervasive odour of camphor mothballs, which were mass manufactured cheaply from this period onward, and/or lavender, both of which are still widely used to protect stored fabric from insect damage.

Since up to two weeks would often pass while the money was found and arrangements made for the funeral (Chadwick 1834: 46ff), and an unenbalmed corpse at room temperature becomes noticeably odiferous as VOC production accelerates from around day four post-mortem (Statheropoulos et al. 2011: 157), further olfactory mitigations were therefore required meanwhile. A readily available, low-cost measure was to scatter aromatic herbs and flowers including rosemary, thyme and southernwood (the latter a natural form of camphor, on which also see above) on or around the corpse and room (Latham 1878: 53; Addy 1903: 180; Parker 1923: 325). The ritual use of rosemary at funerals, and more generally as a purgative and bringer of good luck, is well attested by antiquarian and literary sources from the late sixteenth century onward (Opie and Tatem 1989: 332–333). Victorian accounts vary as to whether the sprigs were given out to visitors upon arrival at the house, or by the 'bidders' who went around the neighbourhood issuing invitations to the funeral. In the latter case, an account from Lancashire, the guests then either wore their rosemary to the funeral 'or carried [it] in the hand' (Harland and Wilkinson 1867: 275). Rosemary was also frequently carried in the funeral procession and throughout the service in order 'to signify the soul's immortality' (Cole 1828: 138). Some accounts state that the rosemary was thrown into the grave afterward, the purpose of this action being 'to make the spirit rest' (Fowler 1909: 293) – a ritualised act of catharsis to encourage it on to its proper place and discourage any malign forces from interfering with this journey.

Salt was another apotropaic widely employed in Victorian and early twentieth century popular funeral customs; a saucer of salt placed upon the corpse's chest whilst it was laid out was 'almost universal amongst the poorer classes' of northern England in particular (Halton 1920: 154; see also Hardwick 1872: 181; Parkinson 1889: 231; Taylor 1929: 123). Some of these antiquarian accounts state that the purpose of the salt was to ward off decomposition; in which case, surely then it should have been placed directly on the corpse? Or perhaps the workings of this ritual went beyond mere biochemistry – perhaps the salt also had to be clearly seen at work combatting this manifestation of spiritual disorder and danger. Salt certainly possesses an extensive history within the Christian para/liturgical tradition of being employed to discourage evil spirits in a funerary context (Duffy 1992: 16ff, 281, 330, 361–362) and for a wide range of magico-religious purposes (Opie and Tatem 1989, 338–343). Even at the turn of the twentieth century, some people still believed firmly in its ability 'to scare the Devil away' (Berkeley 1923: 165) from a vulnerable newly dead soul.

The same rationale also pertained to placing lit candles around the corpse as it was laid out: 'they used to light a candle and leave it in the room with the corpse directly it grew dark, and they'd no more think of not doing it than they would of flying' (Hadow and Anderson 1924: 349; see also Hardwick 1872: 181; Carrick 1929: 281). Beeswax would therefore also have been present within the Victorian and early twentieth century funerary smellscape. This is another old and widespread usage, documented back into the Middle Ages as a means of warding off evil spirits, invoking the forces of light and divining the future in a wide range of funerary and other para/liturgical contexts (Duffy 1992: 281, 330, 361; Opie and Tatem 1989: 53–56) – or, in the modern scientific discourse, burning up VOCs emitted by the decomposing corpse while dispersing the alternative, more agreeable aroma of beeswax.

'Telling the bees' of a death in the household is another aromatic paraliturgical funerary custom, which is again well documented throughout the British Isles during this period. This involved the household hives being formally notified of deaths and other significant events within the family, and in most versions being offered a sample of the funeral food and tobacco (Dyer 1884: 130–131; Nutt 1892; Blakeborough 1911: 115; Parker 1923: 325; Hadow and Anderson: 349–350; Puckle 1926: 79; Taylor 1929: 123; Coote Lake 1956: 110). Several antiquarians who recorded this custom also noted a notion that the bees would cease honey production, fly away or even die if it were not performed. Since bees were widely regarded in folklore as being the souls of the dead (Ransome 1986 [1937]: 218–219), this suggests an effort to move the dead on to their proper place by multisensory means which included the wax and honey scents of the hives themselves – also of the food and tobacco offerings given to the bees in many of these accounts.

Even amongst the poor (Thompson 1918: 85) alcoholic drinks, including wine, ale and spirits, were widely consumed at Victorian and early twentieth century funerals (Fletcher 1908: 309; Blakeborough 1911: 114; Puckle 1926: 110–111; Carrick 1929: 282; Moody 1959: 33), adding their fumes to the olfactory admixture when visiting to view the deceased, and again upon arrival for the funeral service. Some accounts even indicate that alcoholic drinks were exempt for the purposes of teetotalism when consumed at funerals (Thompson 1918: 85; Fairfax-Blakeborough 1935: 110). In a possible echo of the pre-Reformation funeral mass, there are also accounts of coffin-bearers being given glasses of wine which they ceremoniously consumed before 'lifting' the coffin for conveyance to the funeral service (Hope 1893: 392; Frisby 2019: 224). Then at the post-funeral meal the smell of yet more alcoholic refreshment would have mingled with the life-affirming, even celebratory aromas of hot food such as ham, beef and plum pudding, and freshly baked cake (Harland and Wilkinson 1867: 271; Fletcher 1908: 309; Fowler 1909: 293; Thompson 1918: 85; Carrick 1929: 282). These smells would have both physically and symbolically countered the previous smells of death, decay and disorder, replacing them with the good smells of the stuff of ongoing life, and thus embodying a post-mortem rebounding of social, emotional and spiritual good order (Davies 1997: 44).

## CONCLUSIONS

Such is both the subjectivity and the ephemerality of olfaction, that it can never be known for certain how funerals – or indeed anything else – in the past 'really' smelled. Hopefully, however, even this tentative whiff of Victorian and early twentieth century funerary smellscapes indicates how olfaction played a much more prominent and powerful physical, spiritual, social and emotional part in Victorian and early twentieth century English experiences of death, dying and bereavement than it does nowadays.

With the partial exception of Strange in relation to funerals, and for several possible reasons (Jenner 2011: 343–348), olfaction has since been largely neglected by historians generally. However, and as highlighted in this case study, smells are in fact particularly apposite as signifiers for the newly dead and their journey to the afterlife. Like them, smells are invisible yet also of the tangible world; they steal around spaces and penetrate the consciousness of the living unbidden but forcefully; they linger there, whether welcome or not. Like the dead, a smell is difficult to simply ignore – one cannot so easily stop one's nose as one may close one's eyes or ears or refuse to touch (Bauman 1993: 24–25; Harvey 2015: 1, 7).

Not only do smells share these qualities with the newly dead, they – and by extension the spirits or souls they embody – are in the Christian para/liturgical tradition capable of active manipulation from one state to another. Particular mechanisms seen above include catharsis, where an unpleasant smell and what it embodies is 'thrown out' by a pleasant countersmell; fumigation, where disagreeable smells and what they embody are diluted and dispersed by currents of air; and resemblance, in which similar smells are magically deployed in order to baffle and confuse any lurking malign spirits.

Smells are thus important, if hitherto neglected, components of the ritualised somatic codes whose function it is to contain and resolve the disruption engendered by death across multiple levels and dimensions of human experience. Indeed, so effective are they in this respect that, when in the sixteenth century Protestant reformers 'abandoned the manipulation of smells in sacred contexts' (Baum 2013: 336), as with many other seasonal and life-cycle customs, usages of smells would not only survive but continue over time creatively to evolve within the paraliturgical realm (Hutton 1995). Subsequently these usages would be documented, decades and even centuries later, by the antiquarians whose works have largely comprised the evidence base for this case study.

In answering Jenner's call for 'a richer, quasi-ecological, history of smell' combining scientific and humanistic discourses in examinations 'simultaneously [of] both the person or people perceiving *and* the environment that they inhabited' (2011: 349), the otherwise odd 'folk' funerary customs documented by Victorian and early twentieth century antiquarians in England are thus reframed as both subjectively affective and objectively effective acts of ritual choreography in relation to the newly dead and bereaved. Here were some highly creative, spiritually, emotionally and socially impactful, appropriations of everyday materiality by people with limited financial and material resources at their disposal. Perhaps this should prompt us too, in the present day when both life and death have become deodorised and (arguably over-) sanitised, to rediscover the power of olfaction in meeting mortality.

# BIBLIOGRAPHY

Addy, Sidney O. 1903. 'Death and the Herb Thyme', *Folklore* 14(2): 179–180. https://doi.org/10.1080/0015587X.1903.9719354

Baum, Jacob M. 2013. 'From Incense to Idolatry: The Reformation of Olfaction in Late Medieval German Ritual', *Sixteenth Century Journal* 44(2): 323–343. https://doi.org/10.1086/SCJ24245084

Bauman, Zygmunt. 1993. 'The Sweet Scent of Decomposition'. In Chris Rojek and Bryan S. Turner (eds.), *Forget Baudrillard*, pp. 22–46. London and New York: Routledge.

Berkeley, Mary A. 1923. 'Beliefs Regarding Death', *Folklore* 34(2): 164–166. https://doi.org/10.1080/0015587X.1923.9720270

Blakeborough, Richard. 1911. *Wit, Character, Folklore and Customs of the North Riding of Yorkshire*. Saltburn: W. Rapp & Sons.

Britten, James. 1878. 'Plant-Lore Notes to Mrs. Latham's West Sussex Superstitions', *The Folk-Lore Record* 1: 155–159. https://doi.org/10.1080/17441994.1878.10602548

Carrick, T.W. 1929. 'Scraps of English Folklore, XVIII. Cumberland', *Folklore* 40(3): 278–290. https://doi.org/10.1080/0015587X.1929.9716889

Chadwick, Edwin. 1834. *Report on the Sanitary Conditions of the Labouring Population of Great Britain*. London: Her Majesty's Stationery Office.

Classen, Constance, Howes, David and Synnott, Anthony. 1994. *Aroma: The Cultural History of Smell*. London and New York: Routledge.

Cole, John. 1828. *Wit, History and Antiquities of Filey in the County of York*. Scarborough: published by the author.

Coote Lake, E.F. 1956. 'Folk Life and Traditions', *Folklore* 67(2): 109–113. https://doi.org/10.1080/0015587X.1956.9717534

Corbin, Alain. 1996. *The Foul and the Fragrant: Odour and the Social Imagination*. London and Basingstoke: Papermac.

Cuffel, Alexandra, di Giacinto, Lucia and Krech, Volkhard. 2019. 'Senses, Religion and Religious Encounter: Literature Review and Research Perspectives', *Entangled Religions* 10. https://er.ceres.rub.de/index.php/ER/article/view/8407. https://doi.org/10.46586/er.10.2019.8407

Davies, Douglas. J. 1997. *Death, Ritual and Belief: The Rhetoric of Funerary Rites*. London and Washington: Cassell.

Duffy, Eamon. 1992. *The Stripping of the Altars: Traditional Religion in England 1400-1580*. New Haven and London: Yale University Press.

Dyer, T.F. Thistleton. 1884. *English Folk Lore*. London: W.H. Allen & Co.

Emslie, J.P. 1899. 'Burial Customs', *Folklore* 10(4): 477. https://doi.org/10.1080/0015587X.1899.9720513

Eyre, L.M. 1902. 'Folklore Notes from St. Briavel's', *Folklore* 13(2): 170–177. https://doi.org/10.1080/0015587X.1902.9719676

Fairfax-Blakeborough, J. 1935. *Yorkshire Days and Yorkshire Ways*. London: Heath Cranton.

Fletcher, J.S. 1908. *A Book About Yorkshire*. London: Methuen & Co.

Fowler, Miss M.M.E. 1909. 'Yorkshire Folklore'. In Thomas M. Fowler (ed.), *Memorials of Old Yorkshire*, pp. 285–305. London: Allen & Sons.

Frisby, Helen. 2019. 'Victorian Funeral Food Customs', *Victorian Review* 45(2): 221–226. http://doi.org/10.1353/vcr.2019.0055

Goff, M. Lee. 2009. 'Early Post-Mortem Changes and Stages of Decomposition in Exposed Cadavers', *Exp Appl Acarol* 49: 21–36. https://doi.org/10.1007/s10493-009-9284-9

Hadow, Grace E. and Anderson, Ruth. 1924. 'Scraps of English Folklore, IX. (Suffolk)', *Folklore* 35(4): 346–360. https://doi.org/10.1080/0015587X.1924.9719298

Halton, J.W. 1920. 'Beliefs Regarding Death in Cumberland', *Folklore* 31(2): 154. https://doi.org/10.1080/0015587X.1920.9719144

Hardwick, Charles. 1872. *Traditions, Superstitions, and Folklore (Chiefly Lancashire and the North of England): Their Affinity to Others in Widely-Distributed Localities; Their Eastern Origins and Mythical Significance.* Manchester: A. Ireland & Co.

Hardy, James (ed.). 1895. *The Denham Tracts*, Vol. 2. London: David Nutt for The Folk-Lore Society.

Harland, John and T.T. Wilkinson. 1867. *Lancashire Folklore: Illustrative of the Superstitious Beliefs and Practices, Local Customs and Usages of the People of the County Palatine.* London: Frederick Warne & Co.

Harvey, Susan A. 2015. *Scenting Salvation: Ancient Christianity and the Olfactory Imagination.* Berkeley and Los Angeles: University of California Press.

Hayward, L.H. 1938. 'Shropshire Folklore of Yesterday and Today', *Folklore* 49(3): 223–243. https://doi.org/10.1080/0015587X.1938.9718762

Hope, G. 1893. 'The Sin-Eater', *Folklore* 4(3): 392–393.

Hutton, Ronald. 1995. 'The English Reformation and the Evidence of Folklore', *Past and Present* 148(1): 89–116. https://doi.org/10.1093/past/148.1.89

Jenner, Mark S.R. 2011. 'Follow Your Nose? Smell, Smelling, and Their Histories', *The American Historical Review* 116(2): 335–351. https://doi.org/10.1086/ahr.116.2.335

Kjellmer, Viveka. 2021. 'Scented Scenographics and Olfactory Art: Making Sense of Scent in the Museum', *Journal of Art History* 20(2): 72–87. https://doi.org/10.1080/00233609.2020.1775696

Krebs, H. 1907. 'Opening Windows to Aid the Release of the Soul', *Folklore* 18(2): 215–216.

Latham, Charlotte. 1878. 'Some West Sussex Superstitions Lingering in 1868', *The Folk-Lore Record* 1: 7–67. https://doi.org/10.1080/17441994.1878.10602542

Moody, F.W. 1959. 'Funeral Customs at Addingham', *Transactions of the Yorkshire Dialect Society* 59(10): 32–35.

Nutt, Alfred. 1892. 'Sympathetic Bees', *Folklore* 3(1): 138. https://doi.org/10.1080/0015587X.1892.9720097

Opie, Iona and Tatem, Moira (eds). 1989. *A Dictionary of Superstitions.* Oxford: Oxford University Press.

Parker, Angelina. 1923. 'Oxford Village Folklore, II', *Folklore* 34(4): 322–333. https://doi.org/10.1080/0015587X.1923.9719265

Parkin, David. 2007. 'Wafting on the Wind: Smell and the Cycle of Spirit and Matter', *Journal of the Royal Anthropological Institute* 13(s1): S39–S53. https://doi.org/10.1111/j.1467-9655.2007.00408.x

Parkinson, Rev. Thomas. 1889. *Yorkshire Legends and Traditions as Told by Her Ancient Chroniclers, Her Poets and Journalists.* London: Elliot Stock.

Parsons, Brian. 2018. *The Evolution of the British Funeral Industry in the 20th Century: From Undertaker to Funeral Director.* Bingley: Emerald Publishing.

Puckle, Bertram S. 1926. *Funeral Customs: Their Origin and Development.* London: T. Werner Laurie.

Ransome, Hilda M. 1986 [1937]. *The Sacred Bee in Ancient Times and Folklore*. Bridgwater: Bee Books New & Old.

Reinarz, Jonathan. 2014. *Past Scents: Historical Perspectives on Smell*. Urbana-Champaign, Chicago and Springfield: University of Illinois Press.

Statheropoulos M., Spiliopoulou, C. and Agapiou, A. 2005. 'A Study of Volatile Organic Compounds Evolved from the Decaying Human Body', *Forensic Science International* 153: 147–155. https://doi.org/10.1016/j.forsciint.2004.08.015

Statheropoulos M., Agapiou, A. Zorba, E., Mikedi, K., Karma, S., Pallis, G.C., Eliopoulos, C. and Spiliopoulou, C. 2011. 'Combined Chemical and Optical Methods for Monitoring the Early Decay Stages of Surrogate Human Models', *Forensic Science International* 210: 154–163. https://doi.org/10.1016/j.forsciint.2011.02.023

Stoddart, David M. 1990. *The Scented Ape: The Biology and Culture of Human Odor*. Cambridge: Cambridge University Press.

Strange, Julie-Marie. 2005. *Death, Grief and Poverty in Britain, 1870-1914*. Cambridge: Cambridge University Press.

Tarlow, Sarah. 2011. *Ritual, Belief and the Dead in Early Modern Britain and Ireland*. Cambridge: Cambridge University Press.

Taylor, Mark R. 1929. 'Norfolk Folklore', *Folklore* 40(2): 113–133. https://doi.org/10.1080/0015587X.1929.9716814

Thompson, T.W. 1918. 'Arval or Avril Bread', *Folklore* 29(1): 84–86. https://doi.org/10.1080/0015587X.1918.9719032

'Viator'. 1846. 'Death Bed Superstition in Devonshire', *The Athenæum* 990 (17 October 1846): 1068 col. C.

Vickery, Roy. 1985. *Unlucky Plants: A Folklore Survey*. London: The Folklore Society.

Watts, G.J., Nason, R.M. and Hooper, I. 1899. 'Burial Customs', *Folklore* 10(2): 253–254.

Willander, Johan and Larsson, Maria. 2006. 'Smell Your Way Back to Childhood: Autobiographical Odor Memory', *Psychonomic Bulletin & Review* 13(2): 240–244. https://doi.org/10.3758/BF03193837

**Helen Frisby** is an internationally recognised expert on the history and folklore of death, dying and funerals. Her most recent publication, *Traditions of Death and Burial* (Bloomsbury, 2019), is a history of death, dying and funerals since the Middle Ages. She combined her job as Researcher Development Manager at the University of West of England, with her research interests into death and burial.

# Chapter 6

# The Sense of Smell and the Odour of Death

## WENDY BIRCH

*Note: this chapter contains material that some readers may find distressing.

'Smell', according to the *Oxford English Dictionary*, is 'that property of things which affects the olfactory organ, whether agreeably or otherwise'. The 'smell of death' is undeniably disagreeable to humans. Indeed, students at a London medical school, surveyed over several years, consistently reported that even the anticipation of the 'smell of death' was a significant factor in generating increased levels of anxiety and concern prior to entering the anatomy laboratory for the first time. Furthermore, upon entering the lab and participating in their first human dissection, the same students commented on how relieved they were by the presence of the acrid odour of the embalming fluid used to preserve the donors they were dissecting, and which was considered to be more acceptable than the anticipated smell of a dead body.[1]

After death, the human body undergoes various chemical and physical processes, modified by biological and environmental factors, resulting

---

1 The decomposition of human soft tissue can be temporarily halted by the introduction of chemicals into the body via the arterial system during the embalming process; the odour of the formaldehyde and phenol often used in embalming fluids usually overpowers the smell of the deceased in the anatomy laboratory.

in the breakdown of the organic matter of the body into its fundamental elements. These processes result in the emission of volatile organic compounds (VOCs). These (often pungent) VOCs originating from decomposing tissue are strong drivers of necrophagous and necrophobic behaviours. The attraction of certain insect species to decomposing human bodies and animal carcasses for food or a suitable environment in which to oviposit (lay eggs) is vital for their survival. Meanwhile, the avoidance of dead or injured conspecifics (members of the same species) has been reported in insects, aquatic organisms and small mammals; this has been related to the idea that such avoidance has been selected for by the increased risks of predation and disease often associated with the presence of the dead (Prounis and Shields 2013). It has also been reported that humans can process the smell of putrescine (a chemical compound produced by the breakdown of fatty acids in decomposing tissue), which they interpret as a warning signal that mobilises protective threat management responses, such as heightened alertness and fight-or-flight responses (Wisman and Shrira 2015). In recent years there has been a substantial increase in the interest in VOCs due to their potential use in forensic science, in particular in the location of clandestine burials and the victims of mass disasters, and in establishing the post-mortem interval, i.e. how long an individual has been dead.

This chapter explores the 'smell of death' and decomposition, the effect of this odour on the living, and its practical applications as a tool for assisting in forensic science, search and recovery operations, medical and veterinary science, ecological and environmental science and public health.

## THE 'SMELL OF DEATH'

The distinctive odour usually associated with death occurs during the decomposition process when dead organic matter, such as a human body or the carcass of an animal, breaks down and decays. Decomposition is an essential process that recycles organic matter into the biosphere. The smell of decomposing organic matter is highly complex, and although recognisable, it is challenging to describe. As expected, this scent usually resembles the putrid odour of rotting meat; however, human decomposition also emits a surprisingly distinct fruity-earthy undertone or note. The decomposition of a dead human body can be divided into four stages, and each has its own distinctive odour; these different aromatic stages may go some way to explain why it is so difficult to describe the 'smell of death'.

Although each stage of decomposition produces its own unique scent, when it comes to being able to 'smell death' before someone dies, medical professionals agree that there is no single smell perceptible by humans that can be correlated with the occurrence of impending death. The most common scents often attributed to impending death in terminal patients are associated with poor personal hygiene as a consequence of illness, immobility and decline in cognitive function, as well as the scent of the naturally occurring deterioration of the cells of the body. In some cases, even the clinical antiseptic smell of the hospital/hospice is associated with approaching death and the process of dying. Hirakawa and Uemura identified that healthcare professionals dealing with dementia patients at the end of life, attributed the 'foul smell' associated with their patients to the gradual decline in their patient's independence in performing daily-life activities and incontinence as a result of cognitive function decline (2012: 61). People who claim they can 'smell death', for example, upon entering the hospital room of a terminal patient or a loved one, are not experiencing the actual 'scent of death' as there is no specific chemical compound yet attributed to the scent of the dying process. However, chemical reactions occurring in some dying individuals may give off a particular smell, which may be the scent that most people refer to when claiming they can smell death. The physiological, biological and chemical changes occurring before death are unique to each individual; however, a dying individual may release a distinctive acetone-like odour which is related to changes in their metabolism and which may emanate from their breath, skin or bodily fluids (according to the PubChem open chemistry database,[2] acetone has a 'fruity', 'characteristic odor'). This distinctive fruity smell results from the chemical breakdown of the deteriorating body as the individual nears the end of life. This odour, although not strictly the 'smell of death', may often be representative of the occurrence of death for healthcare professionals, relatives or friends present at the deathbed of their patient or loved one.

The human response to specific scents associated with death may develop through learned associations. Based on these learned behaviours, a healthcare professional working with terminal patients may therefore be predisposed to associating these aromatic cues with an indicator that their patient is nearing the end, or is in the process of dying. Furthermore, they may also associate the smell of a decomposing body with the scent of the deteriorating body of a terminal individual nearing death. As a result, they

---

2  For information about PubChem (part of the National Library of Medicine) see https://pubchem.ncbi.nlm.nih.gov/docs/about

may automatically assume that any distinctive odour given off by the body close to the time of death constitutes the actual 'smell of death'. However, the true definition of the 'smell of death' can only really be defined as occurring after the process of dying has taken place, and the process of decomposition has commenced.

Decomposition of the body commences at the moment of death, and results from two main processes which break down the body tissues and release gases and chemicals. The first process is known as autolysis (self-digestion) and is where the body tissues are broken down by the body's own internal chemicals and enzymes. The second is putrefaction, which is the moist degeneration of the body's tissues by the action of bacteria. These two processes produce the compounds responsible for the putrid odours of decomposition. The distinctive odour associated with human decomposition is primarily caused by the release of VOCs and gases such as putrescine, cadaverine, skatole and various sulphur compounds, which are the by-products of bacterial and enzymatic activities during decomposition. Decomposition is associated with a wide range of VOCs. Although the exact combination of these compounds has yet to be fully established, the classes of these compounds are generally agreed on. The most reported VOCs resulting from decomposition are the polysulphide compounds, namely dimethyl sulphide (according to the PubChem database, this compound has the 'unpleasant odor of wild radish' and is 'cabbage-like'), dimethyl disulphide (PubChem suggests this compound has a 'garlic-like', 'sulfurous' and 'diffuse, intense onion odor'), and dimethyl trisulphide (although PubChem states this compound has a 'powerful odour' unfortunately no further description is provided).

As mentioned above, the decomposition of a dead human body can be divided into four stages, during which different chemical compounds are released, contributing to each stage's specific odour and scent profile. In addition, the decomposition of human tissue is highly dependent upon the surrounding environmental conditions, including temperature, humidity, presence of oxygen and water, as well as access by insects or vertebrate scavengers; each of these factors adds to the complexity and variable chemical make-up of each decomposition stage and the odours produced. These differences and variations may also help explain why it is so difficult to attribute a specific smell to decomposition and to describe this scent. In addition, individual perception of smell may vary; some individuals may have different sensitivity or tolerance levels to certain smells, particularly those specific odours associated with death.

Although the perception of smell may vary from person to person, and the descriptions provided below are generalisations, typically, the four stages of decomposition and their corresponding scents may be described as follows:

1. ***Fresh stage***: This initial stage commences within the first few hours following death; it is characterised by the onset of autolysis in the body. Externally, the body may not appear very different; however, in some cases, although faint, the body may already have a distinctive sweet or fruity scent.

2. ***Gaseous or bloat stage***: This second stage is characterised by the onset of putrefaction and the accumulation of gas in the body. 'Putrefaction is the main cause of decomposition' (DiMaio and Dana 2007: 27); it is the moist degeneration of the body tissues as a result of bacterial action. Bacteria, mostly from the gastrointestinal tract, multiply rapidly after death and consume the devitalised body tissue: as they do so, they produce gas. Consequently, putrefaction is 'accompanied by both visual (bloating) and olfactory (foul ammoniacal odours) features', which are the result of 'the generation of gases (hydrogen sulphide, hydrocarbons) and the release of ammonia', produced by bacterial action (Madea et al. 2014: 91). Hydrogen sulphide, according to the PubChem database, has an 'offensive odor' and has 'a strong odor of rotten eggs'; PubChem also notes that the 'sense of smell becomes rapidly fatigued and can NOT be relied upon to warn of the continuous presence of hydrogen sulfide'. PubChem refers to ammonia as having a 'sharp, cloying, repellent' odour, that is 'very pungent' and 'suffocating', an odour which is 'characteristic of drying urine'.

   As the body bloats due to the accumulating gas produced by the bacteria, pressure is exerted on the internal organs of the body and the aroma of the gas produced by the bacteria may now also be accompanied by the strong and familiar smell of urine, faeces or vomit as the contents of the bladder and digestive tract are pushed out of the body. The rate of putrefaction depends on many factors, but typically within two to three days following death, it will manifest as a discolouration of the abdominal wall; after about a week, the body swells up due to the gas produced by the bacteria, resulting in gross disfiguration in about three weeks (Mason and McCall Smith 1987: 457).

   The scent of this second stage will vary based on environmental conditions (particularly increased heat and access to moisture), as well as variation in the individual body chemistry of the deceased. At this stage, typically, the odour can be described as resembling a combination of rotting meat and a sulphur-like, rotten egg ammonia scent, with a strong garlic, sickly sweet undertone. Overall, the scent during the bloat stage of decomposition can be described as overwhelmingly unpleasant and difficult to ignore.

3. ***Active stage***: This stage of active and rapid decomposition typically has a broad scent profile. Bacteria and enzymes continue to break down the tissues and organs, releasing additional scented compounds. After about a month following death, the body cavities burst open, and the body deflates; the remaining soft tissues progressively liquefy and break down completely (Mason and McCall Smith 1987: 457).

   During this stage, initially, there is a complex odour consisting of a wide array of compounds. As decomposition progresses, the odour intensifies, becoming more offensive, pungent and unpleasant. It can be described as a mixture of putrid meat, faeces and ammonia. Gradually as the remaining soft tissues dehydrate, this odour becomes less intense, although it is still present and complex. The smell during the latter part of this stage can be described as sickeningly sweet, musty and reminiscent of rotting vegetation or boiled cabbage.

   The intensity of the odour of human decomposition can vary depending on environmental conditions, particularly temperature and humidity. Warmer temperatures tend to accelerate the decomposition process, leading to a more rapid release of gases and intensifying the smell. Conversely, colder temperatures can decrease the decomposition process, somewhat reducing the resultant odour.

   The smell of decomposition, particularly during the bloat and early active stages, can be overwhelming, powerful and persistent, especially in enclosed or poorly ventilated spaces. The odour can permeate surrounding materials and may linger for an extended period, making it challenging to eliminate without professional assistance.

4. ***Dry stage***: By this final stage of decomposition, the soft tissue has usually completely broken down, and only skeletal remains and some desiccated tissue may be left. The smell during this stage is reduced and is not as intense as the previous stage; it often has a faint, earthy, musty odour; eventually, this scent will dissipate.

Sir George Scharf (1820–1895) described the smell (and taste) of this final stage of decomposition in his diary dated 1871.[3] In August 1871, alongside several sketches of the skull of Richard II,[4] which had been exhumed during Scharf's visit to Westminster Abbey, Scharf wrote, 'the skull of Richard [II] I had in my hand and pressed to my lips, a small spongy compact substance ... came from inside the skull, is very light; it had no taste nor smell. The bones were quite dry and not at all musty'.

## THE EFFECT OF THE 'SMELL OF DECOMPOSITION'

The odour of decomposition can be described as pungent, foul or nauseating; it is generally considered unpleasant and is undeniably associated with death, decay and the presence of dead human bodies or animal carcasses. The smell of decomposition serves as an important biological and sensory cue to humans and other animals, signalling that organic matter in the vicinity is decaying or rotting. The human olfactory system is highly sensitive to these odours as a natural defence mechanism to help identify potential sources of infection or danger. This odour is deeply ingrained in our evolutionary history as a warning sign of potential dangers, such as the presence of dead animals or spoiled food, which can harbour harmful bacteria and pose health risks. The effect of the smell of decomposition on individuals can vary. Some people may find the smell nauseating and disturbing, leading to feelings of discomfort, disgust or even anxiety, as demonstrated by the medical students mentioned above, who experienced increased anxiety at the anticipated 'smell of death' in the anatomy laboratory. Furthermore, the emotional and psychological impact of this odour may be significant, especially in situations where the smell is associated with traumatic events or the loss of a loved one.

The smell of decomposition may have various effects on an individual. Some of the potential effects of the smell of decomposition include:

1. **Discomfort, disgust and nausea**: The smell of decomposition may be highly unpleasant for most people. It often triggers a strong aversive reaction and may cause discomfort, nausea and even vomiting in some individuals. The smell of decomposition can create a

---

3　Sir George Scharf's diary is currently held by the National Portrait Gallery London (NPG7/3/1/28).

4　For the sketches produced by Scharf see (NPG7/3/4/2/97).

strong feeling of discomfort and unease due to the association of this odour with death, decay and the breakdown of organic matter. The emotional and psychological implications of such associations can intensify this negative reaction and contribute to feelings of discomfort or even distress. Vomiting, or the urge to vomit by some individuals when experiencing the smell of decomposition, is the body's natural response in order to try to expel any potential toxins or harmful substances from the body that may be associated with the decaying matter.

2. ***Biological response***: The smell of decomposition can elicit a biological response in humans. The body's natural defence mechanisms may be activated in response to potential health risks associated with decomposing organic matter, such as the release of harmful bacteria or toxins. This response may include an increased heart rate, heightened senses or an instinctive desire to avoid the source of the odour (also see Wisman and Shrira 2015).

3. ***Emotional and psychological impact***: The emotional and psychological impact of the smell of decomposition can be significant and may vary depending on the individual experiencing the scent and their previous olfactory experiences. As well as evoking the feelings of distress and discomfort briefly discussed above, this scent may also serve as a reminder of mortality, the fragility of life and the inevitability of death. The association with decay and the loss of life may often trigger sadness, unease or even existential angst.

The smell of decomposition can generate feelings of anxiety and fear in some individuals and may trigger anxieties about one's own mortality or the well-being of loved ones. The odour of decomposition is often connected to the death and the loss of a loved one. As a result, it can also evoke deep feelings of grief, sorrow and mourning, particularly if the individual has recently experienced a loss or has had past traumatic experiences related to death. For individuals who have experienced traumatic events involving death, such as witnessing an incident involving a fatal accident or violence, or for those working in death-related professions, such as pathologists, morticians, embalmers, funeral directors or end-of-life health-care professionals, the smell of decomposition may act as a trigger for traumatic memories or post-traumatic stress reactions; in this book, McLachlan's chapter on death and the sense of humour explores how those in the 'Death World' develop coping strategies to deal with this.

4. *Cultural and societal influences*: Socio-cultural and religious attitudes towards death, funeral practices and beliefs about the afterlife
can influence how individuals perceive the smell of decomposition
(Welch's chapter on death and the sense of taste provides some context here). In addition, cultural and personal beliefs about death,
the afterlife and the sanctity of the body can also greatly influence
the emotional and psychological impact of the smell of decomposition, as discussed above. These beliefs and influences may intensify
or alter an individual's response to this pungent odour.

Some cultures have elaborate rituals, ceremonies and beliefs
associated with death and decay and the handling of the deceased
body, which may provide a framework for understanding and
accepting the smell as a natural part of the cycle of life. These rituals may involve specific practices for body preservation or disposal,
which can impact how the smell of decomposition is perceived; for
example, in traditional Buddhism, the smell of decomposition may
be associated with purification or the release of the soul (Hayagriva
undated). In other religions, however, the smell of decomposition is associated with taboo subjects, such as death and decay;
Zoroastrianism is an example here (Williams 1997). Cultural and
societal norms often dictate what is considered inappropriate (or
appropriate) to discuss or experience openly; this can lead to stig-
matisation or social avoidance and a reluctance to openly address
or acknowledge the presence of this particular odour which may
consequently influence an individual to feel uncomfortable or
repulsed by it. In some cultures, this scent may have supernatural connotations (Deathscent 2022). Societal norms and standards
regarding hygiene and cleanliness may also influence the perception of the smell of decomposition. In cultures that place a strong
emphasis on cleanliness, the odour and the bodily fluids associated
with bodily decomposition may be considered highly offensive and
repugnant. In contrast, this odour may be more accepted or even
expected in other cultures with different hygiene practices, as in
the case of the Toraja people of Indonesia, well-known for keeping
their dead relatives within the family home (Coville 2002; Sayoga
2021).

The portrayal of decomposition and its associated smell in the
media and popular culture can also shape societal attitudes and
perceptions. Often depicted in horror films or television crime
dramas, the smell of decomposition is commonly associated with

fear, danger or mystery, most often with accompanying menacing soundtracks, which may influence public perception and reinforce negative emotional responses. These portrayals can influence how people associate the smell of decomposition with fear, disgust or even intrigue, depending on the narrative and context in which it is presented.

Individuals working in death-related professions or pest control who regularly encounter the smell of decomposition as part of their work may receive specific training and exposure to this odour. Their professional context and experiences may influence their reactions, desensitisation or their ability to manage the emotional impact of this odour. In these contexts, the smell may be seen as a professional necessity or even an accepted part of the job. Cultural and societal attitudes toward these professions may also influence how this smell is perceived and managed.

Cultural and societal influences vary significantly across different regions and communities. As a result, individuals within these contexts may have diverse responses and attitudes towards the smell of decomposition based on their cultural background and societal norms. These influences shape individual attitudes, beliefs and responses to the smell of decomposition, highlighting the importance of considering cultural context when examining the impact of odours on individuals and communities.

As well as affecting humans, there are numerous contexts in which VOCs produced as the result of decomposition have been found to interact with the surrounding ecosystem (and reversely), including interactions with vertebrates and invertebrates and various biotic and abiotic factors. Many vertebrates exploit dead human bodies or animal carcasses as a food source; tigers, wolves, dogs, foxes, cats, rodents and birds are among these animals. As a consequence of the competition for food, vertebrate scavengers have evolved to become highly dependent on their senses for the rapid detection and localisation of carrion. Furthermore, some scavengers must be able to detect carrion at a specific stage of decomposition so that they are able to digest it.

## THE APPLICATION OF THE 'SMELL OF DECOMPOSITION'

In the context of fragrance, a musical metaphor is often used to describe the composition and structure of a scent; for example, the expressions top notes, middle notes (also known as heart notes) and base notes are frequently used to describe the ingredients that make up a fragrance. Fragrances, like music, have different notes; just as musical notes combine to create melodies and harmonies, fragrance notes blend to create the overall profile of a scent, with each note performing a specific role and contributing to the overall composition. As discussed above, the process of decomposition produces a complex symphony of scents, with different notes becoming louder or quieter as decomposition progresses. Taphonomy is 'the study of decomposition and the interactions of bodily decomposition with the surrounding environment' (Verheggen et al. 2017: 600). In 2004, Vass and colleagues at the human taphonomy facility in Tennessee introduced the concept of the 'decompositional odor analysis database' to help inform and improve the location of clandestine burials involving human remains; they identified over 400 specific VOCs associated with burial decomposition (Vass et al. 2004). Since then, further studies of human and porcine samples have examined the seasonal variation of grave soil VOCs, early post-mortem VOCs, VOCs from residual decomposition, VOCs from body bags and VOCs from probed graves, see Verheggen et al. (2017) for a more comprehensive list. By 2008, Vass et al. had identified 478 separate compounds, 30 of which were 'identified as key markers of human decomposition' detectable at the soil surface (Vass et al. 2008: 387). Furthermore, Dekeirsschieter et al. have identified more than 800 VOCs from porcine carcasses (2012). Understanding the notes of the decomposition scent profile and how the resultant melody changes throughout the decomposition process is beneficial in several fields. Some practical applications for the use of these scents and their complex profiles include:

1. *Forensic investigations*: The smell of decomposition plays a crucial role in the location and identification of human remains. For example, specially trained 'cadaver dogs' can be utilised to detect and alert their handlers to the presence of the scent of decomposition, assisting the police in the location of concealed or buried bodies. The presence of this odour provides vital evidence for forensic investigators, including anthropologists and pathologists, and it may also be used to help establish the post-mortem interval indicating when an individual may have died, which subsequently may assist in the identification of unknown human remains.

2. *Crime scene investigations*: The detection of the smell of decomposition at a crime scene can provide important clues and evidence for investigators. The presence of this odour at a scene may be an

indicator of the presence of a deceased individual, even in cases where visual or other physical evidence is scarce. This information may provide further insights into the circumstances surrounding the crime, for example, helping to establish a timeline and identify potential suspects. Even when no remains are recovered at a scene, the presence of this scent may guide the search for further evidence and assist in the final location of the deceased.

3. ***Search and recovery operations***: The detection of the smell of decomposition can also be used in search and recovery operations involving missing persons or following mass disasters. When an individual goes missing in a remote area or following natural or man-made disasters resulting in multiple deaths, the smell of decomposition can be used to guide search and recovery personnel who employ 'cadaver dogs'. Cadaver dogs are frequently used to locate the bodies of deceased missing persons who may have succumbed to a fatal accident or other unfortunate circumstance or the bodies of disaster victims who may be trapped or buried under debris.

4. ***Medical and veterinary science***: Medical and veterinary professionals can use the smell of decomposition to identify and diagnose certain medical conditions. In medicine, the presence of a particular odour may be indicative of certain infections or metabolic disorders, necrotic tissue or other underlying health issues. Similarly, veterinarians can use the smell of decomposition to help diagnose diseases or infections in animals; these infections and necrotic tissue may also be accompanied by the presence of blowfly larvae as a result of some blowfly species being attracted to necrotic tissue.

5. ***Agriculture and animal husbandry***: In agriculture and animal husbandry, the detection of the odours associated with decomposition can be utilised to identify and manage issues related to livestock health, crop diseases or the presence of spoiled food. The detection of a foul, putrid odour can prompt further investigation and enable appropriate action to prevent further deterioration or contamination.

6. ***Ecological science***: The smell of decomposition plays a vital role in ecological science, particularly in decomposition ecology. Ecologists study the decomposition process and its resultant odours to understand ecological processes, nutrient cycling, ecosystem dynamics and the role of decomposers in different ecosystems. By analysing the chemicals and gases released during decomposition, researchers

can gain insights into the ecological processes and interactions that occur after an organism's death.

7. ***Entomological science***: Insects, such as blowflies, are highly attracted to the smell of decomposition and are often the first organisms to arrive at a dead body. The smell of decomposition changes with increasing time, and these changes influence the necrophagous insects (and other vertebrate scavengers) attracted to a dead body. By studying the behaviour and life cycle of these insects, forensic entomologists can apply this knowledge to estimate the post-mortem interval of human remains, which can, in turn, assist forensic and criminal investigations.

8. ***Environmental science***: Monitoring the smell of decomposition can provide insights into environmental health. For example, in waste management facilities or landfills, the detection of excessive or abnormal odours associated with decomposition can indicate improper waste management practices or potential environmental hazards. Monitoring and identifying the smell of decomposition in public spaces, such as buildings or public transportation systems, can help identify potential health hazards, such as the presence of decaying organic matter and unsanitary conditions. This monitoring can prompt necessary interventions to maintain public and environmental health.

9. ***Biosecurity and public health science***: While the smell of decomposition itself is not inherently harmful to human health, it is often an indicator of potentially hazardous conditions. The presence of decaying organic matter, whether an animal carcass or spoiled food, can attract scavengers, pests, insects and disease-carrying organisms, each posing potential health risks. Monitoring and identifying the smell of decomposition can help identify areas of concern and prevent the spread of diseases.

Overall, the smell of decomposition has multiple practical applications, including forensic investigations, medical science, search and recovery operations, ecological studies and public health. This distinctive odour and its changing scent profile provide valuable information and can assist professionals in various fields in understanding, diagnosing and addressing different situations and challenges.

## CONCLUSION

The distinctive smell, often emanating from the human body just before death, is associated with the chemical reactions occurring within the body as the organs start to fail and the tissues deteriorate. This specific scent, although often referred to as the 'smell of death', is the natural scent produced by the dying body, and it is not technically what death smells like; no specific chemical compound has yet been identified and explicitly attributed to the process of dying. However, after death, the human body undergoes the process of decomposition resulting in the breakdown of its organic matter into its fundamental elements and the subsequent release of gases and emission of VOCs, which can result in the powerful, unpleasant odours often associated with death and the dead body. Current taphonomic research shows that the decomposition of the human body comprises around 480 different chemical compounds representing the 'smell of death' of the human body during its different stages of decomposition. With the use of human taphonomy facilities to help study the process of decomposition under differing environmental conditions and with the increasing sensitivity, accuracy and repeatability of the analytical tools used for collecting, separating and identifying the VOCs released throughout the decomposition process, new compounds are being added to the growing list of human cadaveric VOCs. This growing list will aid advances in several scientific areas, including the more scientifically rigorous training of 'cadaver dogs' for the detection of clandestine burials and human remains resulting from mass disasters. Identifying and recreating an artificial 'scent profile' for each stage of human decomposition would result in an invaluable tool for the training of 'cadaver dogs'.

Individual responses to the smell of decomposition vary; some people may be more sensitive or have a heightened aversion to the odour, while others may be less affected. The smell of decomposition may present a poignant reminder of death and the natural cycle of life, which may evoke feelings of fear, anxiety, grief, sadness or disgust. For some people, it may trigger traumatic memories or associations.

In conclusion, the smell of decomposition can profoundly impact an individual due to its association with death and decay. This smell can evoke strong emotional and physiological responses; moreover, its recognition and interpretation are highly dependent upon personal experiences, cultural backgrounds and previous exposure to similar odours, which may each influence how an individual perceives and responds to the 'smell of death'.

# BIBLIOGRAPHY

Coville, Elizabeth. 2002. 'Remembering Our Dead: The Care of the Ancestors in Tana Toraja'. In Henri Chambert-Loir and Anthony Reid (eds.), *The Potent Dead: Ancestors, Saints and Heroes in Contemporary Indonesia*, pp. 69–87. Honolulu: University of Hawai'i Press: 69–87.

DeathScent. 2022. 'The Odor of Sanctity: When the Dead Smell Divine', *The Death Scent Project* 12 January 2022. https://deathscent.com/2022/01/12/odour-of-sanctity/

Dekeirsschieter, Jessica, Stefanuto, Pierre-Hugues, Brasseur, Catherine, Haubruge, Eric and Focant, Jean-François. 2012. 'Enhanced Characterization of the Smell of Death by Comprehensive Two Dimensional Gas Chromatography–Time-of-Flight Mass Spectrometry (GCxGC–TOFMS)', *Plos One*: 1–16. https://doi.org/10.1371/journal.pone.0039005

DiMaio, Vincent J.M. and Dana, Suzanna E. 2007. 'Time of Death – Decomposition'. In *Handbook of Forensic Pathology*, pp. 23–28. Boca Raton: CRC Press.

Hayagriva. Undated. 'Introduction'. Hayagriva Buddhist Centre. https://hayagriva.org.au/wheel-of-life-death-process/

Hirakawa, Yoshihisa and Uemura, Kazumasa. 2012. 'Signs and Symptoms of Impending Death in End-of-Life Elderly Dementia Sufferers: Point of View of Formal Caregivers in Rural Areas – A Qualitative Study', *Journal of Rural Medicine* 7(2): 59–64. https://doi.org/10.2185/jrm.7.59

Madea, Burkhard, Henssge, Claus, Reibe, Saskia, Tsokos, Michael and Kernbach-Wighton, Gerhard. 2014. 'Postmortem Changes and Time since Death'. In Burkhard Madea (ed.), *Handbook of Forensic Medicine*, pp. 75–133. West Sussex: John Wiley and Sons Ltd.

Mason, J. Kenyon and McCall Smith, R. Alexander. 1987. *Butterworths Medico-Legal Encyclopaedia*. London: Butterworth and Co. Ltd.

Prounis, George S. and Shields, William M. 2013. 'Necrophobic Behavior in Small Mammals', *Behavioural Processes* 94: 41–44. https://doi.org/10.1016/j.beproc.2012.12.001

Sayoga, Puta. 2021. 'In Indonesia, a Blurred Boundary between the Living and the Dead', *New York Times* 9 January 2021. https://www.nytimes.com/2020/12/14/travel/torajan-death-rituals-indonesia.html

Vass, Arpad A., Smith, Rob R., Thompson, Cyril V., Burnett, Michael N., Wolf, Dennis A., Synstelien, Jennifer A., Dulgerian, Nishan and Eckenrode, Brian A. 2004. 'Decompositional Odor Analysis Database', *Journal of Forensic Science* 49(4): 1–10. https://pubmed.ncbi.nlm.nih.gov/15317191/. https://doi.org/10.1520/JFS2003434

Vass, Arpad A., Smith, Rob R., Thompson, Cyril V., Burnett, Michael N., Dulgerian, Nishan and Eckenrode, Brian A. 2008. 'Odor Analysis of Decomposing Buried Human Remains', *Journal of Forensic Sciences* 53(2): 384–391. https://doi.org/10.111/j.1556-4029.2008.00680.x

Verheggen, François, Perrault, Katelynn A., Caparros Megido, Rudy, Dubois, Lena M., Francis, Frédéric, Haubruge, Eric, Forbes, Shari L., Focant, Jean-François and Stefanuto, Pierre-Hugues. 2017. 'The Odor of Death: An Overview of Current

Knowledge on Characterization and Applications', *BioScience* 67(7): 600–613. https://doi.org/10.1093/biosci/bix046

Williams, Alan. 1997. 'Zoroastrianism and the Body'. In Sarah Coakley (ed.), *Religion and the Body*, pp. 155–166. Cambridge: Cambridge University Press.

Wisman, Arnaud and Shrira, Ilan. 2015. 'The Smell of Death: Evidence That Putrescine Elicits Threat Management Mechanisms', *Frontiers in Psychology* 6: 1–11. https://doi.org/10.3389/fpsyg.2015.01274

**Wendy Birch** an Associate Professor at University College London, where she manages the Anatomy Laboratory and lectures on anatomy and forensic osteology. She works as a forensic consultant, providing advice on human anatomy and the excavation and identification of human remains. Her academic interests include decomposition, taphonomy and trauma research.

Chapter 7

# 'Sounding out Death': Academic and Professional Viewpoints

## SUZI GARROD AND CHRISTINA WELCH

This collaborative chapter explores the sense of sound in connection with death, dying, grief and bereavement. It draws on Suzi Garrod's work as a mental health practitioner and thanatologist, informed both by her clinical practice and by her academic studies during her master's degree in Death, Religion and Culture (DRC). Suzi has worked in end-of-life care since 2009 and her pluralistic death doula practice integrates sound therapy with psychotherapy, psycho-educational and practical interventions, alongside a family systems approach to anticipatory grief (that is, grieving a death or a loss before it physically happens).

This chapter also draws on academic work in the field of death studies and the sense of sound; a field which is notably slight. This is interpreted through the lens of a death studies scholar, Christina Welch. Christina started teaching about the academic study of death in 2008, leading the DRC master's degree programme until 2022. The course attracted a range of students, many of whom were, like Suzi, working professionally with the dying and bereaved; Christina learnt as much from them as they did from her. Given the relative scarcity of writing on death and the sense of sound, this chapter aims to cover a little of both the academic and the professional practice side.

## DEATH AND THE SENSE OF SOUND: IN PRACTICE

Listening is integral to Suzi's work as a psychotherapist, a death doula – someone who spiritually and emotionally assists the dying and their loved ones with the dying process – and a sound therapist. Her pluralistic approaches to death education, end-of-life care and grief support emphasise the importance of the hearing sense, incorporating not just listening and talking but also singing, chanting, even wailing with clients, as well as playing a range of sound instruments. Over the years, this multifaceted approach to death-work and grief-work has evolved into a sound-centric practice which she informally refers to as 'sounding out death'; a concept she has developed to not only help clients express their emotions around death, dying, grief and bereavement, but also to bring into consciousness a wider awareness of the many sounds associated with death. In her work with the dying and bereaved, Suzi explores what is heard or not heard, what is vocalised or simply left unsaid at the end-of-life, all of which can positively or negatively impact a person's experience of dying or grieving.

Douglas Davies in his book *Death, Ritual and Belief*, theorised 'words against death' as being words (often combined with actions) that literally and or metaphorically deny the physical reality of a mortal/finite earthly existence (Davies 2017: 27). Suzi's 'sounding out death' similarly embraces words and sounds embedded within many traditional death rituals that occur in some form across every human culture and religion, such as prayers, blessings, invocations, chants, hymns and eulogies; but here to confront rather than deny the reality of death. It also embraces powerful outpourings of grief, which universally communicate (sound out) death without the accompaniment of liturgical music or words, such as mournful crying, keening or wailing (McLaughlin 2019).

Since the 1900s, death in the urban industrialised world has become a much more private event, quietly hidden away in hospitals, care homes and hospices, rather than being openly embraced and ritually celebrated by families and wider communities (Ariès 1981: 603–605, 611–614); indeed, 'Rose Cottage' is a well-used euphemism in these settings to negate the sting of the mortuary room. Davies describes how this geographical removal of death from the public gaze to the clinical space has led to Western/Westernised society becoming increasingly unfamiliar and uncomfortable with the process and language of death and dying (Davies 2017: 177). As a result, many people have forgotten not only the language of dying but also the importance of hearing life stories, sharing memories, passing on wisdom and settling relationships as part of the 'dying role' (Gawande 2015: 249; Omori et al. 2022: 1).

In her practice, Suzi often comes across families struggling to communicate their fears about death. Whilst a large part of her work involves encouraging clients and their families to actively listen and talk to each other, share their life stories and express end-of-life wishes, her notion of 'sounding out death' encapsulates much more than rekindling our connection with the language of death and the legacy of words alone. 'Sounding out death' reacquaints people with an auditory appreciation of death on a deeper, innate level. It reconnects us directly through the hearing sense with the emotional impact of death-related sounds, including the sound that is silence. Silence can be very powerful, especially in the context of death (as in the lack of sound emanating from a person when they have died), or in the context of dying (when there are often long silent pauses between the final breaths); and even in the context of grief when people may feel unable to express their grief or carry the burden of their pain alone, in silence.

The sense of sound plays an important role in how we experience death. Soft music or gentle sounds can help to create a peaceful and calming environment for the dying person, while the sound of a loved one's voice at the bedside can offer them reassurance and comfort. For those who are present during the dying process, playing their loved one's favourite music, or soothing nature sounds, reading a cherished book or poem, or passing on messages from relatives, can present a meaningful way to support and connect with the dying. In this context, death and the hearing sense can have a positive impact on the dying process to those involved. However, there are also potential negative impacts to consider. Some sounds associated with death, such as the sound of laboured breathing, the moans or screams of a dying person experiencing terminal agitation or even pain, and other death-related sounds, such as alarms activated by hospital monitors or cardiac resuscitation equipment, can be jarring, and upsetting for both the dying person and family members to hear (MC 2022). In Suzi's experience, these death-related sounds can often linger in the memories of the bereaved (or soon to be bereaved), sometimes causing prolonged emotional distress that may lead to complicated grief. Likewise, sounds associated with traumatic or violent deaths, such as gunshots or car crashes, or a final voice message from someone who has taken their own life, can trigger a lasting trauma or a fear response that could lead to Post Traumatic Stress Disorder (PTSD).

A dying person's shallow intermittent gasps for air, or the 'gurgling and wet' sound of their final 'death rattle', further exemplify unpleasant and potentially negative expressions of sound at the end of life. Both are uncomfortable to hear and have been described as a haunting experience for relatives. People who hear this rattling sound, which is caused by fluid accumulation in the upper airway, have used words like 'horrific', 'disgusting' or 'very stressful' to describe the sound that is emitted, with some family members expressing concern that their loved one is 'choking', 'drowning' or even experiencing an 'unworthy' death (van Esch et al. 2020). Conversely, in a study by Wee et al. (2006a) whilst five of twelve relatives interviewed found the death rattle distressing, a further five were unconcerned by the sound. One interviewee, although finding the sound 'horrible', stated that 'cos I knew about ... the death rattle and things ... I just thought oh thank goodness for that, it's near the end ... I felt relieved ... he's going to be out of this pain within an hour or so' (in Wee et al. 2006a: 173). Wee et al. concluded that although 'most health professionals in palliative care are experienced at discussing sensitive issues with patients and their relatives ... talking about the death rattle can be difficult ... and particular emphasis should be placed in dealing with the fears of choking and drowning' (2006b: 180). The psycho-educational side of Suzi's death doula role involves normalising such sounds like the death rattle, as well as explaining the various stages of dying and how families can support their loved one (and themselves) through each phase of the dying process.

Although death education is an important component in her role, Suzi considers listening to be the most crucial aspect of her work. By listening attentively, she strives to understand the unvoiced thoughts and feelings of her clients as death approaches, beyond their spoken words or sounds. Helping families communicate the deeper meaning of their unexpressed emotions to their loved ones can be a powerful tool for easing the dying process.

The rationale behind Suzi attuning both her palliative and bereaved clients to the concept of 'sounding out death' is to facilitate a conscious exploration of sound within their primal human reaction to death and loss. In her clinical practice, she creates a safe and supportive soundscape in which dying people and their loved ones can experience, confront, vocalise or surrender to their feelings about death and mortality. The fundamental purpose of 'sounding out death' is to enable clients to gain an emotional cognisance of dying, death and grief that may not be as easily, or as deeply, attained through the utterance of words alone.

Arguably the expression 'sounding out death' resonates with Davies' theory of 'words against death'. Both terms acknowledge the emotionally confronting yet potentially 'healing' or 'triumphant' power of words within long-held religious ritual or secular death rites (Davies 2017: 18). However, whilst Davies explores how people use words, music, art or architecture to assert power over the finality of death, as a means of 'express[ing] their trust in hope over fear' or 'to motivate ongoing life' (2017: 8), 'sounding out death', explores how the use of different forms of sound can help people access and express the full range of their emotions around death. This includes hope and hopelessness, anger and forgiveness, acceptance, fear and denial. The evolving framework upon which the concept of 'sounding out death' rests is inherently practical and experiential in nature rather than scholarly, and it is this that differentiates it from the concept of 'words against death'.

Suzi's approach to 'sounding out death' has evolved from many years of working as a death doula. This advocacy role, which includes offering emotional, spiritual and practical support to end-of-life clients and their loved ones, is professionally underpinned by many years of training in psychotherapy, and grief counselling. The interweaving of sound and music-assisted relaxation therapy within Suzi's approach to death-work and grief-work, places this element of 'sounding out death' within the realm of music thanatology and music therapy. Music thanatology is a 'form of palliative care [which brings] together music, voice, and medicine to help the dying person's transition from life to death' (Schroeder-Sheker 1994). Music thanatologists play prescriptive 'music vigils' that are intended to bring comfort by harmonising harp music and their voice with a dying patient's breathing rhythms (Freeman et al. 2006: 100). Music thanatologists synchronise their music to the dying patient's fluctuating physiological needs, 'monitoring vital signs like heart rate, respiration, and temperature, to deliver personalized music that eases pain, restlessness, agitation, sleeplessness, and laboured breathing' (Music-Thanatology Association International [MTAI] 2021). This form of prescriptive musical attentiveness at the end-of-life is noted by Vasquez as an approach which brings 'peace and comfort' to the dying individual without requiring their active involvement (2022).

Music therapy, on the other hand, is an established psychological clinical intervention which encourages patients to actively engage in 'appropriate, sensitive and meaningful musical interaction' (BAMT, 2023a) as part of a therapeutic process. It focuses on delivering individual tones, melodies and sounds, with guided visualisation intended to evoke body awareness

and relaxation (Renz 2016: 43). In the UK, music therapy is a legally protected title which is regulated by the Health and Care Professions Council
(NHS HEE: 2022). It aims to enhance communication, improve cognitive
functioning, promote well-being and improve a person's quality of life
through music and sound (BAMT 2023b). If carefully planned, and with
patients' consent, music therapist-led sound interventions at the end of
life can reduce levels of anxiety and depression, and may even 'facilitate
peacefulness, transcendence and appreciation for beauty at the end of life'
(Ryan et al. 2022). By helping to relieve anxiety, aid relaxation and in some
cases even ameliorate pain, music therapy may also assist family and caregivers in coping with bereavement and communicating their grief (Archie
et al. 2013; Graham-Wisener et al. 2018).

Suzi is neither a music therapist nor a music thanatologist. However,
she has trained as a 'sound therapist' and considers that the sound and
music playing element of 'sounding out death' sits somewhere between
these two approaches. Sound therapy is not a regulated profession, which
means that there are no standardised training courses for individuals
who offer sound therapy services. Although feasibly a multidimensional
concept which spans three distinct areas of death-work, 'sounding out
death' is not in any way envisioned as a therapeutic framework, rather
a means of holistically contemplating death and supporting the process
of dying and grieving through the sense of sound. Firstly, in her role as a
psychotherapist, Suzi enables clients to contemplate and 'sound out' their
feelings about death and grief by offering traditional talk therapy, helping her palliative patients and their families navigate, make sense of and
articulate their feelings about dying. Secondly, in her death doula role, she
helps clients contemplate and 'sound out' death' by initiating discussions
about the stages of dying and what to expect; and by establishing dia-
logues between families and health professionals to help the dying person
make practical, informed choices about their end-of-life care. Finally, in
her role as a sound therapist, Suzi holistically 'sounds out death' by using
her voice to sing, tone or chant either for or with clients to help them relax
and reduce anxiety levels, or to help them release pent-up feelings around
their diagnosis. Sometimes she encourages active client involvement by
inviting them to play sound instruments themselves such as gongs, drums,
rattles, singing bowls and/or tuning forks. Many clients experience this
active participation as an uplifting, or a relaxing and meditative process,
though for some it can initiate an emotional release of fear, sadness, regret
or anger that requires careful holding or counselling. This active participation in sounding out the senses is often complemented by passive listening

to soft, soothing music, which is also intended to promote relaxation and reduce stress.

In some ways, this eclectic, unregulated approach has resonance with the 'New Age' movement; indeed terms such as 'sound healing' or 'sound bath' which are commonly used by sound therapists certainly connote such an association. Additionally, the use of sound instruments such as singing bowls, tingsha or gongs, potentially reinforces the quasi-New Age (and possibly appropriative) perception of this musical aspect of 'sounding out death'. Suzi acknowledges that when these instruments are taken out of their religious context, cultural appropriation is a term that could be levelled at this element of her work, although she is careful not to disrespect the originating culture. Exploring this aspect is beyond the scope of this chapter. Here, Suzi presents her practical perspective on death and the sense of sound and describes how she personally incorporates sound therapy at the end of life, even within psychotherapy sessions. In their systematic review of well-being outcomes for music and singing, Daykin et al. (2018) reported that singing, listening to music and/or playing musical instruments reduced negative experiences in palliative and end-of-life care, not only for patients but also for family caregivers and the musicians themselves.

Whilst Suzi's work supports these findings anecdotally, the published works of Monika Renz present a clinical reinforcement of this multidimensional approach to end-of-life care (Renz 2020a, 2020b). Renz holds a PhD in pedagogical psychology, psychopathology and music ethnology from Zurich University and offers psychotherapy and music-assisted relaxation to palliative patients, in addition to delivering regular talks and workshops on her approach to end-of-life care. Renz describes how the atmospheric and vibrational environment created by music-assisted relaxation 'opens us up to transcendence' and, along with psychotherapy, 'offers a healing relationship in which experiences of dignity and processes of maturation, self-awareness, grief and forgiveness can take place' (2020c). In addition to Renz's work, there are a growing number of studies that demonstrate the beneficial role of music and sound in palliative care. Some have confirmed that hearing may be the last sense to function at the end of life, and that even when unconscious, a dying person may respond to different sounds, tones and rhythms (Blundon et al., 2020: 1).

The rapid expansion of the Threshold Choir movement, founded by Kate Munger in 2000, further highlights the transformative power of music and sound at life's thresholds. The focus of these volunteer-led singing groups is on creating a supportive and inclusive space where singers from various musical backgrounds, often with no formal musical training, can contribute their voices and offer a compassionate bedside presence to people who are dying, through song (TC 2023a). Threshold Choirs usually comprise two to four singers, who visit hospices, hospitals and homes to sing or hum gentle, soothing songs in harmony to individuals nearing the end of their lives. Over the last twenty years, this movement for 'sounding out death', which began in San Francisco, has expanded globally. Its choirs increasingly offer harmonised vocals not only for end-of-life situations but also other significant life transitions such as serious illness, grief and caregiving (TC 2023b).

Although compassionate deathbed offerings such as singing and other music or sound-assisted interventions are well-intended, it is important to be mindful of each individual person's auditive sensitivity, to seek consent and to remain vigilant of any verbal or non-verbal indications that the sounds being played may be causing distress. People who are dying become increasingly dependent on the compassion, understanding and empathic listening of those around them. As death approaches, they become weaker, immobile, less vocal, and therefore less able to influence the intensity, variety or monotony of the sounds and vibrations in their environment. People who are dying may not be able to vocalise their feelings about the songs being sung at their bedside or to other sounds around them in the room, including the words spoken by loved ones or healthcare providers. However, subtle body language such as facial expressions, or altered neural responses measured by hospital equipment, may indicate whether they perceive this 'sounding out' experience as positive or negative, comforting or distressing; perhaps even painful (Blundon et al. 2020: 5–6; Renz 2015). Just as the living experience auditory stimuli differently, so do the dying. When contemplating any form of sound stimulus at the end of life, we must consider how an unresponsive dying person, or even a conscious, yet immobilised dying person, might for instance experience the ticking of a clock on the wall, the constant sound of a TV playing in the corner of the room, the sound of traffic or indeed the sound of birdsong through an open window. Sounds that may be comforting for one person may be distressing for another; even silence may be perceived as either 'sustaining or threatening' (Renz 2015: 67). Renz postulates that the dying may even be unable to distinguish outdoor sounds from indoor sounds towards the end of life, and that they may eventually only sense their external world as noise. She further asserts that dying patients have a particularly heightened sensitivity to sounds that relay disharmony, stress and unresolved family tensions (2015: 64).

With growing evidence to suggest that dying people can hear, even when somnolent, and Renz's claims that dying is a transition that is essentially acoustic (2015: 68), it is perhaps no surprise that over the years, Suzi has focused on sound to support her death doula and psychotherapy clients. She has practised 'sounding out death' by singing or humming her clients' favourite songs or lullabies, as they clung to the final hours of life, either on her own, as part of a threshold choir, or alongside relatives who were themselves comforted by singing meaningfully to their loved one. She has played instruments, or recited poems, prayers and chants to ease the dying person's anxiety, support their spiritual beliefs or to comfort families. She has listened to life stories that have been both heart-warming and heart-breaking, heard dying words of forgiveness and release, and expressions of anger, vengeance or regret. She has tuned into the subtly changing sounds of a dying person's final breaths, and silently held space to honour the stillness and peace experienced in the moment of a loved one's death. Most importantly, she has always done so respectfully, remaining vibrationally present to any signs that may subtly indicate disharmony or withdrawal of consent.

Just as sounds are not always experienced as soothing or calming, the process of dying is not always experienced as peaceful and dignified. Suzi has often witnessed people fighting against death in their final moments: ranting and raging, sometimes in response to unresolved business or family tensions, sometimes against perceived medical failures, or against a God they may feel has deserted them; and sometimes because they are terrified of falling into the abyss of no longer being a living sentient individual. In an increasingly secular society, death equates to nothingness. For many people living in the UK, the forgotten language of death, the absence of a religious or spiritual framework to which they can turn for support, and a growing unfamiliarity with the process of dying, may result in feelings of distress rather than comfort when it comes to confronting mortality. Frequently, in those final moments when waiting for someone to die, there can be a deafening silence in the room with family members unable to find the words to express their feelings. Nevertheless, it is possible for the dying person and their loved ones to experience stillness within those final moments and the ensuing absence of sound. There can be an inner peace at the point of death, 'a painless state beyond any distress or disquiet' (Renz 2015: 67), but it would be wrong to assert that this is always the case.

There is so much still to explore about the concept of 'sounding out death', and the way in which music or sound and our hearing sense can impact both the dying and the grieving process. Suzi hopes that, in time, there will be more published work available to draw upon within the academic field of death studies and the sense of sound. In the meantime, she continues to listen empathically to her clients' needs as they approach the end of their lives and offers her multidimensional approach to sounding out death when appropriate.

## DEATH AND THE SENSE OF SOUND: IN THEORY

Moving away from the practical side, this section explores in brief the more theoretical side of death and sound/s. Sounds have been connected to death, dying, grief and bereavement. Johnson notes the power of some sounds to cause death. He observes that the 2009 death by Sudden Arrhythmic Death Syndrome of a young student attending a party was caused by the pitch of the music played (2017: 7).[1] Many other studies, including that of Shadrack in this book, have demonstrated that music associated with the dead has the power to move the living (Dell and Hickey 2017). Music too, as noted above, is used in various therapeutic settings including to help people in their grief where it can be used in continuing bonds with the deceased, and with anticipatory grief at the pre-loss stage (O'Callaghan et al. 2013), as well as to comfort the dying (Blunden et al. 2020). Further, for many people in contemporary Western society where death is not an everyday reality, music provides a connection (albeit it is a second-hand mediated connection) with human mortality (Partridge 2015). Of course, a good deal of music has for a very long time been connected with death; from vernacular laments to formal compositions for funerals (Bennett and Gracon 2020), music can mark the death and remembrance of anyone. But whilst music is sound, so is speech, and as such orality (speaking out loud), in the form of prayers for the dying, the dead and the bereaved, is important to mention. Many of these prayers speak of an afterlife and as such tend to gloss over the deceased being physically absent. One such example is the Jewish Mourners Prayer, the Kaddish; a prayer that helps 'comfort the dying' and is used when burying the dead, and during mourning (Diamont 1998). In Judaism, as in many religions, sacred words need to be spoken

---

1 Kate Bush's 1986 song 'Experiment IV' explores the notion of death by sound; see https://www.musicmusingsandsuch.com/musicmusingsand-such/2020/12/20/feature-death-by-sound-kate-bushs-experiment-iv

when deaths occur because the vibrations of speech can have more than symbolic resonance; they can affect physical change.

The words spoken in connection with death can include eulogies at funerals, but perhaps they have the most importance when the words spoken are someone's last words. The topic of last words appears endlessly fascinating (Gawande 2015: 124; Erard 2019), with many people putting huge store in 'the last utterances of the dying' (Guthke 1992; Mendoza 2017). Often, however, last words are 'not audible or are unintelligible', or do not live up to expectations. This can be distressing for relatives especially in religions such as Hinduism and Buddhism where 'a person approaching death is expected to offer a meaningful farewell statement'. Further, in Christianity repenting sins and affirming faith is considered important (Kastenbaum 2023), whilst in Islam, it is expected that the dying person will utter the declaration of faith, 'Laa ilaaha ill-Allaah', as this will help them attain paradise (al-Munajjid 2011). In religious understandings then, last words have an important legacy.

Sound in connection with death in a religious context is a vast subject with many religions requiring spoken prayers, and others using prayers and music; a notable example being the Roman Catholic mass and the many requiems composed in the medieval and early modern era. Music has the power to move people and to encourage a physical outpouring of grief. But the spoken word too can create an atmosphere that supports the grieving process through the expressiveness of the words used. Thus, both the vibrations of music (Schaefer 2017; Lauria 2023), and the vibrations of verbalisations (what words are spoken and how they are sounded out), are affective (Kamiloğlu et al. 2020); however, this must be tempered by linguistic contextuality (Aryani and Jacobs 2018) as for many cultures, every spoken word is important. The saying 'my word is my bond' speaks to this understanding, with *dictum meum pactum* being the motto of the London Stock Exchange since 1801; although the phrase dates to before it was recorded in John Ray's *Collection of English Proverbs* of the seventeenth century: 'An *honeft* mans word is as good as his bond' (1670: 103). Another example of the importance of the spoken word can be found in Hopi culture.

The Hopi people have lived at Oraibi in Arizona, America, since 1125 CE, and their name, in their language means 'people good of heart, pure of breath' (McCoy 1987). In Hopi understanding there is an important connection between life, breath and moisture, with expressed words holding all three. What one says, speaks to who one is as a person – words (made of breath and showing one's heart) are not wasted. The Hopi are an agricultural people whose reliance on the crops of corn, beans and squash (the three sisters) is expressed in ritual and myth. Breath equates to life in Hopi language and is conceived of as the 'spiritual essence of all creation' (John Loftin in Fulbright 1992: 226). The word for a harvested ear of corn (qutunwu) is the same as for a dead human body, and the name for breath (hikwsi) is the same as the name for a mature ear of corn and for an adult human; life, breath, people and plants are intimately connected in reality as well as linguistically. When breath leaves the human body at death, it passes to the world of the Kachina (spirits or life forces that surround the Hopi), where 'the dead ... continue interacting with the universe' (Wright 2008: 112). The hikwsi of the dead 'is believed to have the ability to return ... in visible forms as clouds ... and act as an animating force in the sensuous world of the living' (Glowacka 1999: 137); the dead then bring the life-giving rain that enables crops to grow and the Hopi to live.

The Kachina in their other world can be asked to act in the human world to bring the rain; this is done via prayers which are attached to prayer-sticks by breathing on them, and the meaning of the words spoken from the heart is conveyed in the moisture of the hikwsi (Fulbright 1992: 223, 224). As such, the words spoken are words that are true and meaningful because the sound of the word carries within it something heartfelt. As linguistically breath (hikwsi) means life, and at death, the hikwsi of the dead brings the essential rains; so, whilst death is the end of a Hopi person in one physical form, their breath continues in another physical form, and both of these forms make sounds.

Beyond music and words, there are other types of sounds closely associated with death; violent sounds such as executions, noises accompanying fatal crimes (i.e. a gun firing), or vehicle crashes – all of which may be preceded by screams or cries of terror, and some of which were re-created for public consumption on a BBC sound effects vinyl recording in 1973 (Hypnogoria 2019). Then there are also the brutal sounds of military conflicts (Collins 2017: 109; Damousi 2017), but silences in times of war can be terrifying too, for example the lack of noise from a once vibrant population. Sometimes even everyday sounds can be associated with death; Hearman reports the noises of trucks being 'like the sound of death' to prisoners during the 1965–1966 Indonesian Anti-Communist Repression (2017: 142, 149), whilst Read recounts how the sounds of the footsteps of military boots, and the opening, but not closing, of a metal door were often followed by the screams of terror from torture during and before mass executions in Chile in 1973 (2017: 166). The effects of these types of sounds echo through the ages, and across continents, and remind us that the sense of sound in connection with death can be unnatural, distressing or downright frightening. But sometimes usually pleasant sounds can be associated with death, such as the music (orchestral and sung music from a range of genres) that accompanied the extermination of Jews at the death camps (see Brauer for details), and as such music was a 'kind of torture in this context' (Brauer 2016: 2).

Quignard in his work *The Hatred of Music* gives a number of mythic examples of music accompanying acts of murder and death, with his 'Seventh Treatise' exploring music in the Nazi camps (2016: 129–156). Quignard focuses on Simon Laks (1901–1983), the Polish musician, composer and conductor who spent time in several camps including Auschwitz-Birkenau and Dachau, and Primo Levi (1919–1987), the Italian chemist and writer of *If This is a Man* (UK version)/*Survival in Auschwitz* (US version) (1959) whose chapter 'Ka-Be' speaks powerfully of music in the camp – the whistle of three notes, and the marching music both of which commanded immediate action from the internees (1996: 50–51). Quignard notes that music played an active part in 'the execution of millions of human beings' (Laks quoted in in Quignard 2016: 132) because 'musical rhythms enthral bodily rhythms ... hearing and obedience are related ... [thus] the primary function ... assigned to the music of the Lagerkapelle [official camp orchestras], was to provide a rhythm for the departure and return of the Kommandos [prisoner labour group]' (Quignard 2016: 133; see Fackler 2007 and Dietz 2022 for more information).

However, music could also a form a form of resistance and strength in the Nazi camps with 'at least seven clandestine choirs founded by the prisoners in [the German concentration camp of] Sachsenhausen; three Polish, two Czech, one Norwegian, and one Jewish' (Brauer 2016: 13). Brauer stresses though, that in contrast to this voluntarily singing, '(en)forced musicality was an attempt to inscribe new meaning to the embodied emotional practice of singing ... forcing the prisoners to express positive emotions that were diametrically opposed to the actual emotions they were experiencing at the time'; here singing was experienced as a form of cruelty (Brauer 2016: 13). Brauer notes the same for the camp orchestras, both male and female, whose role was to greet and welcome newly arrived prisoners who were heading unknowingly, to the gas chambers and their death. Polish musician Halina Opielka, a survivor of Auschwitz II-Birkenau (the extermination camp in German-occupied Poland which features in a chapter in this book on death and the sense of dignity) who was a member of a camp orchestra, recalled that prisoners 'listened eagerly to the music, some even greeted the sounds with the movements of their own bodies.

The sight of the women's orchestra calm[ed] them ... g[ave] them courage and hope' (in Brauer 2016: 19); but again, music in this context was used with malice.

## CONCLUDING THOUGHTS

This chapter has explored death and the sense of sound through both a practical and an academic lens. It has highlighted how hope and courage can be gained through music at the end of life, although music was misused in the death camps of the *Shoah* (Holocaust). As such it is vital to contextually consider music (and the spoken word) in relation to death and dying. Sounds are affective, and music that might be calming for one person, could be terrifying to another if it brings back difficult memories (Shadrack's chapter explores this in more detail). As such, as Suzi notes, it is vital to gain informed consent before using sound as a form of therapy, especially if the subject of the therapeutic intervention has limited orality.

Words too are affective, and as with the Hopi connections between life and death, and this-world and the other-world, through the concept of breath/moisture and associated sounds, 'sounding out death' speaks to the notion that a holistic approach to our human existence is important. Many studies have shown in recent years that pretending death doesn't happen, until it does, is not healthy psychologically (and this can cause physical symptoms too). Speaking about death, dying, grief and bereavement, if done sensitively, is a healthy thing to do (Carpenter 2017; SCH 2017; Pinto 2021). Perhaps, the need to talk about death is where religion, in all its forms, might have something to offer in our increasingly secular world; as Kenny noted in her chapter on vanitas art, the world seems to be ever moving away from the spiritual towards the material. Religions tend to have words that speak of and to death, and include music or sounds in rituals that resonate with something other than our everyday world. They may not be *the* right words, or *the* right sounds for everyone, but most religious traditions and spiritual lifeways have centuries of lived practice behind their myths and rituals and they show that hearing, whether it is of music or words spoken out loud, is an important sense in relation to death, dying and bereavement.

# BIBLIOGRAPHY

al-Munajjid, Shaykh M.S. 2011. 'Exhorting the Dying Person to Say ilaaha ill-Allaah', *Islam Questions and Answers* 30 January 2011. https://islamqa.info/en/answers/36826/exhorting-the-dying-person-to-say-laa-ilaaha-ill-allaah

Archie, Patrick, Bruera, Eduardo and Cohen, Lorenzo. 2013. Music-Based Interventions in Palliative Cancer Care: A Review of Quantitative Studies and Neurobiological Literature', *Support Care Cancer* 21(9): 2609–2624. https://doi.org/10.1007/s00520-013-1841-4

Ariès, Phillipe. 1981. *The Hour of Our Death*. Trans. Helen Weaver. New York: Alfred A. Knopf.

Aryani, Arash and Jacobs, Arthur M. 2018. 'Affective Congruence between Sound and Meaning of Words Facilitates Semantic Decision', *Behavioural Science* 8(6). https://doi.org/10.2290/bs8060056

BAMT. 2023a. 'What Is a Music Therapist', *British Association for Music Therapy*. https://www.bamt.org/music-therapy/what-is-a-music-therapist

BAMT. 2023b. 'Information Leaflet: What Is Music Therapy', *British Association for Music Therapy*. https://www.bamt.org/resources/bamt-information-leaflets

Bennett, Marie J. and Gracon, David (eds.). 2020. *Music and Death: Interdisciplinary Readings and Perspectives*. Bingley: Emerald Publishing.

Blundon, Elizabeth G., Gallagher, Romayne E. and Ward, Lawrence M. 2020. 'Electrophysical Evidence of Preserved Hearing at the End of Life', *Scientific Reports: Nature Research* 10(1): 10336. http://doi.org/10.1038/s41598-020-67234-9

Brauer, Juliane. 2016. 'How Can Music be Torturous? Music in Nazi Concentration and Extermination Camps', *Music and Politics* 10(1). http://dx.doi.org/10.3998/mp.9460447.0010.103

Carpenter, Brian. 2017. 'Speaking of Psychology: Making Talking about Death Easier, with Brian Carpenter, PhD', *Speaking of Psychology: American Psychological Association* 51. https://www.apa.org/news/podcasts/speaking-of-psychology/talking-death

Collins, Diane. 2017. 'Startling Reports: Gunfire as Social Soundscape in Early Colonial Australia'. In Joy Damousi and Paula Hamilton (eds.), *A Cultural History of Sound, Memory and the Senses*, pp. 109–122. New York: Routledge.

Damousi, Joy. 2017. 'Sounds and Silence of War: Dresden and Paris during World War II', in Joy Damousi and Paula Hamilton (eds.), *A Cultural History of Sound, Memory and the Senses*, pp. 123–141. New York: Routledge.

Davies, Douglas. 2017. *Death, Ritual and Belief: The Rhetoric of Funerary Rites*, 3rd edition. London: Bloomsbury.

Daykin, Norma, Parry, Barbara, Ball, Kerry, Walters, David, Henry, Ann, Platten, Bronwyn and Hayden, Rachel. 2018. 'The Role of Participatory Music Making in Supporting People with Dementia in Hospital Environments', *Dementia* 17(6): 686–701. https://doi.org/10.1177/1471301217739722

Dell, Helen and Hickey, Helen M. (eds.). 2017. *Singing Death: Reflections on Music and Mortality*. London: Routledge.

Diamont, Anita. 1998. *Saying Kaddish: How to Comfort the Dying, Bury the Dead and Mourn as a Jew*. New York: Schocken Books.

Dietz, Dirk. 2022. 'Todestango?', *Visual History* 24 October 2022. https://visual-history. de/en/2022/10/24/dietz-todestango/

Erard, Michael. 2017. 'What People Actually Say Before They Die', *The Atlantic* 16 January 2019. https://www.theatlantic.com/family/archive/2019/01/ how-do-people-communicate-before-death/580303/

Fackler, Guido. 2007. 'Music in the Concentration Camps 1933–1945', *Music and Politics* 1(1). http://doi.org/10.400/temoigner.5732

Freeman, Lindsay, Caserta, Michael, Lund, Dale, Rossa, Shirley, Dowdy, Ann and Partenheimer, Andrea. 2006. 'Music Thanatology: Prescriptive Harp Music as Palliative Care for the Dying Patient', *American Journal of Hospice and Palliative Medicine* 23(2): 100–104. https://doi.org/10.1177/104990910602300206

Fulbright, John. 1992. 'Hopi and Zuni Prayer-Sticks: Magic Symbolic Texts, Barter, or Self-Sacrifice?', *Religion* 22: 221–234. https://doi.org/10.1016/0048-721x(92)90018-Y

Gawande, Atul. 2015. *Being Mortal: Medicine and What Matters in the End.* New York: Metropolitan Books.

Glowacka, Maria. 1999. 'The Concept of Hikwsi in Traditional Hopi Philosophy', *American Indian Culture and Research Journal* 23(2): 137–143. https://escholarship.org/uc/ item/6dt3285r

Graham-Wisener, Lisa, Watts, Grace, Kirkwood, Jenny, Harrison, Craig, McEwan, Joan, Porter, Sam, Reid, Joanne and McConnell, Tracey H. 2018. 'Music Therapy in UK Palliative and End-of-Life Care: A Service Evaluation', *BMJ Supportive & Palliative Care.* http://doi.org/10.1136/bmjspcare-2018-001510

Guthke, Karl S. 1992. *Last Words: Variations on a Theme in Cultural History.* Princeton, NJ: Princeton University Press.

HC. 2015. House of Commons Health Committee: End of Life Care. https://publications. parliamcnt.uk/pa/cm201415/cmselect/cmhealth/805/805.pdf

Hearman, Vanessa. 2017. 'Hearing the 1965–66 Indonesian Anti-Communist Repression: Sensory History and Its Possibilities'. In Joy Damousi and Paula Hamilton (eds.), *A Cultural History of Sound, Memory and the Senses*, pp. 142–156. New York: Routledge.

Hypnogoria. 2019. *Sounds of Death & Horror: Torture, Murder, and Monsters on BBC Vinyl.* https://www.hypnogoria.com/orrible_deathandhorror.html

Johnson, Bruce. 2017. 'Sound Studies Today: Where Are We Going'. In Joy Damousi and Paula Hamilton (eds.), *A Cultural History of Sound, Memory and the Senses*, pp. 7–21. New York: Routledge.

Kamiloğlu, Roza G., Fischer, Agntea H. and Sauter, Disa A. 2020. 'Good Vibrations: A Review of Vocal Expressions of Positive Emotions', *Psychonomic Bulletin and Review* 27: 237–265. https://doi.org/10.3758/s13423-019-01701-x

Kastenbaum, Robert. 2023. 'Last Words', *Encyclopaedia of Death and Dying.* http://www. deathreference.com/Ke-Ma/Last-Words.html

Komaromy, Carol. 2000. 'The Sight and Sound of Death: The Management of Dead Bodies in Residential and Nursing Homes for Older People', *Mortality* 5(3): 299–315. https://doi.org/10.1080/713686009

Lauria, Frederico. 2023. 'Affective Responses to Music: An Affective Science Perspective', *Philosophies* 8(2). https://doi.org/10.3390/philosophies8020016

Levi, Primo. 1996 [1959]. *Survival in Auschwitz* (published in UK as *If This Is a Man*). New York: Touchstone.

MC. 2022. 'Agitation in Palliative Care', *Marie Curie* 25 November 2022. https://www.mariecurie.org.uk/professionals/palliative-care-knowledge-zone/symptom-control/agitation#:~:text=It%20can%20be%20linked%20to,of%20life%2C%20or%20terminal%20delirium

McCoy, Ronald. 1987 (2012). 'They Dance for Rain', *The World & I* article 12618, June 1987.

McLaughlin, Mary. 2019. 'Keening the Dead: Ancient History or a Ritual for Today?', *Religions* 10(4): 235. http://doi.org/10.3390/rel10040235

Mendoza, Marilyn A. 2019. 'A Collection of Last Words: Words to Remember', *Psychology Today* 4 April 2017. https://www.theatlantic.com/family/archive/2019/01/how-do-people-communicate-before-death/580303/

MTAI. 2021. *Music Thanatology Association International.* https://www.mtai.org

NHS HEE. 2022. 'Art, Drama and Music Therapists', NHS, England. https://www.hee.nhs.uk/our-work/allied-health-professions/art-drama-music-therapists

O'Callaghan, Clare C., McDermott, Fiona, Hudson, Peter and Zalcberg, John R. 2013. 'Sound Continuing Bonds with the Deceased: The Relevance of Music, Including Preloss Music Therapy for Eight Bereaved Caregivers', *Death Studies* 37(2): 101–125. https://doi.org/10.1080/07481187.2011.617488

Omori, Maho, Jayasuriya, Jude, Scherer, Sam, Dow, Briony, Vaughan, Marie and Savvas, Steven. 2022. 'The Language of Dying: Communication about End-of-Life in Residential Aged Care', *Death Studies* 46(3): 684–694. https://doi.org/10.1080/0748 1187.2020.1762263

Partridge, Christopher. 2015. *Mortality and Music: Popular Music and the Awareness of Death.* London: Bloomsbury.

Pinto, Alex. 2021. 'Let's Talk about Death', Blog: *Evidence-Based Nursing* 20 June 2021. https://blogs.bmj.com/ebn/2021/06/20/lets-talk-about-death/

Quignard, Pascal. 2016. *The Hatred of Music.* Trans. Matthew Amos and Fredrik Rönnbäck. New Haven: Yale University Press.

Ray, John. 1670. *A Collection of English Proverbs.* Cambridge: John Hayes.

Read, Peter. 2017. '"For a Few Seconds, Imagine": An Aural Experience of Six Days of Terror at the Stadium of Chile, 12–17 September 1973'. In Joy Damousi and Paula Hamilton (eds.), *A Cultural History of Sound, Memory and the Senses*, pp. 157–175. New York: Routledge.

Renz, Monika. 2015. *Dying: A Transition.* New York: Columbia University Press.

Renz, Monika. 2016. *Hope and Grace: Spiritual Experiences in Severe Distress, Illness and Dying.* London: Jessica Kingsley Publishing.

Renz, Monika. 2020a. 'About: Professional Background', *Monika Renz.* https://www.monikarenz.ch/Werdegang.php?Sprache=en

Renz, Monika. 2020b. 'Research', *Monika Renz.* https://www.monikarenz.ch/Veroeffentlichungen-und-Projekte.php?Sprache=en

Renz, Monika. 2020c. 'Therapy: Music and Psychotherapy', *Monika Renz.* https://www.monikarenz.ch/Therapie.php?Sprache=en

Ryan, Collee, McAllister, Margaret and Mulvogue, Jennifer. 2022. 'Choirs in End-of-Life Care: A Thematic Literature Review, *International Journal of Palliative Nursing* 28(8): 348–356. https://doi.org/10.12968/ijpn.2022.28.8.348

SCH. 2017. 'A Guide: How to Talk about Death and Dying', St Clare Hospice. https://stclarehospice.org.uk/wp-content/uploads/2020/04/How-to-talk-about-death-and-dying-Guide-Ver-2.pdf

Schaefer, Hans-Eckhardt. 2017. 'Music-Evoked Emotions – Current Studies', *Frontiers in Neuroscience* 11(600). http://doi.org/10.3389/fnins.2017.00600

Schroeder-Sheker, Therese. 1994. 'Music for the Dying: A Personal Account of the New Field of Music: Thanatology – History, Theories, and Clinical Narratives', *Journal of Holistic Nursing* 12(1): 83–99. https://doi.org/10.1177/089801019401200113

TC. 2023a. 'What We Do', *Threshold Choir*. https://thresholdchoir.org/what-we-do/

TC. 2023b. 'How We Started', *Threshold Choir*. https://thresholdchoir.org/how-we-started/

van Esch, Harriëtte, Lokker, Martine E., Rietjens, Judith, van Zuylen, Lia, van der Rijt, Carin C.D. and van der Heide, Agnes. 2020. 'Understanding Relatives' Experience of Death Rattle', *BMC Psychology* 8(62): http://doi.org/10.1186/s40359-020-00431-3

Vasquez, Alejandra. 2022. 'What's Music Thanatology's Role in End-of-Life Care?', *Death and Dying JoinCake Blog* 9 May 2022 https://www.joincake.com/blog/music-thanatology/

Wee, Bee L., Coleman, P.G., Hillier, R. and Holgate, S.H. 2006a. 'The Sounds of Death Rattle I: Are Relatives Distressed by Hearing This Sound?', *Palliative Medicine* 20: 171–175. https://doi.org/10.1191/0269216306pm1137oa

Wee, Bee L., Coleman, P.G., Hillier, R. and Holgate, S.H. 2006b. 'The Sounds of Death Rattle II: How Do Relatives Interpret the Sound?', *Palliative Medicine* 20: 177–181. https://doi.org/10.1191/0269216306pm1138oa

Wright, Barton. 2008. 'Hopi Kachinas: A Life Force'. In Edna Glenn, John R. Wunder, Willard H. Rollings and C.L. Martin (eds.), *Hopi Nation: Essays on Indigenous Arts, Culture, History, and Law* 12. https://digitalcommons.unl.edu/hopination/12

**Suzi Garrod** is a holistic health practitioner and trainer whose work includes supporting people who are experiencing life-limiting illness, bereavement, grief and loss. Trained as a death doula, she also has an MA in Death, Religion and Culture and co-authored a chapter on religion and the sense of touch in relation to her death doula work, for the book *Religion and Touch* (edited by Welch and Whitehead 2021).

**Christina Welch** is an interdisciplinary religious studies scholar. She led the master's degree in Death, Religion and Culture (formerly MA in Religion: The Rituals and Rhetoric of Death) at the University of Winchester from 2007 until 2021, and continues to teach on the programme. She has research interests around visual and material culture, particularly in relation to religion and/or death. She also works on issues around heritage, especially as they relate to religion and/or death in the Caribbean.

## Chapter 8

# Sounding Her Death Ballads: Funeral Songs as My Mother's Final Words

### JASMINE HAZEL SHADRACK

**Equinox** *by Joy Harjo*
I must keep from breaking into the story by force
for if I do I will find myself with a war club in my hand
and the smoke of grief staggering toward the sun,
your nation dead beside you.

I keep walking away though it has been an eternity
and from each drop of blood
springs up sons and daughters, trees,
a mountain of sorrows, of songs.

I tell you this from the dusk of a small city in the north
not far from the birthplace of cars and industry.
Geese are returning to mate and crocuses have
broken through the frozen earth.

Soon they will come for me and I will make my stand
before the jury of destiny. Yes, I will answer in the clatter
of the new world, I have broken my addiction to war
and desire. Yes, I will reply, I have buried the dead
and made songs of the blood, the marrow.
(Tuck and Ree 2013: 648)

Twenty-plus years ago, my mother died in circumstances I would rather not think about. If I do, I will end up with a war club in my hand, much like Harjo states in her poem. I have been unable to crack open the story. I have been unable to even contemplate her: her life and, least of all, her death. When I think about it, all that comes to me is a summons from a grim abyss, a catastrophic wailing that bursts from the depths of the void. I distantly think to myself, what the hell is that noise? Then I realise, my mouth is open, and my throat is raw. There is no benediction. Yet, I know that the songs played at her funeral continue to signify sound and death, and I explore these considerations in this chapter, using autoethnography and musicology as my methodology and theoretical framework.

## THE UNIVERSAL SINGULAR

Sartre stresses that:

> No individual is just an individual; each person is a universal singular, summed up and for this reason universalized by [their] historical epoch, each person in turn reproducing [themself] in [their] singularity. Universal by the singular universality of human history, singular by universalizing singularity in [their] projects, the person requires simultaneous examination from both ends. (Quoted in Denzin 2014: 20)

Due to autoethnography's rigorous infrastructure, recognising this interlocking, cross-permeating, un-siloed understanding of the nature of people's lives means that we can appreciate the multifaceted influences occurring at any given moment. Because of this, my chapter is 'an autoethnography of survival' (Crawley 2014: 222), a flaying of the skin to endurance, to perseverance, to spite. How is it, that after all the trauma was left to rot for over two decades, the only things I can vividly recall are the funeral songs, the benign but well-meaning poem I stumbled through? Oh yes, I did stand at your grave and cry, you are not there, but you certainly did die, my voice catching in the soft folds of the swift, uplifting rush of quiet birds in circle flight, and down, down I fall, onto the cold, unforgiving ground. Alone. Gifted platitudes such as 'those who love us never really leave us' just felt like slaps in the face. I'd angrily spit back 'Yeah? You live with this lacerating cut in your heart then!' I could not hear any of it. Salt in my gaping wound, a wound that felt like it would never heal. Nor has it. Thorns have grown around it over time, but you cut them back and the pain is just as bloody now as it was then.

I've always known that carrying this around with me would be extraordinarily heavy and its weight has not lessened; it has become more sombre perhaps, more melancholic, its fiery edges transmuting into a more muted glow. In an attempt to carve a path through those thorns, I discovered the methodology of interpretive performance autoethnography when I was writing my PhD (later, my monograph, *Black Metal, Trauma, Subjectivity, and Sound: Screaming the Abyss* [2021]), and it proved to be such a helpful way of excavating trauma, that I employ it here too. Through a process of identifying memories as epiphanies or turning-point events, this enables me to locate moments that remain with me and examine them from a safe yet critical distance.

Norman K. Denzin writes:

> Interpretive performance autoethnography allows the researcher to take up each person's life in its immediate particularity and to ground the life in its historical moment. We move back and forth in time, using a version of Sartre's progressive-regressive method. Interpretation works forward to the conclusion of a set of acts taken up by the subject while working back in time, interrogating the historical, cultural, and biographical conditions that moved the person to experience the events being studied. (2014: x)

This then, is autoethnography as praxis, as process, an ever-flowing and evolving methodology that actively facilitates the move forwards. Trauma can leave you stuck in the same time and space in which the events took place, and if you're not careful, it is easy to get left behind, as life speeds on for everyone else. As an academic, I sought to find different ontologies and epistemologies to get me 'unstuck', whilst knowing that pain would accompany me on my autoethnographic journey. According to P. T. Clough:

> [i]n the last years of the twentieth century, critical theory came to focus on trauma, loss, and melancholy .... [I]n taking up trauma, critical theory was able to transition ... to new forms of history often presented at first in autobiographical experimental writings .... [T]hese writings ... call into question the truth of representation, the certainty of memory, if not the possibility of knowledge of the past .... The experimental forms of writing that mean to capture trauma often present the subject in blanks, hesitations – a topographic formulation of forgetting, loss, uncertainty, disavowal, and defensiveness .... [T]rauma makes the past and the future meet without there being a present. The future is collapsed into the past as the past overwhelms the present. (2007: 5–7)

This is universal singularity. The coalescing flows of historical moments, culture, employment, interpersonal relationships for example. Given the complexity of these interconnections, we must recognise that it is not an easy thing to delve into your trauma and not see all of these different lines of your life, to stare deeply at your shadow-self, the cocooned parts of you that were catapulted into survival mode. I think the recognition that your survival strategies are not for the rest of your life, is a kind of progress that isn't acknowledged enough. Turning to this methodology for critical assistance has enabled me to see what my coping mechanisms were/are and what I need to do to move forward, even after all this time. My mother's death changed everything, overnight. It was one of those unforeseen moments where I suddenly knew, in the chaos of that moment, in the sterilised chill of the hospital ward, that nothing would ever be the same for me again.

Here, I offer three vignettes, three epiphanies or turning-point events from the time of her death, that I recall clearly. These are key mechanisms of the methodological framework of interpretive performance autoethnography that stand out to me, twenty-plus years later, that are just as vivid and fresh as the moment they happened.

### Vignette 1

*I run into the hospital ward and see you on the bed, prone, delirious, flanked by white coats and stethoscopes. I reach out past them, dodging their banishing, swatting hands to grab yours, cold and paper-thin. 'Mum?' I say, a desperate question carried on the brisk March breeze, hanging over your drug-induced hysteria. The word, your name, punctures your hard shell, that soft sobriquet slipping through its gap to fall on your ears. Mum. Then, I have your attention, for a few, painfully brief seconds, your eyes a rolling whorl of confusion and bewilderment. But you know my voice. Suddenly, alarms and frantic machine-beeps and a swirl of medical panic all sound in a violent cacophony. I get swiftly ushered from the room and my hand slips from yours. I am made to sit in someone's office. It's a variety of 70s browns and beiges. A doctor comes in, the weight of cessation on his face, to inform me you have died. You'd been waiting for me. And my world comes crashing down.*

### Vignette 2

*He keeps getting our names wrong. So annoying and not the thing I should be concentrating on at your funeral. A vicar really should be better at this. I roll my eyes many times during the service. But then it's time for me, the only daughter, to get up and speak. I read a poem, or at least try to. Stanza one flows and my grief sits like a stone in the pit of my stomach. Solid, unyielding, heavy. Do not stand at my grave and weep, I say, my voice like a sword through the church. I stop midway as the force of my tears slam my throat shut. A vice. Time stands still, in those sharp moments, but I'm sitting in the pew again. I don't recall how I got there. Two songs for you, Mum. Kirsty MacColl's version of 'Days' rings out of the speakers like par-ish bells and my heart splits. I cannot bear it. I want to run out of that place and disappear across the distant hills. But I endure it. Like so much else. The last piece of music is from Bizet's* The Pearl Fishers *and I feel that there is now nothing left of me. Only grief.*

*Vignette 3*

*I burst out of the theatre doors into the bright, golden sunlight, gown on, cap in hand. I am suddenly struck how everything looks the same: the same street, the same buildings, the same everything. I am dumbfounded. How can everything have changed so irrevocably for me, yet this scene holds fast? The last time I was here, was for my undergraduate graduation. Mum was so proud of me, I could see her beaming all the way from the stage, her smile like a shining prism, crystal light searing out across the concert hall. And now I am here once more, graduating from my master's degree, and then from my PhD, and she is not here. She. Is. Not. Here. I cannot comprehend why the street outside looks the same. Because it shouldn't.*

These vignettes are deeply painful to me. Deborah Reed-Danahay writes that 'autoethnography is a form of self-narrative that places the self within the social context. It is both a method and a text' (1997: 6). So, it is here, a method and a text, these vignettes casting their runes before me to help me find a truth, of sorts. I have failed to remain stoic writing them but the overarching ostinato (a rhythm, phrase or motif that persistently repeats) that has determinedly clung to me, tarred and feathered, has been that of the funeral songs. Those two pieces of music exist in different worlds to me now; one a grim, dragging chasm shot through with bright sparks of pain, the other an inspiriting catching of the breath that lifts me up and forwards. Identifying how these compositions function in the context of death, sound and interpersonal grief, means 'believing that words matter and writing towards the moment when the point of creating autoethno-graphic texts is to change the world' (Stacy Linn Homan Jones quoted in Denzin 2005: 124). It has certainly changed mine. To further examine how and why these songs are represented to me in the way that they are, an autoethnographic musicology is required.

## AUTOETHNOGRAPHIC MUSICOLOGY

The English singer-songwriter Kirsty MacColl's track 'Days' from 1989 is an absolute no-go for me, a banished territory shattered with the sounds of death. Every single word, a cascade of a life and love lost. Even though the song is a cover of the original track by the English rock band The Kinks from 1968, there was always something heavier and more melancholic in MacColl's rendition that seems to me, inescapably wrought with remorse and gloom. Of course, this could simply be a matter of personal context, but I always thought it jarring to have such burdensome lyrics in a major key. My mother would sing this song to me in happier times, when she would hug me and intone the soft melody line close to my ear, a prophetic cautioning, heralding a time of collapse that neither of us could have possibly foretold. And still the song remains. In those warm, summer mornings the words would pass from her to me, she the singer and I the receiver. Now, since the song's entombment at her funeral, it is I who sings the words to a woman no longer there.

In the key of A major, sonically the song follows the very simple popular music format of swinging between two main, easily identifiable refrains. However, it does not follow the standard popular music song composition of verse, chorus, verse, chorus, bridge, chorus, end. This song's verses and chorus segue into each other, with only slight variations in the vocal melody and instrumentation and what would usually be considered the bridge. The sung female vocals are mostly situated within pop but with a layering of folk. Instrumentally, a semi-acoustic guitar is accompanied by a paired-down drum kit, very light in its application throughout, and the bass following the root note structure of the main chords. If anything, the song operates in a similar way to punk inasmuch as the vocals and lyrical message are the main focal point, not the instrumentation. The song itself offers a standard, relatively simple chordal structure, with finger-picked variational ostinati on the semi-acoustic guitar. The chords follow A (tonic, otherwise the most stable note of the song) to E (the fourth underneath, the subdominant otherwise known as the lower dominant, so named because it is the same distance below the tonic as the dominant, or the fifth above the tonic, is above it). This is followed by D, A, D, A, E, A. This forms the basis of the main ostinato of the song. The bridge that, unusually, has more than one refrain, harmonises between F and A, creating a new tonic of F major, and hits A as a major third and then modulates to C major. Sonically, it presents as completely tonal, diatonic and manageable. There is nothing overtly complex about the song structure or its execution.

Now, this is completely a diversionary tactic on my part, that autoethnography and, more broadly, academia have taught me: critical examination from a distance. I have not listened to this record in over twenty years. And yet I have listened today for the purpose of this analysis. And I am hardening my heart in order to do so. I am glossing over the lyrics, I am filtering out her voice and diving into the intricacies of keys and modulations and ostinati, because quite honestly that is easier, safer. The musical analysis is concrete and solid, and I am able to get to the truth of the matter of the music by being structured in my musicological analysis. But that's not all there is. Now I must be brave. I include the lyrics here:

> Thank you for the days
> Those endless days, those sacred days you gave me
> I'm thinking of the days
> I won't forget a single day, believe me
> I bless the light
> I bless the light that lights on you, believe me
> And though you're gone
> You're with me every single day, believe me
> Days I'll remember all my life
> Days when you can't see wrong from right
> You took my life
> But then I knew that very soon you'd leave me
> But it's all right
> Now I'm not frightened of this world, believe me
> I wish today could be tomorrow
> The night is dark, it just brings sorrow, let it wait
> Thank you for the days
> Those endless days, those sacred days you gave me
> I'm thinking of the days
> I won't forget a single day, believe me
> Days I'll remember all my life
> Days when you can't see wrong from right
> You took my life
> But then I knew that very soon you'd leave me
> But it's all right
> Now I'm not frightened of this world, believe me
> Thank you for the days

Those endless days, those sacred days you gave me
I'm thinking of the days
I won't forget a single day, believe me
I bless the light
I bless the light that shines on you, believe me
And though you're gone
You're with me every single day, believe me.
('Days' by The Kinks, *The Kinks Are the Village Green Preservation Society*, Pye
Records, 1968).

My experience of the sounds of her death are not held captive in the guitar
chords or the drum fills or the bass lines. They are here, in the words. This
song at her funeral made me feel like she was singing for me one last time,
from beyond the veil. I knew it, even as I sat there in the church, swathed
in my grief, that this was her goodbye, '*but then I knew that very soon you'd
leave me*' was every beat of my broken heart. Denzin writes:

> There are no experiences outside the text, only glossed, narrative reports of
> them. The use and value of the autoethnographic method lies in its user's
> ability to capture, probe, and render understandable problematic experi-
> ence. If this cannot be done, if subject representations of lived experiences,
> as given in stories, cannot be represented, then the method ends up produc-
> ing the kinds of documents I have [vocally] criticized .... (2014: 36)

I suspect, then, that I must dwell between these two renditions: half capturing the trauma, half shying away from it. Although I must take heart to
some degree, that I have been strong enough to even write this chapter.

The French romantic composer Georges Bizet and his composition, on
the other hand, have not caused me quite so much anguish and, whilst I
am not fully sure of the reasons for this, I was able to have two members
of my choir perform this in 2013. We worked on this piece for the whole
academic year and whilst it was painful for me, being part of their learning
and resituating myself inside the music assisted me in seeing the duet in all
its beauty, allowing me to see the piece with the same heart as my mother
did. Perhaps it's because it is considered high culture, that it offered me
more of a buffer. This was not sung to me on quiet mornings at home. The
MacColl piece is popular music and is, in musical terms, considered more
low-brow, yet that is the one I cannot brook. The Bizet is most certainly
considered high culture, performed in opera houses, and as such, perhaps
there is a class divide here that assists me in my separation.

I reference a particular recording of this duet, the 1951 Jussi Björling and Robert Merrill version which, to my mind and ears, is a superior performance. Taken from Bizet's opera *The Pearl Fishers*, this duet for tenor and baritone incorporates dramatic melodic and harmonic lines attributable to the Romantic era it was composed in, yet the two voices sing together in dyadic counterpoint, a compositional format more commonly found in Baroque and early Classical. As the lyrics are in French, this also offers me a barrier against the pain. In this example, my grief is present, but it transmutes into something other that is carried on swift wings by the harmonic ostinato. The manner in which the two voices interlace with one another is, for me, where the true beauty of this piece rests. Not in the instrumentation nor in the lyrical content (in complete opposition to the previous example), but in the emotional performance of Björling and Merrill.

The duet 'Au fond du temple saint' tells of the friendship between Nadir (tenor) and Zurga (baritone) which becomes threatened by their love for the same woman. The piece is in E-flat major, opening with a call and response between Nadir and Zurga. This is, however, simply a prelude to the chorus. And, I am able to identify the exact moment where my emotions collapse.

**Image 8.1** Bars from Les Pêcheurs de Perles by Georges Bizet, 1863. Open source at https://imslp.org/

The second half of bar 1 in Image 8.1, with the B-flat in the tenor line accompanied by D in the baritone line held as minims and performed as legato means the tension of this interval is maintained for two whole beats of the bar. For both voices, these notes are high, and sit right at the top of their tessituras or vocal ranges. When notes such as this are sung in this manner, it facilitates a particular resonance to the vibrato, sounding both beautiful and anguished simultaneously. This is precisely what Björling and Merrill accomplish and why their rendition has always been so deeply popular, with writing on the Classical Music and Musicians website stating: 'this duet has been sung by many different people. I have selected this recording because I have never heard it sung better' (Pearl Fishers Duet – Bizet: Jussi Björling and Robert Merill). The same harmonic pairing comes at the end of the piece, the B-flat and D held with a fermata (conductor's pause). This revisits the beauty and anguish of its previous incarnation. It is one of those enigmatic moments in opera, full of tension and elegance, that holds the listener's breath for as long as the fermata lasts. The piece concludes in E-flat major, coming back to its home, tonic key.

What is it about this duet that lifts me out of my grief, instead of compounding it like the MacColl track? Offering a compare and contrast of these two pieces of music simply because they are music, is like comparing apples and oranges. Yet, there are ghosts that link them, inextricably, to my moment of collapse. It strikes me as strange that the more transparent of the compositions is the one that causes me the most pain. I wonder if the complexity of the Bizet assists in cushioning my anguish, rather than exposing it. Derrida suggests that 'voice is often taken to be the true measure of presence, that is, the voice simulates presence' (1973: 15) but the ways in which these singers exist within these musical examples differ greatly. Arguably the MacColl track requires just a normal singing voice with no training. It would be a struggle to sing the Bizet properly without training.

## SOUNDING HER DEATH BALLADS

I argue that it is the lyrical content of the MacColl performance that carries the shadow of my mother's voice back to me, not the music. Diametrically, it is the main melodic ostinati of the Bizet that triggers my tears. And so, I am caught between the two universes colliding against me, in this performative, symbolic ritual of emotive transference, of transmutation, of transfiguration. I am forever changed by these pieces of music, by their contextualised significance and their ability to carry my grief within them. We perform them all together, for 'performances are constitutive of experience. They are practices that allow for the construction of situated identities in specific sites. They are embodied co-performatives that actually do something in the world' (Conquergood 1998: 32). I sing with MacColl, Björling and Merrill, I become crushed under the weight of words and soar in the cradle of ascending crescendi.

Autoethnography reminds me that experience is performance, that 'this view of experience and the performance makes it difficult to sustain any distinction between appearances and actualities' (Schechner 1988: 362), meaning that with their inclusion in my story, these pieces of music coalesce with my trauma. They have merged together in a fractalised yet monolithic embodiment of autoethnographic musicology that when recalled through epiphanic moments, as exampled in the vignettes, offers me a window into that time. If, as Judith Butler notes (1993: 141), 'there are no original performances', then 'every performance establishes itself performatively as an original, a personal and locally situated production' (Denzin 2014: 43). My trauma and these songs interweave as one, a danse macabre, the sounds of her death ballads ringing across the decades. Tami Spry writes that 'the body in performance is blood, bone, muscle, movement. The performing body constitutes its own interpretive presence. It is the raw material of a critical cultural story. The performed body is a cultural text embedded in discourses of power' (2011: 18–19).

This musical engagement and representation encapsulate my memories at the moment of her death, becoming a hardened carapace against my performing body. Performance against performance, sound against death, hearing against loss. These pieces live on where she does not and as much as I wish my autoethnographic analysis to have offered me catharsis, like it has done before, this time the wound is just too deep. Prior to writing this, I have been operating from an 'unshareable position' (Denzin 2014: 55) inasmuch as it has been a locked door, an oubliette, a barren territory where the unforgiving sun beats down and nothing grows. I have rarely talked about her death or the manner in which she died because 'a story that is told is never the same story that is heard' (Denzin 2014: 55) and I could not risk miscommunication and the opening up of old scars. What I offer here is, instead, a 'performance text … of suffering, loss, pain' (Denzin 2014: 54) all elbowing their way against melody, harmony, poetry and intervals. It is not a comfortable coexistence, far from it. It is an antagonistic, argumentative grief that falls upon my head.

I hear her voice from outside of me, from somewhere else, from distant shores where the wet sand sucks at her toes and the sea breeze dances in her hair. Her sweet, earthy cry gets trapped in the void, escaping only through these two pieces of music. The E-flat and A major keys, the words thanking me for the days, it is altogether just too much.

I have had to be brave, to put on my battle armour to write this, to be willing to discuss sound and death. I imagine I have only been marginally successful because I am blocked, so confoundedly, by grief and trauma, still. Autoethnography has helped me gain some rare access, but I am unwilling to delve deeper. This is a key issue to acknowledge with this type of methodology; you have to know when to stop. Denzin writes:

> there is no simple retelling of lived experience ... the text creates its view of the world, language is used self-reflexively ... in emphasizing the personal, a new kind of theorizing occurs. Narratives are filled with biographical and not [necessarily] disciplinary citations. A minimalist theoretical text is sought, a text unmediated by complex theoretical terms and concepts. The text is meant to speak for itself, a site where the writer carries on a dialogue with herself and with the reader. (2014: 40–41)

And so, I cut this from me and give it to you, the sound of her death through these compositions. It has created a new text, a new view, a different ontology and epistemology and I can now say goodbye.

*And though you're gone*
*You're with me every single day, believe me ...*

## BIBLIOGRAPHY

Butler, Judith. 1993. *Bodies That Matter*. New York: Routledge.

Clough, Patricia T. 2007. 'Introduction'. In Patricia T. Clough and Jean Halley (eds.), *The Affective Turn: Theorizing the Social*, pp. 1–33. Durham, NC: Duke University Press.

Conquergood, Dwight. 1998. 'Beyond the Text: Toward a Performative Cultural Politics'. In Sheron J. Dailey (ed.), *The Future of Performance Studies: Visions and Revisions*, pp. 25–36. Annandale, VA: National Communication Association.

Crawley, Rex L. 2014. 'Favor: An Autoethnography of Survival'. In Robin M. Boylorn and Mark P. Orbe (eds.), *Critical Autoethnography: Intersecting Cultural Identities in Everyday Life*, pp. 222–233. Walnut Creek, CA: Left Coast Press.

Denzin, Norman K. 2005. 'Interpretive Autoethnography'. In Tony E. Adams, Stacey H. Jones and Carolyn Ellis (eds.), *Handbook of Autoethnography*, pp. 123–142. Walnut Creek, CA: Left Coast Press.

Denzin, Norman K. 2014. *Interpretive Autoethnography*. Los Angeles: Sage.

Derrida, Jacques. 1973. *Speech and Phenomena*. Evanston, IL: Northwestern University Press.

Pearl Fishers Duet – Bizet: Jussi Björling and Robert Merrill. https://classicalmusicand-musicians.com/2018/02/14/pearl-fshers-duet-bizet-jussi-bjorling-and-robert-merrill/ (accessed 27 July 2022).

Reed-Danahay, Deborah. 1997. *Auto/Ethnography: Rewriting the Self and the Social*. Oxford: Berg.

Sartre, Jean-Paul. 1963. *In Search for a Method*. New York: Knopf.

Schechner, Richard. 1988. *Performance Theory*. New York: Routledge.

Shadrack, Jasmine H. 2021. *Black Metal, Trauma, Subjectivity, and Sound: Screaming the Abyss*. Bingley: Emerald Publishing Ltd.

Spry, Tami. 2011. *Body, Paper, Stage: Writing and Performing Autoethnography*. Walnut Creek, CA: Left Coast Press.

Tuck, Eve and Ree, C. 2013. 'A Glossary of Haunting'. In Tony E. Adams, Stacey H. Jones and Carolyn Ellis (eds.), *Handbook of Autoethnography*, pp. 639–658. Walnut Creek, CA: Left Coast Press.

## DISCOGRAPHY

'Days'. Kirsty MacColl. 1989. *Kite*. Virgin KMA2.

'Days'. The Kinks. 1968. *The Kinks Are the Village Green Preservation Society*. Pye Records.

'Au fond du temple saint'. Georges Bizet. 1863. *Les Pêcheurs de Perles*. Recording with Jussi Björling and Robert Merrill, 1951. Nimbus Records.

**Jasmine Hazel Shadrack** is a musician, composer, psychoanalyst and feminist autoethnographer with over twenty years of teaching, lecturing and research experience. She is adjunct professor at the Don Wright Faculty for Music Research and Composition, Western University, Canada, and a member of the National Coalition for Independent Scholars. She sits on the editorial boards for the International Society for Metal and Music Studies and Intellect's new series entitled *Advances in Metal Music and Culture*. Her monograph *Black Metal, Trauma, Subjectivity and Sound: Screaming the Abyss* was published by Emerald in 2021.

Chapter 9

# Food for the Dead, Food for the Living

BEVERLEY ROGERS

Food nourishes us, comforts us, gives us energy and provides sustenance to our bodies. Food is vital to our life, but it plays a major role in our deaths too (Mendoza 2021). All around the world, food rituals have been a fundamental response to loss since early times – edible responses to the act of processing the spiritual and sacred nature of death and in assisting the bereaved to steer through the painful and disorientating nature of their newly altered state (Thursby 2006: 79). These responses take on their own individual meaning and symbolism depending on religion, geography and cultural significance, but what is a universal factor is the way food rituals are loaded with multilayered emotions and multidimensional significant meanings. Through food, communal, ethnic and religious identities are communicated, conveyed and reinforced, strengthening kinship bonds and providing comfortable and familiar emotional support during a major period of stress (Holtzman 2006: 361).

Food can represent positivity, life-affirmation and celebration, such as the choice to serve the deceased's favourite food as a wake; it can also be hugely symbolic of transition and passing over, such as the last meal before the execution of a condemned prisoner. In this chapter, I explore the role that food plays in death and mourning, using examples from a variety of different world cultures and covering a span of differing time periods.

As a historian I want to explore how some cultures undertake to care for their dead with food, whereas others remember them through food

(Walter 2009: 216). I also want to detail how food is the medium through which a shared ritual space is created; where the bereaved come together to support each other and reimagine a life after loss. I hope to show that food, and as such the sense of taste, can be a comfort when dealing with death.

## FOOD RITUALS TO CARE FOR THE DEAD

At the heart of a number of food rituals lies the belief that the living can exert some control over the destiny of the deceased's soul. Food rituals to care for the dead help the dead move on to the next realm and be supported there. Italians, for example, hang a *cornicelli* – similar to a red pepper hence its translation as 'little red horns' – as an amulet over the doorway or near the bed of the very ill or dying, with the belief that it will ward off evil spirits (Thursby 2006: 94). In Islamic tradition, honey is placed on the lips of the dying to sweeten the moment of death and so aid the soul onwards (Thursby 2006: 94). In ancient Egypt, the corpse was mummified for forty days with natron salt to ensure the body was preserved in readiness for the afterlife. A well-preserved body meant its associated soul would recognise, and thus return to it – a necessary component for a successful afterlife. But food rituals go beyond being used to try to exercise control over death to food traditions that purify the soul. For instance, Japanese Buddhism holds a traditional religious service seven days after a death that involves the sprinkling of salt dissolved in water to purify the corpse (Thursby 2006: 87), and food and drink have also been widely used to cleanse the soul of material sins throughout history. The ancient Greeks believed that the only way that the gods would forgive their sins was by the amount of food that friends and family consumed after the funeral. The more you ate, the better the chance for the soul to reach the afterlife (Mendoza 2021).

In Pre-Reformation Europe, Roman Catholics were haunted by the prospect that their deceased loved one could suffer long periods in purgatory or even be punished in hell. To encourage prayers for the dead, food offerings were made by the relatives. Although a different tradition of Christianity, in Greece today this type of food use is evident in the Greek Orthodox special service for departed souls called *mnemonsinon* which reminds the bereaved to make a special appeal to pray for the departed's salvation. *Kollyva* (or *koliva*) – a boiled wheat dish made of sugar, currants, flour, oil, spices, sesame seed and walnuts with the shape of a cross on top, is offered in the Church three days, nine days, forty days, six months and one year after death (Thursby 2006: 95). A Japanese tradition is to give a small packet of salt, as well as rice, sugar, onions and garlic, to the Buddhist monks as they leave to return to their home or temple after a Japanese burial service. The gifts are donated in thanksgiving for their presence and prayers on behalf of the deceased.

A variation on these gifts can be found in the funeral custom practised in the United Kingdom, Europe and North America during the eighteenth to early twentieth century, where a funeral token, called a 'funeral biscuit', sometimes served along with burnt wine, was given to all attending a funeral (Houlbrooke 2020: 25–42). By Victorian times, as funerals became more lavish and abundant, and offering of food and drink to the mourners reflected the demonstration of means and status, the biscuit transitioned to a sponge-like cake. It was wrapped in paper with details of the deceased printed on the wrapper alongside various symbolic symbols and motifs, commonly hourglasses, coffins, skulls, crossbones or cherubs. Sealed with black wax, the biscuit/cake became a symbolic reminder to the living that a valued member of their circle had died, and called upon the mourners to remember the dead in their hearts (Thursby 2006: 84).

Food traditionally used in Morocco functions as a conduit to seek God's blessings and forgiveness. Mourners believe that serving food to family members and strangers brings merit to the dead, allowing for misdeeds to be forgiven (Oualaalou 2019: 136–137). Muslims in other countries also believe that the act of feeding others at the funeral is connected with God forgiving some of the deceased's minor misdemeanours. As to what types of misdeeds are forgiven, only God can decide. An extreme example of this type of ritual known as sin-eating was enacted in Wales from the sixteenth century to the early nineteenth century. On a sudden and unexpected death, a 'sin-eater' was called to the home of the deceased where he was paid a small fee to eat a simple meal over the corpse. It was believed that the sin-eater consumed and transferred the sins of the dead to himself, so allowing the departed soul to enter heaven with a cleansed soul. This custom may have been designed and adapted in response to the Reformation removal of purgatory assisted rituals. The concept of a spiritual transfer from the corpse to the living can also be found in the medieval funeral tradition of eating 'corpse cakes' in Germany. Historically, after the body had been washed and laid in its coffin, the woman of the house prepared leavened dough that was placed to rise on the linen-covered chest of the corpse. It was then eaten by the nearest relative in the belief that the dough 'absorbed' some of the deceased's personal qualities that were, in turn, passed on to mourners (Hoag Levins, in Cann 2019a: n12). This symbolic act can still be found in Upper Bavaria today and in the Balkan peninsula, where a small bread image of the deceased is made and eaten by the survivors of the family.

Caring for the dead also involves nourishing them. Early evidence of cultures that cared for the deceased in this way include the San Francisco Bay Area shell mounds which date to the Early Period (c. 3000–500 BCE) and the Middle Period (c. 500 BCE–500 CE) (Luby and Gruber 1999: 96). The positions of the shell mounds surrounding multiple burials indicate that humans from the time of the Neanderthals concerned themselves with the provisioning of the dead (Luby and Gruber 1999: 105). The ancient Egyptians left food and drink within tombs believing that the food would nourish the deceased in the afterlife. To ensure that nourishment would never run out, images of food and drink were also painted and carved on the tomb walls, often as part of a scene showing the deceased enjoying a banquet with their family. In Roman times, funeral feasts were held with a belief that the dead needed not only sustenance, but a break from the tedium of the tomb. These feasts were often riotous and drunken occasions, and the dead were believed to derive both pleasure and advantage from these offerings (Yoder 1986: 150). Ancient Romans also developed a system where tubes, attached to the top of graves, were lowered directly into the deceased's mouth so that the mourners could continue to supply the deceased with bread and wine to sustain them (Rowell 1977: 10).

Other examples include the Mayan civilisation, where the dead were buried with maize in their mouths to ensure they never went hungry (Mendoza 2021) and in the American West, where the Hopi use maize as the dominant symbol of their spiritual life: two ears of blue maize accompany the deceased on his or her journey beyond life (Thursby 2006: 82). In all these examples, food functions as a symbolic conduit between the living and the dead. The rituals underlie the belief that these substances somehow become transformed from a material object to a spiritual essence, allowing the dead to nourish themselves and to ensure they receive a continuing supply of food. For these cultures death is not regarded as a termination, but rather an advancement to another level of being where the dead are re-accommodated as ancestors who watch over the living who in turn have an obligation to ensure their ancestors are cared for.

In Chinese culture, following a death, there is intense chanting, food offerings and numerous gatherings of family and friends in honour of the deceased for forty-nine days. Minimally processed food is also offered to the ancestors via an ancestral shrine and then made into cooked dishes to serve at the family gathering (Wu 2019: 17). Thereafter, family members continue making offerings at the newly cleaned and tended graves of ancestors on the anniversary of the deceased's death, at Chinese New Year, and at the annual Qing Ming festival (Cann 2019b: 74). These offerings, which continue to be undertaken in most of rural China and even in urban areas, keep the ancestors consistently revived and continually included in the community. Despite the Communist Cultural Revolution, a strong sense of continuity between the living and the dead is maintained (Lalande and Bonanno 2006: 307). In return for the offerings the living expect reciprocal benefits from the ancestors such as their power to influence their luck, wealth and protection. To displease the dead by not caring for them means they will return and haunt the living with bad luck (Wu 2019, 29). The Mesquaki (Fox Nation) Indians ensure they are 'firm with their dead', making them understand that they have lost nothing by dying by regularly giving offerings of tobacco and food. They expect the deceased to compensate the living by guaranteeing them long life, clothes and plentiful food in their role as a 'protective spirit' (Levi-Strauss 1983: 31). In Asian countries rooted in Buddhism, bereaved relatives typically engage in ancestor worship at home. A Buddha altar is constructed where they place incense burners, bells, candles, photographs of the dead and offerings of food. The deceased play ongoing and significant roles in the life of the living and may become dangerous when no ritual is performed for them (Klass 2001: 742, 747). This belief is also seen in Zulu culture (an Nguni ethnic group), where the spirit of the deceased is fetched from the grave and brought home to enjoy a series of food and drink related rituals. If these extensive and expensive rituals are ignored, there is a fear of the dead bringing bad luck to the family (Ntsimane 2019: 178–180). In all these food rituals, this continued exchange between generations ensures that every member of the family – alive or deceased – is treated as a necessary link in the family chain (Wu 2019: 19, 30). Continuity with the traditional past remains strong through the medium of food and the well-being of the living and dead remain mutually dependent (Klass 2001: 749). Walters understands these rituals as helping to renegotiate the deceased's new status in the community, allowing the living to maintain an active relationship with the dead and creating a continuing bond between the two parties (2009: 216–219).

Ancestor food rituals are by nature a communal affair, as demonstrated by the Korean festival of Young San Jae where hundreds of people perform a food ritual together and innumerable dead souls are summoned and invited (Wu 2019: 52). Koreans believe that the souls of the dead visit their families on holidays and on the anniversaries of their deaths, so families offer food for the dead to eat during their visit, as well as material goods such as money and shoes for the soul's return journey (Wu: 2019, 41). Food delicacies are offered in an artistic way – three towers of offerings are made: one composed of nuts and fruits, another of oil and honey pastries and the third of rice cakes (Wu 2019: 46). The monks collect all the water used for washing the dishes and throw it away as a means of giving food to hungry ghosts – the beings who live in hell, struggling with hunger no matter how much they eat (Wu 2019: 49). Young San Jae demonstrates a liminal blurring of the boundary between the living and the dead, and the secular and the sacred (Wu 2019: 51). It symbolically re-enacts the last festival that the historical Buddha had with his disciples and emphasises new life through transformation, connection and joy, and the combating of negativity over decay, separation and bereavement (Park 2019: 37). The feast is considered one of the most powerful ways to empower the soul so that it gains Nirvana where the deceased can step out of the cycle of rebirths and is set on a path of enlightenment (Wu 2019: 43; Klass 2001: 744–745). Through Young San Jae, food is utilised as an expression of gratitude and family devotion. It also becomes the agent through which descendants offer the teaching of the dharma to their ancestors (Wu 2019: 52).

The most colourful, convivial and festive example of food being used in ancestor veneration is the Mexican Day of the Dead (Dias de Muertos). All over Mexico, during the period 30 October to 2 November, specific days are set aside for welcoming the souls of the deceased. An *offrenda* – a cloth-covered table – is constructed in every household with an arch, festooned with palm or green leaves decoration and stalks of sugarcane, and embellished with flowers, fruits and ornaments. Placed on the table are photos of saints, a Virgin or Christ statuette, candles, vases of flowers, incense and photos of the deceased (Carmichael and Sayer 1991: 19–20). Food and drink are central to this celebratory welcome for the souls of the dead, which involves hours of preparation and cooking (Carmichael and Sayer 1991: 10). The souls absorb the essence of the food and drinks, and when they have had their fill, it is the turn of the family members to take their share of the *offrenda*. Vigils take place at flower-adorned graves, accompanied by candles, decorations and a large amount of food, whilst copal incense sanctifies the ceremony (Brandes 1998: 360; Carmichael and Sayer 1991: 10). The family feast with the extended family members – both alive and dead – is an enjoyable celebration where present family members tell stories about the dead family members and say prayers for their souls. Friends arrive, food is eaten and the souls return to enjoy for a few brief hours the pleasures they once knew in life (Brandes 1998: 364; Carmichael and

Sayer 1991: 9–10). The boundaries between the living and dead are erased through the preparation and consumption of the food which becomes a bridge between the two realms. In turn, the grave site is transformed into a social space through the act of decoration and eating (Cann 2019b: 74–76). Alongside the *offrenda*, symbolic food such as sculptured sugar candies in the form of skulls, skeletons and caskets are displayed and eaten; their humour and gaiety suggest an almost irreverent, macabre confrontation with mortality (Brandes 1998: 360–362). They act as a symbolic reminder that, though we all must face the reality of death, there are still aspects of life that are sweet and should be savoured (Cann 2019b: 69). All play humorously on the theme of death whilst acting as reminders that life is short (Brandes 1998: 360). Food and drink offerings of the living for the dead are interwoven with theological understandings of salvation and the afterlife. Amongst the communal joviality there can be seen the Spanish Catholic belief brought to Mexico in colonial times, in the requirement of prayers and offerings to help the soul meditate through purgatory and then on to heaven. The symbolism of Pan de Muertos (Bread of the Dead) – a rich coffee cake decorated with a bone-shaped cross with a knob or a teardrop in the centre – which is often carried to the grave site, underlies this. The yeast is symbolic of life's ultimate ability to overcome death and the rising of the bread is a symbolic re-enactment of the resurrection of the soul in the afterlife (Cann 2019b: 70).

## FOOD RITUALS TO CARE FOR THE LIVING

Immediately following a death, food can also be employed as a strong symbol of love and condolence to the living, especially within many close-knit ethnic groups or communities. Simple meals are prepared and cooked as nourishment for the grieving families to help them navigate the distress of losing a loved one (Thursby 2006: 99). These comforting and sustaining dishes – which are easy to transport and reheat – help the bereaved adjust to their new circumstances without having to worry about day-to-day planning of meals (Yoder 1986: 150). In the American South, for example, an abundance of foods such as casseroles, biscuits, fried chicken, baked ham and deserts provide familiar cuisine, whilst also sending an underlying message of emotional support from the gift giver to the griever (Yoder 1986: 150). Sometimes this can be a traditional obligation based on religious practice (Graham 2019: 91). For two or three days, it is customary for a Muslim family to rest and begin to adjust to the change in their lives, supported and nourished emotionally and physically by friends and relatives. Gifts of fruit, desserts and a variety of well-loved dishes are provided alongside a fragrant sweetmeat called *halma* or *helva*, consisting of pine nuts, walnuts, sesame seeds, honey, flour, semolina and butter or margarine. Often the food is culturally related and is often prepared with influence from the nature of origin (Thursby 2006: 106). Another example is Shiva, an intense seven-day period of mourning in the Jewish religion, which is undertaken with the support of the community and includes a meal of condolence – Seudat Havra'ah – which is served by friends and neighbours (Thursby 2006: 90; Crocker and Fuller 2019: 119). Highly symbolic, the meal is primarily made up of foods that are symbolic of the wheel of life such as lentils, peas, eggs, rolls and bagels (Thursby 2006: 96). During the Hindu mourning period, the family cannot cook any food when they return to their home. Family members subsist entirely on foods given by others for the period of mourning (Thursby 2006: 87). The food which is provided follows traditional spiritual rules such as the avoidance of salt, certain vegetables and any meat. Some other foods are also avoided, such as garlic and onion, as they may create bodily odours and could offend both humans and other living creatures, creating disharmony (Thursby 2006: 109). The time-intensive labour of preparing and presenting wholesome foods, acts as a way to honour the deceased whilst also strengthening the bond of love and support of the community for the family left behind (Thursby 2006: 97). At a time when it is difficult to know what to say, the gift of food says 'I am sorry for your loss' (Brien 2003).

Soothing nourishment for the living also takes centre stage at a funeral meal, usually held after the interment or cremation. Borne from the past necessity of having to refresh mourners who had travelled considerable distances to attend the ceremony, funeral feasts allow the community to come together, either at the bereaved's home, the home of the deceased, or at a suitable venue such as a community hall or restaurant. Alongside the need to feed those who attended the funeral, the meal acts as a significant way to remember the dead. When held at the home, the private space of the bereaved temporarily transforms into a 'public space' where the deep sorrow of the separation of death becomes softened by the presence of family and friends who use the event to embrace the past and share memories of the deceased. The purpose of the food and drink at these events is ultimately to sustain the living – they are not intended to be shared with or consumed by the deceased, unlike the case of an ancestor meal. As Cann asserts, 'the dead linger in the living rooms through stories, memories, shared meals, and recipes, passively invoked but not active participants'

(2019b: 63). The anthropologist van Gennep viewed the funeral meal as a rite of incorporation, and believed that its purpose was 'to reunite all the surviving members of the group with each other ... in the same way that a chain which has been broken by the disappearance of one of its links must be re-joined' (1960: 149). Through the sounds of conversation and laughter evoked by fond remembrance of the deceased, the deep sorrow of the separation by death is softened. The deceased become placed in social memory and the bereaved can achieve some kind of moving on (Shimane 2022; Holtzman 2006: 371).

There is tremendous diversity in the form post-funeral meals take around the world, and the foods served can vary depending on the culture, geography and individuality. Food preparation can often be ceremonial and ritualistic; they may be favourite foods of the deceased, or traditional recipes passed down through the family. Often, they are simple, porta-ble, comfort foods which evoke nostalgic memories (Thursby 2006: 115). Traditional, culturally appropriate meals may be served such as at African American funerals, where dishes such as greens, fried chicken, corn bread and yams, steeped in southern flavours, are common. Some foods are tra-ditionally only seen at funerals, such as a potato cheese casserole called 'funeral potatoes', a lemon tart known as chess pie in the American South, or the Amish sweet raisin 'funeral pie'. These staple foods help bond mourn-ers together in comfort and familiarity (Thursby 2006: 82). Often there can be a dish served which is iconic to the memory of a long-deceased family member (Graham 2019: 94, 101). The use of their recipe causes that person to be socially remembered once again. The consumption of starch staples in funeral feasts, such as rice, wheat and corn, is symbolic of their central place in life, as is the inclusion of sugary foods which can often be found on the menu. As an added benefit, sugar is known to create a measurable chemical pleasure response in the body which helps deal with the stress and the difficult emotions of mourning (Cann 2019b: 59).

Sugar can also be used symbolically. Those who attend Chinese funerals are given candy made of brown rock sugar to 'sweeten the sting of death'. The candy is meant to be consumed before going home to prevent negative thoughts or sad spirits from following one home from the funeral (Cann 2019b: 74). Alcohol as part of the feast has been used in rituals pertaining to death for centuries, albeit in a variety of culturally specific ways (Shusko 2019: 152). The 'tension reducing effect of alcohol' can have the effect of altering emotions when consumed (Shusko 2019: 154). It can console the living and turn the meal into 'a celebration of the ties between living fam-ily members and friends, times of reunions and renewed relationships'

(Jellinek 1977: 849). Food as a symbolic element can also be seen in the simple Moroccan funeral feasts where couscous is served, which represents unity with and support to the grieving family. This is further emphasised by the community members eating from a shared bowl (Oualaalou 2019: 129). The communal element of the feast acts as a symbolic representation of compassion, love and relationships held together by community (Wu 2019: 41). The simplicity of the Moroccan funerary meal, which also usually includes simple bread, honey, and butter, reminds the bereaved that no matter what and how much one eats and accumulates when alive, the day will come when one leaves behind the physical world. In this way, the funeral feast becomes not only a social arena but incorporates religious and mindful reflections as well (Oualaalou 2019: 129).

Whilst contemporary behaviours and traditions are rooted in legacies from the past, there has been a gradual decline in some cultures in the practice of the old customs in regard to funerary feasts (Thursby 2006: 86). Younger people tend to view death through cultural and social lenses that are very different from those of past generations, and as society changes, new needs grow and take over old ones (Oualaalou 2019: 134). For example, while their funerals were once traditionally subdued, with little conversation or conviviality taking place after burial or cremation, many contemporary Native Americans are now using mortuary services and allowing standard funerary ritual practices (Thursby 2006: 93). Also, within the Japanese culture, rites have become relaxed and the feast of fish and wine – *sho-nanoka* – held on the seventh day after death, may now take place on the same day as the funeral (Thursby 2006: 114). However, whilst cultures have experienced a gradual demise of formal funerary ritual, the immediate bereaved, together with the larger social community, still benefit from a funeral meal as it functions as a group experience in a familiar structured setting which enables the living to make significant progress in handling their grief (Yoder 1986: 149). The funeral meal provides an important support service to those who are mourning. No more poignantly was this highlighted than during the Covid-19 pandemic (2020–2021) when the inability in many cases to hold a communal funeral feast caused much distress.

Cultural distinctiveness constantly undergoes transformation from generation to generation, as do new consumer expectations, causing old rituals to be lost, revived or reinvented in an ever-changing fluidity of circumstances, social dynamics and necessity (Long 2004: 119). Yet, food and drink continue to play a major part in how we cope with death and loss universally. Whilst its use in specific customs may change and adapt, the need for nourishment for both the living and the dead remains consistent in our ways of dealing with death.

## CONCLUDING WORDS

The very act of eating reminds people that they themselves are very much alive (Cann 2019b: 77). Food is a transformative activity – when cooked, prepared and consumed it nourishes us but in the context of loss it represents so much more. Food honours and respects the ancestors, providing them with sustenance in the afterlife, and promises reciprocal support for the living, maintaining important continuing bonds between the living and the dead. Through the medium of food, the bereaved are strengthened with purpose, bonding and support so that the smaller grieving family becomes part of an extended family of supporters in the wider community (Thursby 2006: 81, 84). The sensuality of eating transmits powerful mnemonic cues, principally through smells and tastes, making it a particularly intense and compelling medium for evoking recollection on a cognitive, emotional and physical level (Holtzman 2006: 372, 378). It has a strengthening power to emotionally alter the way we feel and is a conduit for sharing valuable memories (Thursby 2006: 84). Food and drink also help us to express our community, ethnic and religious identities, reflecting and shaping a culture, and affirming kinship, security and belonging in an uncertain time of bereavement (Long 2004: 119; Cann 2019a: 7). Overall, food is a powerful conduit in carrying meaning. Its use as part of death rituals provides comfort, symbolic communal expression and ritual links between the mourners and the deceased and provides the bereaved with the motivation to move forward in life.

## BIBLIOGRAPHY

Brandes, Stanley. 1998. 'The Day of the Dead, Halloween, and the Quest for Mexican National Identity', *The Journal of American Folklore* 111(442): 359–380. https://doi.org/10.2307/541045

Brien, Donna Lee. 2003. 'Concern and Sympathy in a Pyrex Bowl: Cookbooks and Funeral Foods', *M/C Journal* 16(3). https://doi.org/10.5204/mcj.655

Cann, Candi K. 2019a. 'Starters: The Role of Food in Bereavement and Memoralization'. In Candi K. Cann (ed.), *Dying to Eat: Cross-Cultural Perspectives on Food, Death, and the Afterlife*, pp. 1–13. Lexington, KT: University Press of Kentucky.

Cann, Candi K. 2019b. 'Sweetening Death: Shifting Landscapes of the Role of Food in Grief and Mourning'. In Candi K. Cann (ed.), *Dying to Eat: Cross-Cultural Perspectives on Food, Death, and the Afterlife*, pp. 55–85. Lexington, KT: University Press of Kentucky.

Carmichael, Elizabeth and Sayer, Cloë. 1991. *The Skeleton at the Feast*. Austin: University of Texas Press and British Museum Press.

Crocker, Lacy K. and Fuller, Gordon. 2019. 'Memorializing and Sustaining Faith'. In Candi K. Cann (ed.), *Dying to Eat: Cross-Cultural Perspectives on Food, Death, and the Afterlife*, pp. 107–124. Lexington, KT: University Press of Kentucky.

Graham, Joshua. 2019. 'Funeral Food as Resurrection in the American South'. In Candi K. Cann (ed.), *Dying to Eat Cross-Cultural Perspectives on Food, Death, and the Afterlife*, pp. 89–106. Lexington, KT: University Press of Kentucky.

Holtzman, Jon D. 2006. 'Food and Memory', *Annual Review of Anthropology* 35: 361–378. https://doi.org/10.1146/annurev.anthro.35.081705.123220

Houlbrooke, Ralph. 2020. 'Death, Church, and Family in England Between the Late Fifteenth and the Early Eighteenth Centuries'. In Ralph Houlbrooke (ed.), *Death, Ritual and Bereavement*, pp. 25–42. London: Routledge.

Jellinek, E.M. 1977. 'The Symbolism of Drinking: A Culture-Historical Approach', *Journal of Studies on Alcohol and Drugs* 38(5): 852–866. https://doi.org/10.15288/jsa.1977.38.852

Klass, Dennis. 2001. 'Continuing Bonds in the Resolution of Grief in Japan and North America', *American Behavioural Scientist* 44(5): 742–763. https://doi.org/10.1177/00027640121956476

Lalande, Kathleen M. and Bonanno, George A. 2006. 'Culture and Continuing Bonds: A Prospective Comparison of Bereavement in the United States and the People's Republic of China', *Death Studies* 30(4): 303–324. https://doi.org/10.1080/07481180500544708

Levi-Strauss, Claude. 1983. *The Raw and the Cooked: Mythologiques*, Vol. 1. Trans. J. Weightman and D. Weightman. Chicago: University of Chicago Press.

Long, Lucy M. 2004. 'Learning to Listen to the Food Voice', *Food, Culture and Society* 7(1): 118–122. https://doi.org/10.2752/155280104786578067

Luby, Edward M. and Gruber, Mark F. 1999. 'The Dead Must be Fed: Symbolic Meanings of the Shellmounds of the San Francisco Bay Area', *Cambridge Archaeological Journal* 9(1): 95–108. https://doi.org/10.1017/S0959774300015225

Mendoza, Marilyn A. 2021. 'The Role of Food in Death and Grief', *Psychology Today* 20 July 2021. https://www.psychologytoday.com/gb/blog/understanding-grief/202103/the-role-food-in-death-and-grief

Ntsimane, Radikobo. 2019. 'Eating and Drinking with the Dead in South Africa'. In Candi K. Cann (ed.), *Dying to Eat: Cross-Cultural Perspectives on Food, Death, and the Afterlife*, pp. 285–312. Lexington, KT: University Press of Kentucky.

Oualaalou, David. 2019. 'Moroccan Funeral Feasts'. In Candi K. Cann (ed.), *Dying to Eat: Cross-Cultural Perspectives on Food, Death, and the Afterlife*, pp. 125–149. Lexington, KT: University Press of Kentucky.

Park, Jung Eun Sophia. 2019. 'The Eating Ritual in Korean Religiosity'. In Candi K. Cann (ed.), *Dying to Eat: Cross-Cultural Perspectives on Food, Death, and the Afterlife*, pp. 37–54. Lexington, KT: University Press of Kentucky.

Rowell, Geoffrey. 1977. *The Liturgy of Christian Burial*. London: S.P.C.K.

Shimane, Katsumi. 2022. 'Special Bonds with the Dead: How Funerals Transformed in the Twentieth and Twenty-first Centuries', *Philosophical Transactions of the Royal Society* 373: 20170274. https://doi.org/10.1098/rstb.2017.0274

Shusko, Christa. 2019. 'Alcohol Consumption, Transgression, and Death'. In Candi K. Cann (ed.), *Dying to Eat: Cross-Cultural Perspectives on Food, Death, and the Afterlife*, pp. 151–169. Lexington, KT: University Press of Kentucky.

Thursby, Jacqueline S. 2006. *Funeral Festivals in America: Rituals for the Living*. Lexington, KT: University Press of Kentucky.

Van Gennep, Arnold. 1960. *The Rites of Passage*. Chicago: University of Chicago Press.

Walter, Tony. 2009. 'Communicating with the Dead'. In Clifton D. Bryant and Dennis L. Peck (eds.), *Encyclopedia of Death and the Human Experience*, pp. 216–219. Los Angeles: Sage Publications.

Wu, Emily S. 2019. 'Chinese Ancestral Worship'. In Candi K. Cann (ed.), *Dying to Eat Cross-Cultural Perspectives on Food, Death, and the Afterlife*, pp. 17–36. Lexington, KT: University Press of Kentucky.

Yoder, Lonnie. 1986. 'The Funeral Meal: A Significant Funerary Ritual', *Journal of Religion and Health* 25(2): 149–160. https://doi.org/10.1007/BF01533245

**Beverley Rogers** is a freelance researcher, historian and folklorist based in the Gower Peninsula in Swansea, Wales. She has an undergraduate degree (Hons) in Egyptology, and a master's degree in Death, Religion and Culture.

# Chapter 10

# Tasting the Dead

## CHRISTINA WELCH

This chapter explores the sense of taste in relation to death. The sense of taste is tricky to define as there are cultural differences in the profiles of recognised flavours, but in this chapter, the sense of taste concerns something being put into the mouth to be consumed. Taste is inherently related to other senses: anything being put into one's mouth is also usually seen and/or smelt, when eating the sounds of chewing and munching can be heard, and when drinking the gulp of liquid entering the throat makes a sound. Further, food or drink when brought to the mouth utilises the sense of proprioception (body awareness that includes movement and balance), and the thing being tasted touches the tongue and palate. As such David Howes has argued that taste cannot be understood in isolation (2007: 10) and therefore whilst this chapter relates primarily to taste, it must be remembered that tasting is a fully somatic experience.

There are several ways that taste and death are related and this chapter explores three examples: first, the food traditionally eaten at funerals (funeral foods), and here is some overlap with the previous chapter; second, the deliberate ingestion of dry human remains (which in this chapter focuses on the consumption of mumia/mummia as a medicinal cure in Europe); and third, the deliberate ingestion of wet human remains, i.e. cannibalism in the form of ritualistically consuming dead human flesh. The use of 'dry' and 'wet' as terms is adapted from Hertz (1960) who differentiated between funeral rites for dry skeletal human remains or cremated human remains (cremains), and rituals around the disposal of the dead wet fleshy body. In this chapter, the first two examples are mainly European in focus, but the third moves to the Americas. It is important to note in regard to the second example of death and the sense of taste, mumia/ mummia consumption was normal in Europe in the early modern period despite technically being a form of cannibalism (and thus related to the third example), but was understood as medical cannibalism and thus just medicine (Sugg 2016). Further, in regard to the third example, whilst cannibalism today is often placed in the realm of horror movies, this practice, although rare, continues into the present day with Wikipedia helpfully listing examples (Wiki cannibalism).

Perhaps the most notable example of cannibalism in the past fifty-odd years is the 1972 Uruguayan plane crash in the Chilean Andes. With very little food on board, the crash survivors discovered the search for them had been terminated after only eight days, and despite trying to eat parts of the airplane, a mutual decision was made by the survivors that cannibalism of the dead would be the only way to stay alive. The crash initially killed 12 of the 45 crew and passengers, but starvation, exposure and avalanches left just 16 to be rescued 72 days later (Wiki Uruguay Flight). However, not all acts of contemporary cannibalism come from desperate circumstances. In 2003, Armin Meiwes advertised that he wished to meet a man to kill and eat. Bernd Brandes answered the advert and was duly killed, butchered and cooked, with Meiwes eating several portions of Brandes's flesh (Harding 2004 [online]). Then, in 2012 Mao Sugiyama cooked and served up his own genitals (with button mushrooms and garnished with parsley) at a $250-a-plate banquet, having advertised the meal via a blog (Campbell 2012 [online]). These three examples of contemporary cannibalism do not inform this paper but serve to demonstrate that even when it is a cultural anathema, cannibalistic acts still take place. However, what is far more normal in regard to death and taste, is food at funerals.

## INGESTION OF FUNERAL FOOD

Eating as a form of commemoration of the dead, and a sociable act of condolence with the bereaved or comfort between mourners is very common, with wakes or funeral buffets being globally normative. This is perhaps of no surprise given that relationships between the living typically need reinforcing during the time of a close bereavement; as Whinfrey-Koepping notes, *Food, Friends and Funerals* go hand in hand (2008). In Judaism and

Islam, the family of the deceased traditionally receive food from neighbours. In Judaism a special meal (Seudat Havra'ah) is given to the mourners. It customarily consists of hard-boiled eggs and other round-shaped foods such as bagels and lentils, which symbolise the ongoing cycle of life, of which death and suffering are part (JFG 2021). In Judaism traditionally mourners are not expected to prepare food, and the same occurs in Islam although here it is forbidden under Sunnah regulations (*al-feqh*). In Christianity too there is a strong relationship between food and funerals, with Jesus serving a meal knowing he soon would be dead, this Last Supper being enacted in the Eucharist (Stewart 2017). Hindus and Buddhists have funeral rites that involve food, with traditional dishes served for mourners but also food provided for the dead to ensure the right relationships between ancestors and decedents (see Williams and Ladwig 2012: *passim*; McDaniel 2019: 296). Traditional funeral rituals around food take a central place not only when the funerals occur in the place where the religion developed but also continue when people move, with death rites and afterlife beliefs adapting to diasporic locations (Meyer-Rochow 2009; Manian and Bullock 2016; Cann 2019). However, reiterating the normative is not the aim of this chapter, as that has been covered by Rogers. Here I aim to highlight two examples of food rituals related to death rites in Northern Europe that are less typical.

The first less usual example of thinking about the sense of taste and death is sin-eating. It is unclear whether sin-eating stories are based in fact or folklore, but in Wales, as well as in Scotland, England and Ireland, during the late-1800s claims are made that bread would be eaten off a corpse by a poor person paid to take on the 'Sinnes of the Defunct, and free him (or her) from walking after they were dead' (Hartland 1892: 146). One example of this story comes from the book *The Sin-Eater and Other Tales* (1895) by Fiona MacLeod (the literary pseudonym for William Sharp, d. 1905) who wrote about the Western Isles of Scotland. The Sin-Eater story was based on the island of Iona and includes the following information: the act was 'a good Christian act' undertaken by a person who was a stranger to the deceased (1895: 38), the food and water had to be placed on the naked breast of the individual (1895: 40), the sin-eater would add a pinch of salt to the bread and the water before ingesting them and the deceased's sins (1895: 43). Other tales speak of the custom in Hereford using a loaf of bread, and beer, both of which were placed on the funeral bier rather than the body of the deceased, and mention that 'sixpence in money' was paid to the sin-eater (Simpson and Roud 2003).

An early example of the myth, from medieval Wales, notes that the bread was eaten by the sin-eater directly off the body of a dying person (Naro 2021: 472). Because of the date of this tale, the understanding was that by having their sins consumed (eradicated) before death, the dying person would die sin-free rather than have their sins painfully purged (eradicated) in purgatory. Although this suggests a somewhat simplistic grasp of complex Roman Catholic post-mortem theology, the theological context does help makes sense of sin-eating, and it may well be that the later examples are, as Roger has noted, hangovers from a time when the country was Roman Catholic. Although the veracity of all the folk rituals concerning sin-eating are unclear, there is oral testimony suggesting that Irish and Welsh immigrants took the practice to the Appalachian region in America and that the practice continued into the 1950s (Beliveau 2017: 171). However, sin-eating is not the only myth connecting the consumption of food with death.

Whilst sin-eating was about someone ingesting food to remove the sins of the deceased, in the Bavarian Highlands, it was the socially acceptable qualities of the dead that were transmitted to the eater via food. Called corpse cakes, dough was placed on the corpse and once it had risen (proved through the heat emitted from the fresh corpse) it was baked into special cakes for the mourners. It was believed that the dough absorbed the good qualities of the deceased and these were transmitted these to those left behind through the eating of the cakes (Hartland 1892: 146). Whilst proving dough on a dead body sounds implausible, a fresh corpse could give off enough heat, as at about 24 hours after death maggots take hold of the body, heating the corpse to the temperature required for proving dough (24–36 degrees C, or 75–95 degrees F);[1] of course, the ambient temperature would affect this and the corpse would need to be located in an area where flies could gain access. However, eating (tasting) bread believed to contain a dead stranger's sin, or consuming cakes where the dough was risen on a fresh corpse, are not the same as ingesting parts of a dead human being, which is the topic of the following sections.

## INGESTION OF DRY HUMAN REMAINS

Human flesh in the form of mumia/mummia/mummy (dried and powered human remains) was regularly ingested in early-modern Europe as a

---

1 E-mail conversation with forensic anatomist, Dr Wendy Birch, University College London.

medicinal cure. The earliest extant evidence for this practice dates to the thirteenth century, with the noted sixteenth century physician Paracelius (1491–1541) terming it the noblest of medicine (Noble 2003). To give a brief context to this, it is important to note that humorism, the Greek-derived understanding of the body, and medicine until the mid-nineteenth century and the rise of empirical science, posited that one's life-force was contained in the blood and that an imbalance in the four fluids contained in the body (blood, phlegm, yellow bile and black bile) caused illnesses (Lagay 2002 [online]). It was also believed that taking into one's own body the blood of another could extend your life span, especially if that other person was not yet at the end of their natural life. At the time this was understood as three-score years and ten (Psalm 90:10), so under seventy years of age. A notable example of this belief is that the ailing Pope Innocent VIII (Giovanni Cibo), was transfused with blood of three 10-year-old shepherd boys sometime between 1490 and his death in 1492; not only was there was no change in the Pope's condition, but all three boys died (Reardon 2004: 167). Mummia though was less blood and more human flesh, fat and bone which were also thought to have curative powers through their connection with humorism (Sugg 2016). With mumia/mummia believed to be hot and dry in essence, it was sold to help counteract ailments associated with coldness and wetness and as such was common in England, a notably cold and damp country. However, getting hold of mumia/mummia was not always easy. A recipe for making mummia appeared in the English *Pharmacopoeia Londinensis* by William Salmon published in 1678; the recipe included getting hold of a fresh dead body and perhaps somewhat worryingly it was not until the 1824 edition of the book that corpse medicine no longer featured in this *Pharmacopoeia*.

In his early life William Salmon (1644–1713) had been apprentice to a mountebank (a charlatan who sold medical panaceas), with the pair travelling widely including to New England in what would become the United States of America. By 1671 Salmon had established a medical practice in London and in 1684 published a *London Almanac*. He also published a number of works on various topics including on religion, philosophy, metaphysics and alchemy. He co-wrote a surgical observation in 1687, and in 1689 translated *The Anatomy of Human Bodies* from Dutch into English. However, whilst he had an extensive personal library, most of his writings came from the sources noted above, with, as Wilson states, little evidence that he made any original contribution to medical knowledge (2021). As such, Salmon was drawing on already established medicinal techniques and cures when he wrote his *Pharmacopoeia Londinensis*. One chapter of this work is devoted to the use of animals in curing disease and dis-ease, with a sub-section on the use of parts taken from human bodies, both living and dead. In this sub-section Salmon lists five types of mummia: 1. Pissasphaltum; or Bitumen (a mineral), 2. the flesh of a human carcass dried in the sun (such bodies would largely be those of pilgrims and other travellers who had died in the desert sands), 3. Egyptian (being a liquor coming from a human carcass embalmed with bitumen), 4. Arabian (being a liquor coming from a human carcass embalmed with myrrh, aloes and balsam), and 5. Artificial. He noted that the Arabian and Egyptian mummies were the best as they had sweated out the liquor, but highly recommended the artificial mummia or mummy for which he provided the recipe (quoted below for interest only):

- Take the carcass of a young man (some say red hair'd) dying not of a disease, but killed [note: the red hair indicated the youth had more hot humour and at this time the male body was understood to be more potent in terms of humorism than a female body]
- Let it lie 24 hours in clean water in the air
- Cut the flesh into pieces and add powered myrrh, and a little aloes and myrrh [aloes was a sweet-smelling resinous wood which would help counter the stench of putrefaction, and myrrh was an aromatic resin or natural gum which would also assist to stem the stink of a dead body in the early stages of decomposition]
- Imbibe [soak] it 24 hours in the spirit of wine and turpentine [spirit of wine was a distilled wine such as brandy and was known as *aqua vitae*, water of life]
- Take it out and hang for 24 hours
- Imbibe it again for 24 hours in fresh spirit
- Hang up the pieces in a dry air and a shady place to dry and not stink

Whether anyone used this recipe to make a mummy is not known, but given it pre-dates the somewhat loose 1836 Registration of Death Act (tightened up in 1874)[2] in English history, one could possibly get away with such an act provided the victim was a stranger.

Reports about when the trade in mummies for medical use extended to England is unclear. European reports date it to 1516 and talk about mumia

2 For a brief history on registering a death see; https://www.parliament.uk/about/living-heritage/transformingsociety/private-lives/death-dying/dying-and-death/registeringdeath/

being 'an exudation from corpses' (Tomé Pires in Dannenfeldt 1985: 165–166), although entire bodies were also imported, both Egyptian ritually buried bodies and Arabic desiccated bodies dried in the sand and sun of the desert. The first recorded case of mumia arriving on British shores dates to 1586, when there was a shipment of over 600 pounds in weight of Egyptian or Arabic mummies. Given the trade in mummies was illegal it is likely that they were shipped to Britain in far greater quantity than records show, with a perhaps unsurprising lack of written evidence.

Mumia as a medicinal cure was not just a British phenomenon and Dannenfeldt (1985) in his article on Egyptian mumia notes that historical reports suggest a flourishing European trade in mummies dates to far earlier than 1586. Indeed, mumia was used by the Italian physician Matthaeus Platearius (d. circa 1161), whilst Derricourt highlights a legal case in Cairo dating to 1424 which exposed 'the use and treatment of recent corpses as fake mummy to sell to the European market' (2015: 77). By 1564 there was a thriving market for mummies with one Jewish trader in Alexandria showing Guy de la Fontaine (d. 1695), the physician to the King of Navarre, a good number of so-called false mummies – the bodies of dead slaves filled with bitumen, bandaged and left to dry in the sun (Patai 1964: 8).

So respected was mumia as a medicinal cure that it was recommended by the surgeon of Queen Elizabeth I, and by the philosopher and statesman Viscount Francis Bacon (d. 1626), but its use had not always been uncontroversial given that it was in effect medicinal cannibalism. In 1538 the physician Aloysius Mundella asserted that bitumen was far more preferable to the 'abominable and detestable mumia in prescription' (Dannenfeldt 1985: 172). This response is perhaps unsurprising given that in 1564 a physician in Alexandria discovered that the mummies were in fact not the embalmed bodies of ancient Egyptians as expected but deceased and often diseased slaves, some even dying to the pox, the plague or leprosy, as well as the corpses of criminals, whose bodies and limbs had been filled with bitumen, tightly bound and left in the sun to dry. Most writing notes that these false mummies were not as potent as the real historic Egyptian and Arabic ones, although Salmon, as noted, suggested otherwise. By the time of Samuel Pepys (d. 1703), the noted London diarist, mummies were available in merchant's warehouses with Pepys noting he could see 'all the middle of the man or woman's body, black and hard' and was given 'a little bit, and a bone of an arme' (1668). The commercial aspect of the trade led a contemporary commentator to note that whilst time had spared the Egyptian mummies, avarice had not (Smith 1914: 190). Indeed, so common was the medicinal mummy by the Renaissance that references were made to it in plays and poems; Shakespeare's *Macbeth* (1606) includes mummy as an ingredient in the witches' cauldron (Scene 4 act 1), and John Donne (d. 1631) makes reference to mummy in his poem *Love's Alchemy* (published 1633). Mumia was even to be found in the medical remedies of Puritan New England (Gordon-Grube 1993). However, beyond the medical profession, everyday people also attempted to cure themselves using parts of a human corpse. In Germany, and Denmark in the nineteenth century, warm blood would be collected from dying criminals and drunk in order to cure epilepsy (Sugg 2016: 8), whilst ground up human skull was consumed to help with migraines (Sugg 2016: 17).

The notion of ingesting the dried remains of humans as a medicinal cure is relegated firmly to the past in Europe and America, although this statement has to be tempered by acknowledging that the ingestion of cremains (cremated remains) is still reported in contemporary society. This can happen accidentally during their scattering (McGeehan 2015 [online]), or deliberately in two ways – as a form of connection with a deceased loved one (Limer 2011 [online]; Quigley 2005: 101) or as cremainlining, the snorting of cremains (Griffiths 2017 [online]). However, a further example that combines the accidental and deliberate happened in 1975 with the cremains of Wally Hope, founder of the Stonehenge People's Free Festival. Harvey notes that during the ritual scattering of Wally's ashes, 'a small child dipped his finger in the ashes and put it in his mouth', this was accidental; the previous ash-scatterers (mostly adults) had all taken a small amount of the cremains and let them go free, but the child was young and did not know what to do. Others, again mostly adults, followed the child's lead and ingested some of the cremated remains ... 'or at least, this is the story told in later years' (2004: 257). The mythic quality of this twenty-first century tale demonstrates the rarity of the act, and the general unusualness of cannibalism in all its forms today, so strange that every known occurrence hits the headlines. But whilst ingesting human remains may be highly unusual in the Westernised world, this is not the case globally. In parts of Africa, people with Albinism, including children, have been 'murdered or mutilated' for their body parts, which according to some local traditions are 'believed to be magical' (Brilliant 2015). Bones, which are believed to 'contain gold', and internal organs processed for use (White 2017) function as medicines and/or charms to bring good fortune or ward off dis-ease (Mwiba 2018). This form of cannibalism has some notable resonances with mumia-medicine from medieval and early-modern Europe, particularly in the lack of concern for the consumed person, but this is not the case for the examples in the following section which explores funerary cannibalism.

## INGESTION OF WET HUMAN REMAINS

This section explores cannibalism as practised through the deliberate ingestion of human flesh. Just as sin-eating has clear connections to Christianity, the tasting/eating of human body parts still enfleshed has been a socio-culturally appropriate way that the dead are religiously or spiritually interacted with. This use of a dead human as food made acceptable through 'culinary and ritual transformation' (Classen 2012: 97) has occurred in a number of cultures, and for various reasons. Excluding dietary reasons from extreme survival situations such as noted with the 1972 air crash, there are a number of motives for ritual human cannibalism – notably cannibalism as an act of aggression, and cannibalism as act of compassion. Much of the ethnographic information which details ritual cannibalism has been mediated through a Christian lens, placing the act and the cannibalistic peoples as religiously and morally opposed to the norms of the Christian colonisers (Forsyth 1983; Bôas 2008). This perception was often enhanced by graphic illustrations and some of the most well-known images were of the Tupinambá of Brazil (Metcalf 2005).

The Tupi were agricultural tribal peoples, who engaged in inter-tribal warfare where selected captive warriors were eaten. Cannibalism in the Tupi context therefore can be considered an act of aggression against a foe; however, such a binary division is overly simplistic. For the Tupi, ingesting the strongest and bravest warriors from the opposing tribe could negate the weaknesses and enhance the vitality of those who partook of the flesh (Conklin 2001: 153). This war-based cannibalistic ritual-increase in vigour was based on the Tupi understanding that displaying courage during battle, or in the rituals that led up to the human sacrifice, was considered appropriate and honourable behaviour. The capturing warriors gained increased social status and on the day of the ritual killing, they gained prestige through name changes and skin tattoos (Metcalf 2005: 72–73). However, the Tupi also practised cannibalism as an act of compassion. They believed that by eating deceased members of one's family group, the memories of that person became incorporated into the ongoing life on the tribe, and thus funerary cannibalism acted as a way of transcending death (Conklin 1995: 97). The captured warrior became a relative because as part of the ritual preparations before the act of killing, he was married to a woman within the community and became an affine; a non-genetic relative by marriage (Conklin 1995: 83). As such, in Tupi culture, the two ethnographic reasons for cannibalism blur.

The affine-making understandings of the Tupi resonate with another Amazonian community, who until recently engaged in similar acts of cannibalism – the Wari'. Indeed, so recently have the Wari' given up cannibalism that anthropologist Beth Conklin was able to interview members of the community who had once engaged in both exo- and endo-cannibalism; that is, the ingestion of human flesh from a community that is not one's own (exo-cannibalism) and the ingestion of human flesh from deceased members of one's own community (endo-cannibalism). Conklin was informed that cannibalism for the Wari' was specifically for funerary purposes, as there was no need for human flesh to quell hunger, and indeed Conklin noted that most of the potentially edible parts of the dead body were discarded whilst the parts eaten were often quite decomposed and tasted unpleasant (Conklin 2001).

For the Wari', exo-cannibalism was understood as an act of aggression with warriors eating body parts of their defeated enemies as a form of ritual abuse. The flesh was unceremoniously torn from the bone with bare teeth, and eating was deliberately accompanied by rude comments and grunting noises (Conklin 2001: 90–96). Although it was the adult men who ate the flesh of the vanquished foe, the entire community benefited from the act as it was believed that the fat from the eaten enemy passed into the semen of the warrior, and then entered into the body of the first woman he had sexual intercourse with post ingestion. The killing and eating of the foe, therefore, through a series of acts of touch, added to the 'collective social body' (2001: 153). Here then the conquered foe was incorporated into the community, strengthening it rather than defeating it as was the enemies' aim.

Endo-cannibalism for the Wari' was understood as an act of compassion, helping to eradicate the corpse from the world of the living and sever ties between those still alive and those passed on (Conklin 2001: 97, 104). This form of ritual cannibalism was highly regulated with no one ingesting flesh from a consanguine (someone they were genetically related to); only affines (those related by marriage) would carry out the ingestion act. With affines providing funerary cannibalism services between families, bonds of debt helped cement the Wari' social order (2001: 122). Interestingly, although cannibalism in any form was an integral part of normative Wari' life, the human corpse itself was considered polluting. But by roasting the flesh, the corpse would be less of a contaminant (both physically and mythically), and after ingesting the flesh, eaters would bathe to remove the 'odor of death' (2001: 125).

It is only since the 1960s that the Wari' have buried their dead and this has brought about concerns over burial being an act that keeps the memory of the deceased alive, rather than cannibalistically ingesting the dead and letting them go. That members of the community still alive when Conklin did her fieldwork in the 1980s had ingested human flesh, meant that they were able to inform Conklin that there was no 'fundamental difference between human and animal flesh' in terms of taste and texture (2001: 89).

The deliberate ingestion of human flesh was not confined to the Americas, however. Hertz mentions the Aboriginal Australian Binbinga practice of endocannibalism, from which women were excluded. Here, rather like with European corpse medicine and the notion of humorism, for the Binbinga the 'living incorporate[d] into their own being the vitality and the special qualities residing in the flesh of the deceased [as] if this flesh were allowed to dissolve, the community would lose strength to which it [was] entitled' (1960: 44). Davidson noted that there were different methods for preparing the corpse; 'cooked in a trench or earth oven ... or chunk[ed] for individual roasting'. He argued that the human corpse was understood 'as just another kind of food [but] may be consumed as showing contempt for a slain enemy, or ... as a mark of respect for the dead ... and a means of acquiring [their] qualities' (1949: 77). An Australian magazine article exploring historical cannibalism amongst Aboriginal societies was recently published noting that the reports were largely first-hand (Rubenstein 2021). However, given the colonial history of this society, it is unclear if some of the reports are fabricated; unlike Conklin's ethnographic approach, some of the earlier anthropological reports are distinctly lurid.

## CONCLUDING WORDS

When it comes to death and the sense of taste, most people today would find sin-eating and eating corpse-cakes a strange and possibly slightly distasteful custom due to the direct contact between the food consumed and the dead body. However, they may also want to make a strong distinction between these acts of ingestion, and the direct ingestion of human remains (outside cannibalism essential for the direct preservation of life such as with the 1972 plane crash survivors). Yet, as noted, for some cultures, cannibalism of the dead was the ultimate kindness. If pushed further, many contemporary people would most likely understand the ingestion of dry human remains as less problematic than wet human remains. Although not a direct comparison, the number of people having memorial tattoos that incorporate some cremains in the ink tattooed into their skin is rising across Europe and North America (McCormack 2015; Visser 2018), and as such the notion of incorporating some bit of a dead loved one into one's own body appears to be relatively normal.

However, there are differences between the ingestion of dry and wet human remains, although both corpse medicine and Binbinga cannibalism work on the principle of taking strength and vitality from the deceased to ensure the health of the living so perhaps these differences are smaller than one might initially assume. In these forms of cannibalism, we find neither an act of aggression, nor an act of compassion towards the deceased, but a utilitarian appropriation of a deceased person's life essence. However, when this shifts to the deliberate killing of someone for human body parts, such as with Albino people in parts of Africa, and the case of Meiwes (although this was legally considered to be manslaughter rather than murder) this is a different matter, and although an analysis of ethics is beyond the scope of this short chapter, doubtless the recipients of the body parts would have gained some benefit from this form of cannibalism; in the Albino example they would perceive benefit from a cure or charm, and for Meiwes, benefit from carrying out an act long dreamt of.

Meanwhile, for the Wari', and Tupi, cannibalism was a ritual that cemented or created bonds between the living and the dead, and we can find a resonance here with deliberate ingestion of the ashes of a loved one, and the ritual tasting of Wally Hope's ashes. As such, when considering the sense of taste in relation to death, and the dead, context is key.

# BIBLIOGRAPHY

*al-feqh*. Undated. 'Serving Food as Sadaqah on the Occasion of Somene's Death'. https://www.al-feqh.com/en/serving-food-as-sadaqah-on-the-occasion-of-someone-s-death

Beliveau, Ralph. 2017. 'A Hunger for Dead Cakes: Visions of Abjection, Scapegoating, and the Sin-Eater'. In Cynthia J. Miller and A. Bowdoin van Riper (eds.), *What's Eating You? Food & Horror in Screen*, pp. 169–186. New York: Bloomsbury.

Bôas, Luciana V. 2008. 'The Anatomy of Cannibalism: Religious Vocabulary & Ethnographic Writing in the Sixteenth Century', *Studies in Travel Writing* 12(1): 7–27. https://doi.org/10.3197/136451408X273817

Brilliant, Murry H. 2015. 'Albinism in Africa: A Medical and Social Emergency', *Int Health* 7: 723–225. https://doi.org/10.1093/inthealth/ihv039

Campbell, Andy. 2012. 'Mao Sugiyama Cooks, Serves Own Genitals at Banquet on Tokyo', *Huffpost* 27 May 2012. https://www.huffingtonpost.co.uk/entry/asexual-mao-sugiyama-cooks-serves-own-genitals_n_1543307

Cann, Candi K. 2019. *Dying to Eat: Cross-Cultural Perspectives on Food, Death, and the Afterlife*. Lexington, KT: University Press of Kentucky.

Classen, Constance. 2012. *The Deepest Sense: A Cultural History of Touch*. Urbana-Champaign: University of Illinois Press.

Conklin, Beth A. 1995. '"Thus Are Our Bodies, Thus Was Our Custom"': Mortuary Cannibalism in an Amazonian Society', *American Ethnologist* 22(1): 75–101. https://doi.org/10.1525/ae.1995.22.1.02a00040

Conklin, Beth A. 2001. *Consuming Grief: Compassionate Cannibalism in an Amazonian Society*. Austin, TX: University of Texas Press.

Dannenfeldt, Karl H. 1985. 'Egyptian Mumia: The Sixteenth Century Experience and Debate', *Sixteenth Century Journal* 16(2): 163–180. https://doi.org/10.2307/2540910

Davidson, Daniel S. 1949. 'Disposal of the Dead in Western Australia', *Proceedings of the American Philosophical Society* 93(1): 71–97. https://doi.org/10.2307/2792826

Derricourt, Robin. 2015. *Antiquity Imagined: The Remarkable Legacy of Egypt and the Ancient Near East*. London: I.B. Tauris.

Dole, Gertrude. 1974. 'Endocannibalism among the Amahuaca Indians'. In P.J. Lyons (ed.), *Native South America: Ethnology of the Least Known Continent*, pp. 302–308. Boston: Little, Brown and Co.

Forsyth, Donald W. 1983. 'The Beginnings of Brazilian Anthropology: Jesuits & Tupinamba Cannibalism', *Journal of Anthropological Research* 39(2): 147–178. https://doi.org/10.1086/jar.39.2.3629965

Gordon-Grube, Karen. 1993. 'Evidence of Medicinal Cannibalism in Puritan New England: "Mummy" and Related Remedies in Edward Taylor's "Dispensatory"', *Early American Literature* 28(3): 185–221.

Griffiths, Mark D. 2017. '"Cremainlining" Explained', *Psychology Today* 25 July 2017. https://www.psychologytoday.com/gb/blog/in-excess/201707/cremainlining-explained

Harding, Luke. 2004. 'Cannibal who Fried Victim in Garlic is Cleared of Murder', *Guardian* 31 January 2004. https://www.theguardian.com/world/2004/jan/31/germany.lukeharding

Hartland, Sidney E. 1892. 'The Sin-Eater', *Folklore* 3(2): 145–157. https://doi.org/10.1080/0015587X.1892.9720101

Harvey, Graham. 2004. 'Endo-Cannibalism in the Making of a Recent British Ancestor', *Mortality* 9(3): 255–267. http://doi.org/10.1080/13576270412331272866

Hertz, Robert. 1960. *Death and the Right Hand*. Trans. Rodney and Claudia Needham. Aberdeen: Cohen & West.

Howes, David. 2007. *Sensual Relations: Engaging the Senses in Culture and Social Theory*. Ann Arbour: University of Michigan Press.

JFG. 2021. 'Jewish Mourning – The First Week', *Jewish Funeral Guide*. http://www.jewish-funeral-guide.com/tradition/condolence-meal.htm

Lagay, Faith. 2002. 'The Legacy of Humoral Medicine', *American Medical Association Journal of Ethics* 4(7): 206–208. Retrieved from https://journalofethics.ama-assn.

org/sites/journalofethics.ama-assn.org/files/2022-06/mhst1-0207.pdf.  https://doi.org/10.1001/virtualmentor.2002.4.7.mhst1-0207

Limer, Eric. 2011. 'Woman is Addicted to Eating the Ashes of Her Late Husband', *The Mary Sue* 9 August 2011. https://www.themarysue.com/woman-eats-husbands-ashes/

MacLeod, Fiona. 1895. *The Sin-Eater and Other Stories*. Chicago: Stone & Kimball.

Manian, Sabita and Bullock, Brad. 2016. 'Sensing Hinduism: Lucian-Indian Funeral "Feast" as Glocalized Ritual', *Religions* 7(8). http://doi.org/10.3390/rel7010008

McCormack, Samantha. 2015. *Ashes to Art, Dust to Diamonds: The Incorporation of Human Cremation Ashes into Objects and Tattoos in Contemporary British Practices*. PhD dissertation, Manchester Metropolitical University. https://e-space.mmu.ac.uk/608773/

McDaniel, June. 2019. 'From the Underworld of Yama to the Island of Gems: Concepts of afterlife in Hinduism'. In Candi K. Cann (ed.), *Dying to Eat: Cross-Cultural Perspectives on Food, Death, and the Afterlife*, pp. 293–301. Lexington, KT: University Press of Kentucky.

McGeehan, Kevin. 2015. 'That Time He Accidentally Swallowed His Mother's Ashes', *Menshealth* 28 July 2015. https://www.menshealth.com/trending-news/a19545588/accidentally-swallowed-mothers-ashes/

Metcalf, Alida C. 2005. *Go-Betweens and the Colonization of Brazil*. Austin, TX: University of Texas Press.

Metcalf, Peter. 1987. 'Wine of the Corpse: Endocannibalism and the Great Feast of the Dead in Borneo', *Representations* 17: 96–109. https://doi.org/10.2307/3043794

Meyer-Rochow, Victor B. 2009. 'Food Taboos; Their Origins and Purposes', *Journal of Ethnobiology and Ethnomedicine* 5(18). http://doi.org/10.1186/1746-4269-5-18

Mwiba, Denis M. 2018. 'Medicine Killings, Abduction of People with Albisim, Wealth and Prosperity in North Malawi: A Historical Assessment', *Proceedings of the African Futures Conference* 2(1): 30–49.

Naro, Gillian R. 2021. 'Sin-Eaters', *Journal of the Association of American Medical Colleges* 96(3): 472. http://doi.org/10.1097/ACM.0000000000003895

Noble, Louise. 2003. '"And Make Two Pasties of Your Shameful Heads": Medicinal Cannibalism and Healing in the Body Politic in "Titus Andronicus"', *ELH (English Literary History)* 30(3): 677–708. Retrieved from https://doi.org/10.1353elh.2003.0029

Noble, Louise. 2011. *Medicinal Cannibalism in Early-Modern English Literature & Culture*. New York: Palgrave Macmillan.

Patai, Raphael. 1964. 'Indulco and Mumia', *The Journal of American Folklore* 77(303): 3–11. https://doi.org/10.2307/538014

Pepys, Samuel. Tuesday 12 May 1668. https://www.pepysdiary.com/diary/1668/05/

Plumwood, Val. 2008. 'Tasteless: Towards a Food-Based Approach to Death', *Environmental Values* 27: 323–330. https://doi.org/10.3197/096327108X343103

Quigley, Christine. 2005. *The Corpse: A History*. London: McFarland.

Reardon, Wendy. 2004. *The Death of the Popes: Comprehensive Accounts, Including Funerals, Burial Places and Epitaphs*. Jefferson, NC: McFarland & Co.

Rubenstein, William D. 2021. 'The Incidence of Cannibalism in Aboriginal Society', *Quadrant Online* 25 September 2021. https://quadrant.org.au/magazine/2021/09/the-incidence-of-cannibalism-in-aboriginal-society/

Simpson, Jacqueline and Roud, Steve. 2003. 'Sin-Eating'. In *A Dictionary of English Folklore*. Oxford: Oxford University Press. https://www.oxfordreference.com/view/10.1093/oi/authority.20110803100507834

Smith, G. Elliott. 1914. 'Egyptian Mummies', *The Journal of Egyptian Archaeology* 1(3): 189–196. https://doi.org/10.2307/3853641

Stewart, Benjamin M. 2017. 'Food and Funerals: Why Meals Matter for Christian Mortality and How We Might Respond Gustatorily to Changing Death Practices', *Liturgy* 32(2): 52–61. https://doi.org/10.1080/0458063X.2017.1262654

Sugg, Richard. 2016. *Mummies, Cannibals and Vampires: The History of Corpse Medicine from the Renaissance to the Victorians*. New York: Routledge.

Visser, Renske. 2018. 'Ashes to Ashes: Continuing Bonds in Young Adults in the Netherlands'. In Candi K. Cann (ed.), *The Routledge Handbook of Death and the Afterlife*, pp. 219–228. London: Routledge.

Walens, Stanley. 2014. *Feasting with Cannibals: An Essay on Kwakiutl Cosmology*. Princeton, NJ: Princeton University.

Welch, Christina. 2020. 'Images of Death in Art and Literature in Late Medieval and Early Modern Europe (1300–1700)'. In Elizabeth Tingle Elizabeth and Phillip Booth (eds.), *Brill Companion to Death, Burial and Remembrance in Late Medieval and Early Modern Europe 1300–1700*, pp. 272–299. Leiden: Brill.

Whinfrey-Koepping, Elizabeth. 2008. *Food, Friends and Funerals: On Lived Religion*. Berlin: Transaction.

White, Charles. 2017. 'Albinos Are Being Hunted in Africa and "Harvested" for Their Body Parts', *The Metro* 20 February 2017. https://metro.co.uk/2017/02/20/witch-doctors-are-harvesting-albinos-body-parts-for-medicine-6460173/

Williams, Paul and Ladwig, Patrice (eds). 2012. *Buddhist Funeral Cultures of Southeast Asia and China*. Cambridge: Cambridge University Press.

Wiki Cannibalism. 'List of Incidents of Cannibalism', *Wikipedia*. https://en.wikipedia.org/wiki/List_of_incidents_of_cannibalism

Wiki Uruguay Flight. 'Uruguayan Air Force Flight 571', *Wikipedia*. https://en.wikipedia.org/wiki/Uruguayan_Air_Force_Flight_571

Wilson, Philip K. 'Salmon, William (1644–1713)', *Oxford National Biography*. https://doi.org/10.1093/ref:odnb/24559

**Christina Welch** is an interdisciplinary Religious Studies scholar. She led the master's degree in Death, Religion and Culture (formerly MA in Religion: The Rituals and Rhetoric of Death) at the University of Winchester from 2007 until 2021, and continues to teach on the programme. She has research interests around visual and material culture, particularly in relation to religion and/or death. She also works on issues around heritage, especially as they relate to religion and/or death in the Caribbean.

Chapter 11

# Crafting as a Continuing Bond: Linking Handicrafts and Lost Loved Ones

## ENYA HEALEY-RAWLINGS

*26/6/2022 – As I write this essay [for the Death, Religion and Culture master's degree], my grandmother, the matriarch of our family, the reason I craft, lays in hospital unlikely to make it through the week. It feels important to note this, because this entire chapter exists because of her, and in some cruel twist of fate, I'm preparing to experience this essay first hand.*

*3/7/22 – Update: A week later and that cruel twist of fate has become reality, as my mother sits vigil in hospital watching her own mother depart, the crafting matriarch of our family is leaving us.*

*8/7/22 – Update 2: She's gone. I hope my crafting will provide solace and comfort in the coming weeks and months.*

Death and taxes, the two argued certainties in life; but I propose a third, art. I argue that life and art are intrinsically intertwined, as it is human nature to create in times of joy, but also times of sadness (Carroll 2004; Dissanayake 1988). This urge to create finds many forms, for some it is poetry or literary works of art, for others the stroke of a brush on canvas or pencil on paper. But for some, like myself, it is to sew, knit, crochet, embroider and create other kinds of craft that have been historically relinquished to femininity. While it is widely acknowledged that partaking in crafts is not especially gendered unless there are socio-cultural reasons for one particular craft to be so, for the purpose of this essay I will relate to Turney's statement that 'when one first thinks of knitting, one thinks of women' (2012: 8).

The understood femininity of crafts such as knitting, embroidering and sewing, is rooted in social history which will be explored below. But it is because of this view that crafting in the modern world is mostly passed on through the maternal familial line, with daughters learning from mothers and grandmothers. This was the case within my own family, and thus, as well as academic work, this chapter will draw on my own personal crafting and notably focus upon the relationship between crafting and continuing bonds. It will begin by examining continuing bonds as a theory, and then move to discuss how crafting ties in with continuing bonds and grief. Here the importance crafting holds within grieving for maternal figures who also crafted, is foregrounded before moving on to discuss the ritualistic and meditative form crafting can offer during a grieving process, and lastly covering the historical importance of handicrafts as well as the necessity of continuing these traditional crafts.

## CONTINUING BONDS

The Continuing Bonds theory was first put forward by Klass, Nickman and Silverman in 1996 and addressed what they believed to be a new way of coping with grief and loss. The main theories of the time centred around cutting off ties with the deceased, moving on from the loss and leaving the relationship with the deceased in the past. Klass, Nickman and Silverman's theory proposed that actually, what they were experiencing in their careers was 'people altering and then continuing their relationship to the lost or dead person' (1996: xviii). At the time this sort of continuing relationship was referred to as 'unresolved grief' and was seen as a psychiatric issue and not a healthy coping mechanism. The Continuing Bonds theory offered an alternative, that actually it was healthy to maintain a sort of relationship with someone who had impacted your life enough for you to be grieving. The Continuing Bonds theory suggests that rather than a death ending an entire chapter of one's life connected to the deceased, it instead forms a new chapter, with all the relevant characters still forming dialogue, just now of a different kind. The relationship has changed but does not simply end for those left behind. Klass, Nickman and Silverman's (at the time) unorthodox model of Continuing Bonds offered an alternative approach to grief, where the relationship with the deceased still affects the life of the bereaved: 'while the intensity of the relationship with the deceased may diminish with time, the relationship does not disappear. We are not talking about living in the past, but rather recognizing how bonds formed in the past can inform our present and our future' (Klass et al. 1996: 17).

These relationships can continue in a multitude of ways, from simply maintaining an inner connection to the deceased or writing physical letters to them, to having out loud conversations for instance at a grave site. Fisk (2019) states that another way of continuing this bond is by crafting; if a bond was created in life surrounding a craft it can take on new meaning when the loved one has passed. Most crafters begin their lessons at the knee of their mothers, who in turn have learnt from their mothers, and this familial connection can be helpful within the grieving process of losing a maternal figure. The bond of crafting created in life can hold new meaning after death and provide a source of comfort to the bereaved.

Klass, Nickman and Silverman state that 'memorializing, remembering, knowing the person who has died, and allowing them to influence the present are active processes that seem to continue throughout the survivor's entire life' (1996: 17). As I and many other crafters will attest, hand crafts like knitting, crochet, sewing and embroidery will often provide a constant throughout our lives, something we can always fall back on. It is also because of the familial bond that it offers a form of communication and bond with our kin. When my mother phones me, or grandmother phoned me, a constant topic of conversation is/was whatever we are/were working on at the time, also known as a WIP (Work in Progress). This constant form of conversation offers another point of bonding and provides another meaning to crafting.

## CONTINUING BONDS AND CRAFTS

The relationship between crafting and continuing bonds has been most prominently written about by Fisk. In her article 'Stitch for Stitch You Are Remembering', she asserts that for crafters, their crafts form a central aspect of their identity and as such crafting can help 'in both maintaining continuing bonds with dead loved ones and finding new ways of coping with loss' (2019: 573). Fisk also argues that the act of crafting is usually taught to us by our foremothers and that the act of teaching and maintaining the skills of a craft can help establish and continue a bond between kin:

> Being taught to knit by another person is not an immediate, one-off process: the mothers and grandmothers who may have shown them how to form

stitches are also likely to have been repeatedly asked for help in remembering what to do, and untangling knotty problems. The learning and teaching
of knitting is something that takes time and a degree of commitment and
intimacy. (2019: 555)

I, personally, was taught to crochet, knit and sew by my mother, who in
turn learnt all manner of crafting from her own mother. This legacy of
crafting is important to note in a number of ways; not only in the historical context of continuing a skill, which will be discussed further below,
but also due to the bond this can form between kin. Knitting has predom-
inately been associated with women and as such many of the finished
objects have been products of 'grandmothers, mothers and aunts making
gifts to clothe their families' (Fisk 2019: 562). Turney describes this act of
making as 'associated with both familial and romantic love: of time spent
thinking of someone whilst making, with the made object an expression
of the sacrifice of time, of thoughtfulness, and the embodiment of feminine "virtues" of caring and nurturing' (Turney 2012: 303). This feminine
'ideal' of caring and nurturing is seen further in discussions surrounding
crafting as a whole; descriptions of frumpy jumpers and blankets gifted
by a well-meaning great-aunt, a jumper made from wool that is far too
itchy to wear but too beautiful to part with, or a quilt that was made with
love for the sole purpose of making you feel better when you were lonely
during your first year of university (Image 11.1). Turney goes on to explain
that 'equally, one can see the knitted object, when it is a garment or a toy,
as close to the body, further extending its potential for intimacy' (2012:
303). This intimacy is present in almost all finished objects, especially ones
given as gifts. She goes on to state, 'all knitted objects are tainted with the
sentimental: to make something for someone else is indicative of doing
something that might be described as an act of love and self-sacrifice.
Leisure time is reorganised to focus on another person, an act of altruism
rather than a means of merely whiling away hours' (Turney 2012: 309).

Equally important in the process of crafting and continuing bonds, is
the act of crafting through grief. As previously stated, for crafters, the act
of crafting forms a central pillar through life. Kangól argues: 'Knitting as
a remedy helps women deal with the difficulties of daily life, which are
considerably more challenging in those moments when one is experiencing loss and grief' (2021: 2). For most crafters, the steadying act of crafting
with its ritualistic and meditative nature offers respite from not only any
overwhelming grief they may feel but also any routine or daily challenges
they face such as stress. Kangól goes on to state that 'although knitting
does not abbreviate the process of mourning, it offers comfort during the

journey through grief. Knitting cannot eliminate the emptiness of daily life, but it fills the hands and mind for at least some part of the day' (2021: 16). Fisk furthers this idea in her study of a group of Scottish knitters who have used their knitting to help them cope with grief. Within the interviews many of the women bought along items, or images of items they had created while going through a period of mourning or anticipatory grief (the grief one faces when dealing with an impending death, a phrase coined by Lindemann in 1944).

**Image 11.1** A pieced quilt made of pink, white and pale blue cotton fabrics. The patch on the back reads: 'Every breath you take, every move you make, we will be watching you. Given to Enya Healey our lovely Granddaughter from Nanny and Poppy Lines. Made with love by Dorothy Lines 2012.' © Healey-Rawlings 2022.

One such participant, Nalle, presented a bright green shawl which she had knitted during the time of mourning her mother-in-law, a fellow knitter. While making the shawl she found the process offered her a space to contemplate her mother-in-law as the pattern was repetitive and didn't require much thought, mainly muscle memory. As well as the process of creating the shawl being therapeutic, the final product 'became a way of maintaining the presence of the deceased in material form' (Fisk 2019: 570). The final product of crafts, especially fibre crafts such as knitting, crochet and sewing, offer a comforting and soft fabric that when worn close to the body can feel like a comforting hug from the person the crafter had in mind when making it; the tactile nature of these finished items holds a special value in the process of mourning. Regarding finished objects made during times of grief, Fisk goes on to state:

> They are objects that are special – made by hand with skill – yet, at the same time, everyday. They are carried with the bereaved owner; public in the sense of being on display on the wearer's body, yet also private in that their relation to the deceased and to mourning is not obvious from the object itself. Yet their material properties – color, tactility and function – remain significant. (2019: 571)

Turney agrees with Fisk in the importance of knitted or crafted fabric and the sense of touch: 'the concept of touch informs its construction and consumption: it becomes more than itself, a symbolic object, representative of time spent touching (making), emotion, and ultimately, love' (Turney 2012: 308).

## RITUAL/MEDITATIVE

As well as offering a familial comfort, crafting can offer a ritual and meditative comfort to those grieving.

### Ritual

The nature of rituals is a widely researched field, and many have offered different definitions of the term 'ritual'. Bell argues that some myth-and-ritual theorists suggest that ritual can be used to describe the phenomena called 'religion', whilst some theorists use ritual to analyse 'society', but more recently, 'symbolic anthropologists have found ritual to be fundamental to the dynamics of "culture"' (2009: 4). The ritual of crafting as passed down culturally would fit Bell's remit. Stephenson argues that ritual is one of the key elements in being a human, along with language, tool use, symbolism and music (2015: 1). From this we can understand that a wide variety of things can be seen to be ritual.

The waggle dance of bees and the genuflections of a priest; wearing colours at a football match and the coffee break at the office; hospital birth and speaking in parliament; watching television and tending the garden; waiting at a bus stop in Wichita or attending Kabuki in Tokyo; birthday parties and Fourth of July parades – all these, and more, have been conceptualised, analysed and theorised as ritual. Ritual it would seem, is all around us (Stephenson 2015: 1).

From all of these assertions, it is understood that rituals take many forms. To a lot of crafters their art is unashamedly a ritual, and for bereaved crafters like me, it can be a ritual of mourning.

In relation to craft and mourning, Fisk argues that knitting can be a form of memorial ritual, as 'the arms, hand, eyes and mind are all engaged in what is thus a long-term sensory process of memorialisation. There is also a material product to "show" for the time spent; as material memorials, knit and crochet objects physically manifest the time spent as well as providing a corporeal focal point for memory' (2019: 569). Scrutton furthers this idea and states that 'rituals are typically narratives that are sensorily rich' (Scrutton 2018: 215). Crafting holds a host of sensorily rich factors, from the feel of soft wools which create comforting fabrics, to the cool metal or wood of knitting needles and crochet hooks. The importance of these sensory aspects within grieving are highlighted by Wojtkowiak: 'The material and sensory dimensions are important considerations during the grieving processes because they create a connection with the deceased' (2017: 168).

## Meditative

As well as being identified as ritualistic behaviour, crafting can also offer many meditative qualities that can help in processing the trauma of losing a loved one. The act of crocheting, embroidering, knitting and sewing all offer repetitive movements and soothing sounds, which Corkhill, Hemmings, Maddock and Riley studied as offering meditative qualities. They found that knitting offered 'repetitive tasks that require physical and cognitive skills' (2014: 36). *Comfort: A Journey Through Grief* written by

American author Ann Hood describes how she dealt with the death of her daughter, and the space that knitting offered her for reflection and meditation:

> There were many days when all I did was knit. Once, after nearly eight hours of knitting, I could not even open my cramped fingers. I knit scarves and hats and socks, and as I knit, every part of me calmed. The quiet click of the needles, the rhythm of the stitches, the warmth of the yarn and of the blanket or scarf that spilled across my lap, made those hours tolerable. (2009: 47)

When discussing Hood's description of knitting through her grief, Kangól states: 'Hood does not seem to have considered knitting a solution for her sorrow. Knitting was neither meant to move the mourning process forward nor to heal the "illness"; instead it was intended to ease the symptoms' (2021: 4). This meditative state that crafting creates was backed up by research by Corkhill et al. who argue, 'the movements involved in knitting are bilateral, rhythmic, repetitive and automatic. Bilateral, coordinated movements engage more brain capacity than unilateral ones and appear to facilitate a meditative-like state more readily than unilateral movements' (2014: 40). For most experienced crafters, there is no need to focus on each individual stitch, muscle memory takes over at a certain point. It is during these moments that peace can be found for those grieving, even for those with no prior understanding or practice of meditation. As Corkhill et al. establish, 'a meditative-like state appears to happen as a natural side effect of knitting and requires no conventional understanding or learning of the meditative process' (2014: 40–41).

## NARRATING WITH KIN

As well as the act of knitting offering a space for reflection and memorialisation, there is a lot to be said for the role relatives offer when mourning a maternal figure. Most who learn a craft learn from their mothers, or at the very least show an interest in the craft because a maternal figure introduced them to it. Fisk furthers this point by stating: 'in mourning maternal figures, knitting and crochet may have a special role because the crafts were learnt from and practised with the deceased foremother/s. There is also in contemporary knitting culture a wider valorization of textile crafts as a means of connection with the uncelebrated lives of women in history' (2019: 574). The act of knitting during a period of mourning a maternal figure offers an opportunity to remember the conversations, lessons and shared memories surrounding the craft. With the recent passing of my grandmother, I was offered the opportunity to write something for her funeral. She was quite the wordsmith, so I chose to honour her through a poem akin to one she had written. A running theme throughout the poem relates to the many crafting lessons we have shared over the years; a stitch in time saves nine, measure twice and cut once, your thread will always run out one inch from the end of your final seam, and so on. This shared history and love of craft not only allowed us to strengthen our bond in life but is helping me mourn and honour her in death.

Along with the opportunity to remember lost loved ones during the process of crafting there is also the opportunity to remember a lost loved one in the final product. Many who craft will inherit materials from their kin, or from friends who have lost a loved one but don't craft themselves. The use, even sometimes re-use (in the case of unfinished projects or out of style items of clothing), of these materials can provide comfort for those bereaved. Fisk argues, 'knitted and crochet fabric bring not only an instinctive sense of comfort in the face of grief, but also an embodied sense of presence and memory' (2019: 573). As stated earlier in the case of Nalle, the final object offered both a private and public space for remembering. Private in the sense that if no one asked about the object, she could wear it and quietly honour her loved ones. Public in the sense that if anyone asked about it, she could share the stories of her mother-in-law. Wojtkowiak suggests that this public opportunity allows 'the bereaved ... to share a story about the object and in this way talk about their relationship with the deceased' (2017: 168).

## HISTORICAL IMPORTANCE OF CRAFTS

While discussing the relationship between maternal figures and craft, it is important to note the historical context which carried a lot of these crafts through to the modern day. While knitting, embroidery and sewing are seen as a women's crafts today, historically in England they were undertaken by both men and women. During the fifteenth and sixteenth centuries women were permitted to work alongside men in Embroidery Guilds of master craftsmen; however, 'increasingly rigid regulations did circumscribe their access' (Parker 2021: 67) and by the seventeenth century 'the place of needlework in a women's education was to become primary' (Parker 2021: 73). This shift in views regarding crafts was to be cemented for decades to come. It is still present in society today and owing to varying waves of feminism has been seen to be both in and out of vogue. However, it is important to note that without women continuing these crafts there would likely be much less information regarding them today. As well as remembering a direct relative in the process of creating, the maker is also remembering a history of women who curated the craft and kept the tradition alive. Fisk states: 'There is also, in contemporary knitting culture, a wider valorisation of textile crafts as a means of connecting with the uncelebrated lives of women in history' (2019: 574). She further notes that 'there is a recurrent theme of how quilting, embroidery and knitting provide material witness of the lives of women and earlier generations' (Fisk 2019: 564).

Without our foremothers and the women in history who learnt and carried on the skills associated with traditional craft we would likely not have access to them today. This has proven the case with several crafts such as cricket ball making, gold-beating, and mould and deckle making, all of which have fallen out of fashion and thus the skills and techniques inherent in their production have been lost. In March 2017, The Heritage Crafts Association (HCA) published The Red List of Endangered Crafts. An update in March 2019 was published which showed a change of 'one new extinct craft, 16 new critically endangered crafts and 20 new endangered crafts added' (HCA 2019). Currently Gansey Knitting, a form of cable-knitting of jumpers worn predominantly by fisherman around the coasts of Britain, is the only form of knitting HCA listed as Endangered, the group second most at risk of becoming extinct, while Crochet, Knitting and Embroidery are all listed as 'currently viable'. Continuation of these crafts serves not only as a way to honour our kin but also to honour the generations who have worked to master the craft and have kept the traditions alive. As Walter states, we as 'postmodern humans march into the future connected to and enriched by, not detached from, their (diverse) pasts and their dead' (2018: 394). When describing her own relationship with knitting Debbie Stoller offers:

> Whenever I would take up the needles I would feel myself connected to not only my own mother, grandmother and great-grandmother, but also to the women who had developed the craft, the women who had known, as I did, the incredible satisfaction and sense of serenity that could come from the steady, rhythmic click-click-click of one's knitting needles. (2003: 9)

## CONCLUDING THOUGHTS

Throughout the lifetime of a crafter, their crafts will provide solace and comfort in sad times, and joy and peace in happy ones. From blankets for new babies, to helping with grieving during loss, crafting offers a space for reflection and contemplation. Klass, Nickman and Silverman suggest that grieving is neither a linear nor time constrained process: 'The process does not end, but in different ways bereavement affects the mourner for the rest of his or her life. People are changed by the experience; they do not get over it, and part of the change is a transformed but continuing relationship with the deceased' (1996: 19). This continuation of a bond throughout life can present itself in a variety of ways, and they 'propose that it is normative for mourners to maintain a presence and connection with the deceased, and that this presence is not static' (Klass et al. 1996: 18).

I have proposed that crafting can offer many outlets when grieving along with offering a space for remembering and continuing a bond with a deceased loved one. When it comes to knitting, 'the needle is used to repair damage. It's a claim to forgiveness. It is never aggressive, it's not a pin' (Parker 2021: xix).

## BIBLIOGRAPHY

Bell, Catherine. 2009. *Ritual Theory, Ritual Practice*. Oxford: Oxford University Press.

Carroll, Noël. 2004. 'Art and Human Nature', *The Journal or Aesthetics and Art Criticism* 62(2): 95–107. https://doi.org/10.1111/j.1540-594X.2004.00143.x

Corkhill, Betsan, Hemmings, Jessica, Maddock, Angela and Riley, Jill. 2014. 'Knitting and Well-Being', *Textile: The Journal of Cloth and Culture* 12(1): 34–57. https://doi.org/10.2752/175183514x13916051793433

Dissanayake, Ellen. 1988. *What is Art For?* Seattle: University of Washington Press.

Fisk, Anna. 2019. 'Stitch for Stitch, You Are Remembering: Knitting and Crochet as Material Memorialization', *Material Religion* 15(5): 553–576. https://doi.org/10.1080/17432200.2019.1676621

HCA. 2019. *The Radcliffe Red List of Endangered Crafts*. Heritage Crafts Association. https://heritagecrafts.org.uk/redlist/

Hood, A. 2009. *Comfort: A Journey Through Grief*. New York: W.W. Norton & Co.

Kangól, Marta. 2021. 'Knitting as a Remedy: Women's Everyday Creativity in Response to Hopelessness and Despair', *Cultural Studies* 1: 1–19. https://doi.org/10.1080/09502386.2021.2011933

Klass, Dennis, Nickman, Steven and Silverman, Phyllis. 1996. *Continuing Bonds: New Understandings of Grief*. New York: Routledge.

Klass, Dennis and Steffen, Edith M. 2018. *Continuing Bonds in Bereavement*. New York: Routledge.

Lindemann, Eric. 1944. 'The Symptomatology and Management of Acute Grief', *The American Journal of Psychiatry* 101: 141–148.

Parker, Rozsika. 2021. *The Subversive Stitch*. London: Bloomsbury.

Scrutton, Anastasia Phillippa. 2018, 'Grief, Ritual and Experimental Knowledge: A Philosophical Perspective'. In Dennis Klass and Edith M. Steffen (eds.), *Continuing Bonds in Bereavement*, pp. 214–226. New York: Routledge.

Stephenson, Barry. 2015. *Ritual: A Very Short Introduction*. Oxford: Oxford University Press.

Stoller, Debbie. 2003. *Stitch'n'Bitch: The Knitter's Handbook*. New York: Workman Publishing Company Inc.

Turney, Jo. 2012. 'Making Love with Needles: Knitted Objects as Signs of Love?', *Textile: The Journal of Cloth and Culture* 10(3): 302–311. https://doi.org/10.2752/1751835 12X13505526963949

Walter, Tony. 2018. 'The Pervasive Dead', *Mortality* 24(4): 389–404. https://doi.org/10.1080/13576275.2017.1415317

Wojtkowiak, Joanna. 2017. 'Sensing the Dead; The Role of Embodiment, the Senses and Material Objects in the Ritualization of Mourning'. In Jeltje Gordon-Lennox (ed.), *Emerging Ritual in Secular Societies: A Transdisciplinary Conversation*, pp. 158–170. London: Jessica Kingsley Publishers.

**Enya Healey-Rawlings** has a master's degree in Death, Religion and Culture from the University of Winchester. Her lifelong passion for crafting and the arts began at a young age with a world-renowned artist for a grandfather and an equally talented quilter for a grandmother. This familial history of crafting fuelled her desire to study Costume Design & Making for her undergraduate degree, with her MA focusing on her passions for crafting and the study of death and death rituals around the world.

Chapter 12

# The Sense of Touch in Relation to Working with Archaeological Human Skeletal Remains

HEIDI DAWSON-HOBBIS

The idea for this chapter came from a discussion with one of the editors concerning her previous work exploring religion, touch and death (Welch 2021). Whilst this mostly reflected on touch related to the recently deceased, there was a short section on 'dry remains' where the bones of the long deceased became used as relics or for ancestor worship. As a biological anthropologist I regularly work with human skeletal remains, with the time of death varying from thousands of years ago to just over one hundred years ago, and touch plays an important part of the process of analysis. Unlike relics these remains are mostly of unknown individuals and the role of osteology is to 'read the skeleton' to reconstruct something about the life and identity of the person to whom they belonged. Whilst the phrase 'to read' implies the importance of a visual sense (Sofaer 2012), touch is also a key part of any osteological examination. Handling human remains is an essential part of the training process for students in human osteology/bioarchaeology. As a biological anthropologist/osteoarchaeologist, I, and other tutors, tend to initially present students with plastic replicas of complete skeletons to hone their identification skills before allowing them to handle the real archaeological human remains. Often there is initial surprise expressed by the students about how different the real archaeological human remains both look and feel in comparison to the plastic models. I therefore decided to explore the sense of touch in relation to human skeletal remains from the perspective of students/early career trainees to determine what their reactions were to handling human skeletal remains for the first time, including any emotions that they may have undergone in this initial experience.

This chapter will first discuss how touch is important when analysing human skeletal remains, followed by a discussion of the various factors that can cause differential preservation of bone, and therefore affect both the look and feel of the skeletal remains, related to the burial environment, and the age-at-death and biological sex of the deceased. Finally, the chapter will reflect on how human skeletal remains are perceived by students and professionals who work with them through the sense of touch. A questionnaire was devised and sent out via email to current students at the University of Winchester, UK, whom I had trained in human osteology/bioarchaeology, as well as to the email list for members of the British Association of Biological Anthropologists and Osteoarchaeologists. The questions were designed to gain an insight into the initial experiences of students and trainees within the laboratory or the field in handling human remains which had different taphonomic histories. As most students start by learning skeletal anatomy using plastic models of the skeleton, the questionnaire was also designed to gain an impression of how well these models prepare students in working with the real remains. The final area of exploration was on any positive or negative emotions that were felt when handling human remains and aimed to determine how an individual's own emotional or spiritual concerns may impact on their experience.

## TOUCH AND HUMAN SKELETAL REMAINS

Whilst sight may be the most recognised factor in the analysis of human remains, touch also plays an important part in their recording and interpretation, and is paramount in the learning experience for human osteology/bioarchaeology students. Sofaer (2012) describes how touch is key to both age and sex determination methods. In adult ageing methods, surface changes of joints, such as the pubic symphysis, are graded utilising model casts and images as a reference. The casts allow a more three-dimensional exploration of the changes and allow the use of touch to aid in comparisons of the grading system. For sex determination, assessing the prominence of bony projections such as the ventral arc (something only present on the female pelvis), the thickness of the supraorbital rim (the top of the eye orbit, which is thinner in females) and rugosity of areas such as the nuchal crest (a muscle attachment at the back of the skull, which is more pronounced in males) are key methods (Buikstra and Ubelaker 1994; White and Folkens 2005). Being able to feel these areas aids in the assignment of presence/absence or of the grading systems used. Touch is also important in terms of recording the density of the remains, as the weight of an object cannot be determined by sight. Touch can aid in determining how robust the remains are and therefore any issues that may relate to future handling of the remains so as to ensure avoidance of damage.

Seik (2014) explores how the use of touch is an important part of osteological examination by exploring the vocabulary used in guidance manuals, such as Buikstra and Ubelaker (1994), and core textbooks, such as White and Folkens (2005). These are standard texts used by teachers, students and professionals within the field. Seik (2014) also reflects on how students are taught to interact with skeletal remains using the tactile senses as well as vision.

A key area where touch is important for our interpretations of the lives of people from the past is in the recording and diagnosis of pathological lesions where texture of the bone is often a valuable diagnostic tool. Pathological conditions that these once living individuals may have suffered from can cause changes to the bones in life which remain apparent in their skeletal remains, such as loss of bone density, increase in bone formation, and deformation, that will affect the feel of the remains to those who analyse them. Periosteal new bone formation (PNB) can occur for various reasons, with normal growth processes in infants (Lewis 2007: 135), dietary deficiencies such as scurvy (Mays 2008) and processes associated with infectious disease or trauma (Waldron 2009: 116). The feel of the bone in PNB will differ depending on the state of organisation or healing, with active woven bone being raised on the surface with more irregular edges than the more organised or healing lamellar bone, which will feel smoother to the touch (Roberts and Manchester 2005: 8). Eburnation, a polishing on the joint surface of bones, and an indicator of osteoarthritis (Waldron 2009: 28), is another condition that is aided in diagnosis through touch, especially when present on the small carpal bones of the wrist.

## FACTORS AFFECTING PRESERVATION

Both the look and feel of archaeological human skeletal remains will be dependent on a variety of factors. Taphonomy is the study of the processes that occur to modify an organism after its death and can involve both natural and cultural processes. Natural processes within the burial environment can have a marked effect on how archaeological skeletal remains look and feel.

Taphonomic processes involving the geology of the cemetery site, and rates of fluctuation in groundwater, can cause differences in the permeability and chemical nature of the sediments in which the body is buried (Lyman 1994: 405), the pH value of the sediment (Mays 1998: 17) and the decomposition rate of the body (Roksandic 2002: 101).

Bone consists of both organic (collagen) and inorganic (hydroxyapatite) components, with the inorganic making up around 70% of the material (Lyman 1994: 72). In skeletal remains it is the organic component that has mostly decayed leaving the mineral component, therefore skeletal remains often feel lighter than is expected, which is why they can be prone to becoming brittle and liable to breakage if not handled with care. The time since burial may therefore also play a role in differential preservation, explaining why remains of more recent date tend to feel more robust (heavier) than those that have been buried for hundreds of years. The well-preserved nature of the nineteenth century remains from St George's cemetery, Bristol, UK (Dawson-Hobbis and Davis forthcoming), compared to the more fragile and fragmented nature of the twelfth–fifteenth century remains from Taunton Priory, Somerset, UK (Dawson 2014), is in part down to the time spent in the burial environment.

However, Batten (2019) found no significant difference in the weight of long bones from four cemetery sites in the Winchester (UK) area spanning from the third to the sixteenth century CE. This is likely because the underlying geology of the burial environment is a factor in how rapidly the organic component decays and in the de-mineralisation of the remains. At pH values less than 6 (acidic) the mineral component of bone becomes highly soluble (Mays 1998: 17) and in extreme cases this can lead to the loss of bone material altogether such as at the acidic sandy environment of Sutton Hoo, Suffolk, UK (Witcher 2019). The fluctuation of groundwater will also be a factor in skeletal preservation, as the poorly preserved remains from an alluvial floodplain at Sea Mills, Bristol illustrate (Young 2014). Chalk has a high pH value good for bone preservation; however, due to the free draining nature of this geology, remains will rapidly decay and bone can become de-mineralised and feel very light, as can be seen within the skeletal collection of the St Mary Magdalen excavation from Winchester (Roffey and Tucker 2012) curated at the University of Winchester. The sediments in which remains are buried will also be a factor in the colour of the skeletal remains, with those from a chalk site such as St Mary Magdalen being a chalky white colour whilst those from the iron rich sandstone deposits at cemetery sites in Bristol have a distinct reddish-brown hue (see Image 12.1).

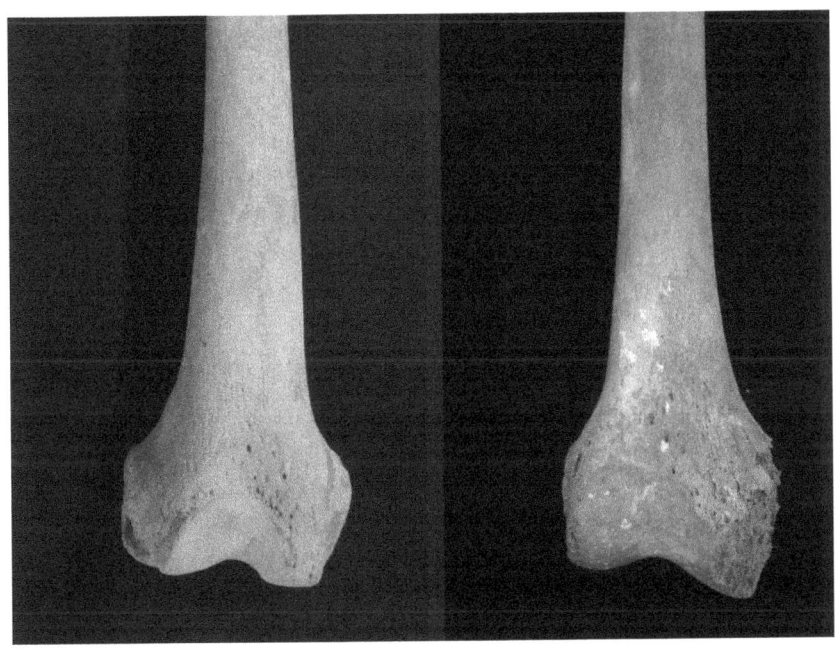

**Image 12.1** Image of distal right femur of SK107 from St Mary Magdalen, Winchester (left) and distal right femur of SK63 from Howland's burial ground, Bristol (right) illustrating colour from soil staining from different geological areas of the UK.
© Dawson-Hobbis.

The type of funerary ritual will also create differential preservation, such as internment within stone cut or lined graves, coffins or shrouds (Daniell 1997; Gilchrist and Sloane 2005), as well as the depth of burial (Buckberry 2000). Tightly shrouded bodies in earth-cut graves can be more likely to remain in place due to the soil being packed around them during the decaying process. Burial within stone lined graves or wooden coffins can allow for movement of the body during decomposition and potential damage to bones as coffins collapse over time.

The age of the skeletal remains, both in terms of how long the remains have been interred as well as how old the individual was when they died, will also factor into the preservation and therefore the feel of the remains. Whilst it had been suggested (Walker et al. 1988) that infant remains might not preserve as well as adult remains, research suggests that infant remains (under the age of 2 years) do preserve well (Saunders et al. 1995) and in fact better than those of some older children (Guy et al. 1997; Manifold 2015). The biological sex of the skeleton may also be a factor in differential states of preservation and especially in the loss of bone density and therefore feeling lighter and more fragile to the touch. The porosity of cortical bone increases with age especially in females (Jackes 2011: 126) and therefore skeletal remains of older females may generally feel much lighter than male remains as well as be less likely to preserve well in the archaeological record. Certain pathologies can also cause loss of bone mineral density, such as osteoporosis, and therefore may also be a factor in bone preservation (Walker et al. 1988).

## SURVEY RESULTS

To explore how handling human remains for the first time can be a surprising and sometimes emotional experience for students/trainees, a survey was devised which was sent initially to students who had studied human osteology/bioarchaeology at the University of Winchester and then to the email list of the British Association of Biological Anthropologists and Osteoarchaeologists. The survey consisted of 14 questions aiming to get an idea of what people found unexpected the first time they handled human remains as well as any emotional reactions experienced. The aim was also to gauge how useful students found the plastic model replicas of skeletons in preparing them for working with real human skeletal remains. As discussed earlier, because skeletal remains will vary in terms of their preservation, weight, de-mineralisation, organic component and colour, the respondents were asked to provide some information about the location that the human remains they first handled came from, if they could remember.

The questionnaire was designed to be completely anonymous with no identifying data collected and the project was approved by the RKE ethics committee at the University of Winchester. Of the 14 questions six had options to choose from and eight were free-text boxes. The results of the survey are presented here with each related question as a subheading. The final question simply asked 'If you wish please add any further comments on your experiences with touch and human remains' so these comments will be mentioned where relevant within the different sections.

*1. In what situations have you come into contact with human skeletal remains*

Sixty-three (93%) of the 68 respondents stated they had worked with human remains as university students, with 37 (54%) noting they had come across human remains in archaeological settings, 20 (29%) as anthropologists and 16 (24%) in museum settings.

*2. What is your current role? student, archaeologist etc.*

Of the 68 respondents, 36 currently identified as students (with 12 of these indicating they were PhD candidates) or recently graduated students (2). Eight respondents identified as academics (in teaching of research roles), 18 had roles associated with commercial archaeology, four related to the museums sector, three were retired, two identified as independent researchers and one was about to start a PhD. Some students also held associated employment and therefore checked two of the categories, hence the discrepancy in numbers.

*3. How long ago did you last handle human skeletal remains?*

Fifty per cent of the respondents had handled human remains in the last month, 30% within the last year and 20% more than a year ago.

*4. When you first handled human skeletal remains what surprised you about the feel or look of the remains?*

Most respondents commented on at least one thing that surprised them about the remains they handled for the first time, with only 12 of the 66 (18%) respondents stating that the remains were entirely as they had expected them to feel. That the remains were lighter than expected was noted most often by 35 respondents (53%), followed by the colour 24 (36%), that they were heavy to hold 18 (27%), and then comments on them being smooth 16 (24%) or rough 15 (23%) to touch.

*5. Any other comments on what you noticed about the feel of the remains?*
*6. If you remember, state the site where the remains were excavated from.*
*7. If you remember, state the time period the remains were from.*
*8. If you remember, comment on the geology of the site, i.e., chalk, clay, sand etc.*

Of seven respondents who remembered the geology being chalk, all noted that the remains were light to hold. Other types of soils gave more varied answers with three respondents who noted the remains were heavy to the touch remembering clay soils, although Respondent 47 noted that the remains from *London c(l)ay sediments from the Thames overlaid with modern silt and sand deposits* were light to hold, and three who noted soils as sand or 'sand and silt' being light to hold, with one (Respondent 33) noting the remains from 'sandy middens' as heavy to hold. Two respondents (34 and 40) could not remember the type of soils but noted the colour of the soils and how the bones took on that colour (orange-brown and yellow respectively).

Of the 59 responses detailing the time period that the remains were from, the majority 19 (32%) came from the later medieval period (1100–1600 CE), nine (15%) were from the early medieval period (600–1100 CE), 11 (19%) from the post medieval period (post 1600 CE), eight (14%) from periods BCE (before common era, including the neolithic to the Iron Age), six (10%) were noted as modern material, four (7%) as Roman/late antiquity/Moche, and two (3%) noted they had worked with material from various periods. In terms of geographical location, the majority (31 respondents) noted the remains had come from sites in the UK, another 13 noted they were from sites within Europe, one from Turkey, one from China, three from south or Mesoamerica, and one from North America.

Those who had worked with more recent human remains in forensic settings commented on how different archaeological bones were to fresh bone. Respondent 14 noted: *My first encounter with skeletal remains was in a forensic setting and the bones were noticeably 'oily' and smooth. Then when I encountered archaeological skeletons, I was amazed at the taphonomical changes and how those differed between bones from different time periods and geographic regions.* Two respondents also commented on how fresh bone or working with cadavers was more *unsettling* (Respondent 32) than working with dry bone. *Despite knowing they were human skeletal remains, it was odd how quickly they felt fine to hold. It is much different to the feel of a cadaver, which takes getting used to* (Respondent 52).

The difference perceived between working with archaeological skeletal remains and more recent human bodies was reflected on by Respondent 28: *I felt no emotional feeling of the skeletal remains, which I was very surprised, as I have always been afraid of blood and soft tissue since my childhood and even gave up to study medicine ....* Respondent 32 also focused on the evidence for disease: *Seeing severe pathological conditions invokes immediate empathy, as you can imagine the suffering the person may have gone through. Also the first time I saw preserved soft tissue (nails, hair, desiccated brain) I was immediately grounded in the fact that they were once a unique living person, whereas it was more of a slow burn realisation with all the dry bone remains I'd dealt with previously. Soft tissue is more tangible.*

The texture and fragility of the bones were also commented on by Respondent 46: *How the texture changes across different bones, how easily/ quickly they can disintegrate and become damaged*; and Respondent 54, who *hadn't realised that bone could chip and delaminate. I was surprised by how delicate the texture of the cortex could feel.* The varied nature, in terms of weight and colour, outlining the importance of having an understanding of taphonomy and the burial environments from which the remains have been excavated, was also commented on: *I still enjoy when I open a box and a bone surprises me with its weight or colour* (Respondent 59).

9. *In your training had you had previous experience with plastic models of human skeletal remains?*
10. *If you answered yes above, how did the plastic models compare to the feel and look of the real skeletal remains?*

Sixty-three per cent (43/68) of respondents had undergone training with plastic models prior to working with human skeletal remains and, other than in relation to the shape of the bones for identification purposes, most (98%) made some comment that suggested they were not a good comparison to real skeletal remains in terms of weight, colour, texture and anatomical details (such as identifying landmarks). Respondent 11 notes *how different they were in look and feel to 'plastic' replicas.*

This aligns with the recent research by Goodison and Aris (2022) who presented details of a survey which asked respondents whether they thought it was viable to use replicated bones for teaching instead of real human bones using a Likert scale of 1–5 where 1 and 2 were responses that thought it was not viable, 3 uncertain and 4 and 5 were responses that thought it was viable. From 477 responses the mean scores which were calculated separately by gender identity all fell between 1 and 3, indicating the vast majority thought replacement for teaching with plastic replica bones was not a viable solution. Interestingly, females gave the lowest mean score, with individuals identifying as gender fluid giving the highest.

Respondent 31 commented on the positive that you *never have to worry about breaking them.* This is one of the key reasons that most teachers, including the present author, choose to train students with plastic models in identification skills before moving them on to actual human remains. This helps to ensure students know what to expect (at least morphologically in becoming more familiar with the different bone elements) before handling the more fragile archaeological remains, so as to avoid any damage.

Respondent 33 reflected: *You cannot learn about remains from a plastic cast. Doesn't inform on osteoporosis, or 'unusually' heavy bones etc. I've also used gloves when required, totally get that (we're greasy) but it's a barrier.* The use of gloves in handling human skeletal remains can be a necessity, to avoid cross contamination if they are to be sampled for aDNA (ancient DNA) for example, and are probably more likely to be used by students today than in the past. Respondent 39 also reflects on the use of gloves: *I believe that most people do not realise it, but touch is actually one of the most important factors when working with human remains (also, the fact that many people prefer to wear gloves when working with them, needs to be taken into account). Personally, I find the feel a very familiar one and I think touch can actually help with several things such as the evaluation of preservation/taphonomy, as well as siding and identification of pathologies.* I have worked on collections where gloves have had to be worn, and those where this was not necessary, and personally feel that gloves can be a barrier to engaging fully with the material and can make interpretations more difficult. Whilst in some cases gloves will protect the material as the tactile senses are not as engaged, wearing gloves can actually lead to a higher likelihood of damaging very fragile remains as the sense of the feel of the bone is lost. As Respondent 50 says, *Handling skeletal remains is very tactile and they can convey such a lot from the touch of them and particularly so in association with pathological processes/changes.*

In terms of learning anatomy, a difference was also noted between learning from standard textbooks and from being able to handle skeletal remains. Respondent 37 commented on *all the details you could feel to the touch but not see in pictures,* and Respondent 39 said *The feel was much more pleasant than I expected given their nature (human remains). I was surprised by how many things you could understand just by holding them (e.g. the different landmarks, even though I did not know how to identify them yet).*

11. *Did you feel any emotional response when handling the human skeletal remains?*
12. *Did you have any spiritual/religious emotions when handling human remains?*
13. *Did any emotional feelings brought about by handling the human skeletal remains influence how you felt about working with them?*

The results showed that most respondents had overwhelmingly positive experiences in handling human remains, with 35 out of 67 respondents (52%) stating they had a positive emotional response when working with human remains, and only two of them (3%) reporting a negative response, while the rest marked a neutral response. To gain qualitative data as well as purely quantitative I allowed space for respondents to comment on their experiences, which indicated how diverse individual experiences can be, and how we may need to be more prepared for negative emotional reactions when training students in human remains identification and research, or when presenting findings to the public. One of the negative responses from a current student (Respondent 17) stated that it was the skulls and jaws that *humanised the remains* [and I] *felt very emotional*. Respondent 53, a recent MSc graduate, stated, *It made me a bit sad to see such a large proportion of infants and very young children with lots of pathology in the assemblage.* They went on to comment: *I think it increased the care and respect/responsibility I felt to handle and study them properly.* This was a reflection that came up throughout the comments: that handling the real remains made people more careful and respectful (see below). Respondent 54 reflected that *not all elements create the same emotional effe*[c]*t. Crania and soft tissue definitely spark a stronger reaction, and any pathological elements make me empathise with the individual and their potential pain.*

The responses to question 12 were more mixed with eight out of 68 (12%) respondents indicating a positive religious/spiritual emotion and seven (10%) a negative one. The other respondents marked this section as neutral. Respondent 12 who noted a negative response commented: *Just generally realising you are holding an individual who was once alive. Whether that was for a long or short time, whether they suffered or not. This I think increases how careful you are and how sensitive you need to be in your language. It also makes you think deeply about provenance, ethically should you be studying these remains?* Whereas Respondent 55 who registered a positive response commented: *It was a revelation .... It started a five year journey looking at societal attitudes to death and death denial, attendance at death positive conferences, and a massive help in me coping with the recent death of my mum.*

Out of the 68 respondents, 44 chose to write something about their feelings. The word that was most used was 'respect' with 16 respondents commenting that touching the remains instilled in them the importance of being respectful to the dead, four of these also used the term 'care' or 'careful', five respondents also referred to a 'connection' that they felt with the remains and four noted the 'privilege' they felt in being able to handle them. Six respondents noted that the remains inspired them to further study the bones with the aim to tell their story. Six respondents used terms related to wonder and awe on handling remains for the first time, with 'curiosity' and 'intrigue' being used by a further three. In terms of more negative emotions these were mostly focused around handling the remains of infants and children, noted by eight respondents. Two respondents (33 and 55) noted that handling human remains had positively helped them to deal with their grief over deaths in their own families. One respondent (10) noted they had a clinical approach, with another (31) noting that only violent forensic cases made them emotional. Other terms used by single respondents included 'compassion', 'sympathy', 'sensitive' and 'exciting'.

From my own experience I am aware that people who work with archaeological skeletal remains, especially in the field excavating burials, can start to feel a strong connection to them as individuals. I still remember details of many of the skeletons that I worked with, both in the field and then as research for my PhD, from the cemetery of the Priory of St Peter and St Paul, Taunton, Somerset, UK. In fact, the high numbers of immature skeletons led to my interest in juvenile osteology and to the focus for my PhD on medieval children (Dawson 2014). One of these skeletons, SK2077, was a young child with various skeletal lesions associated with tuberculosis (Dawson and Robson Brown 2012; Dawson-Hobbis et al. 2021) who was buried on the edge of the cemetery. Another young child, SK914, was buried within the nave of the church. Whilst this was a high-status position (Daniell 1997: 95; Gilchrist and Sloane 2005: 56), the remains still showed evidence for stress and/or malnutrition during their short lifetime on both their bones and teeth (Dawson-Hobbis 2017: 220). These skeletons, that I got to know intimately, began to feel like people that I knew, even though they had been deceased for hundreds of years, and whilst to me their remains are nothing more than the mineralised bony structures of the body, the power of osteological techniques allows us to be able to 'read' the skeleton and therefore learn something about that individual's life even long after their death.

Respondent 2 also reflects on this type of connection when they state, *I can still remember certain aspects of the individual that I was assigned to and the availability for me to interact physically with the remains, I believe, has enabled me to retain more information about the individual.* Respondent 59 comments: *Initially I regarded the individuals or bones as 'specimens' and retained my distance through scientific thought, because I needed that distinction. As I have become used to working with human remains I now very much regard each individual as a person, and even occasionally speak to them!*

Comments made on other more personal experiences included Respondent 10's reaction to a particular skull: *I have only once felt any sort of emotional or physical reaction – not my first time holding bones but it was the most complete skull I had seen and was unexpectedly cold, none of the other bones near it were.* However, this respondent marked both the emotional and spiritual responses as neutral in relation to their first experience with human remains.

Reflections on the ethical implications surrounding human remains were also noted, such as final comments from Respondent 55: *I know there are numerous ethical and moral concerns about handling human remains. However, I believe that it is a valuable experience for so many people, who are accepting of visible, handleable human remains in certain contexts e.g. museum displays, archaeology talks, and it performs a valuable service to the living in helping come to terms with mortality.*

Ensuring that students, or new archaeologists in the field, know what to expect can be key in avoiding any issues or discomfort that may be felt from having to handle human remains. Respondent 47 suggests, *The key to feeling comfortable has been previous knowledge of the remains and what to expect, particularly when there was soft tissue preserved. It has felt neutral working with mummies e.g. having seen the site photographic documentation beforehand. Conversely, it was extremely unpleasant to take a skull from a 19th cent. into my hands and discover with touch patches of hair still attached, even though in other circumstances it's never been an issue – it was just unexpected that this skeleton would be so relatable.* Whilst we have become more aware that trigger warnings should accompany any teaching or outreach events so that attendees are made aware of the content, such as images of skeletal remains, there are recent projects where working with human remains, especially in the excavation of burials, is seen to be helpful to the participants' mental health (Everill et al. 2020; Király 2022).

## CONCLUSION

*Handling human remains was a vital part of my studies as it allowed me to recognise and differentiate types of skeletal material. It was also an opportunity to respectfully explore the identity of the individual* – Respondent 57.

As the above quotes show, overall, the response to the handling of human skeletal remains as part of their training in osteology has been overwhelmingly positive and many respondents have commented on how the sense of touch both adds to the connection felt to once living humans, and aids in their interpretations, especially in terms of pathology. It seems that plastic model replicas are not seen as a useful substitute for learning about the variations in anatomy, taphonomy and pathology that are seen across the human skeleton and that understanding this variability is a key element in training students who work with human remains.

## BIBLIOGRAPHY

Batten, Kim N. 2019. *Light of Ages: Assessing How Long Bone Weights Are Affected by Age, Lifestyle and Disease*. Unpublished MSc thesis, University of Winchester.

Buckberry, Jo. 2000. 'Missing, Presumed Buried? Bone Diagenesis and the Under-Representation of Anglo-Saxon Children', *Assemblage* 5: 1–20. https://bradscholars. brad.ac.uk/handle/10454/676

Buikstra, Julia E. and Ubelaker, Douglas H. 1994. *Standards for Data Collection from Human Skeletal Remains*. Arkansas Archaeological Survey, Research Series 44.

Daniell, Christopher. 1997. *Death and Burial in Medieval England 1066-1550*. London: Routledge.

Dawson, H. 2014. *Unearthing Late Medieval Children: Health, Status and Burial Practice in Southern England*. British Archaeological Reports, British Series 593. Oxford: Archaeopress.

Dawson, Heidi and Robson Brown, Kate. 2012. Childhood Tuberculosis: A Probable Case from Late Medieval Somerset, England. *International Journal of Paleopathology* 2: 31–35. https://doi.org/10.1016/j.ijpp.2012.04.001

Dawson-Hobbis, Heidi. 2017. 'Interpreting Cultural and Biological Markers of Stress and Status in Medieval Subadults from England'. In Eileen Murphy and Mélie Le Roy (eds.), *Children, Death and Burial: Archaeological Discourses*, pp. 211–226. Oxford: Oxbow Books.

Dawson-Hobbis, Heidi and Davis, Jocelyn. Forthcoming. 'Uncovering the Lives of Late Eighteenth- and Nineteenth-Century Inhabitants of Bristol through Osteoarchaeological and Documentary Analysis'. In Elizabeth Craig-Atkins and Karen Harvey (eds.), *The Material Body: Embodiment, History and Archaeology in England, 1700-1880*. Manchester: Manchester University Press.

Dawson-Hobbis, Heidi, Taylor, G. Michael and Stewart, Graham R. 2021. 'A Case of Childhood Tuberculosis from Late Mediaeval Somerset, England', *Tuberculosis* 128: 102088. http://doi.org/10.1016/j.tube.2021.102088

Everill, Paul, Bennett, Richard and Burnell, Karen. 2020. 'Dig In: An Evaluation of the Role of Archaeological Fieldwork for the Improved Wellbeing of Military Veterans', *Antiquity* 94: 212–227. https://doi.org/10.15184/aqy.2019.85

Gilchrist, Roberta and Sloane, Barney. 2005. *Requiem: The Medieval Monastic Cemetery in Britain*. London: Museum of London Archaeological Service.

Goodison, George and Aris, Christopher. 2022. *The Efficacy and Practicality of Bone Cast Replicas as Opposed to Real Human Bones in Higher Education*. Poster presentation at BABAO online conference 2022.

Guy, Hervé, Masset, Claude and Baud, Charles-Albert. 1997. 'Infant Taphonomy', *International Journal of Osteoarchaeology* 7: 221–229. https:// edisciplinas.usp.br/pluginfile.php/4634064/mod_resource/content/1/ Guy_Masset_Infant%20Taphonomy.pdf.                https://doi.org/10.1002/ (SICI)1099-1212(199705)7:3<221::AID-OA338>3.0.CO;2-Z

Jackes, Mary. 2011. 'Representativeness and Bias within Archaeological Skeletal Samples'. In Sabrina C. Agarwal and Bonnie A. Glencross (eds.), *Social Bioarchaeology*, pp. 107–146. Chichester: Wiley-Blackwell.

Király, Giselle. 2022. 'Human Remains as a Facilitator for U.K. Veteran Coping Strategies', podium presentation at online BABAO conference, Saturday 18 September 2022.

Lewis, Mary E. 2007. *The Bioarchaeology of Children: Perspectives from Biological and Forensic Anthropology*. Cambridge: Cambridge University Press.

Lyman, R. Lee. 1994. *Vertebrate Taphonomy*. Cambridge: Cambridge University Press.

Manifold, B. 2015. 'Skeletal Preservation of Children's Remains in the Archaeological Record', *Homo* 66(6): 520–548. https://doi.org/10.1016/j.jchb.2015.04.003

Mays, Simon. 1998. *The Archaeology of Human Bones*. London: Routledge.

Mays, Simon. 2008. 'A Likely Case of Scurvy from Early Bronze Age Britain', *International Journal of Osteoarchaeology* 18: 178–187. https://doi.org/10.1002/oa.930

Roberts, Charlotte and Manchester, Keith. 2005. *The Archaeology of Disease*, 3rd edition. Stroud: Sutton Publishing.

Roffey, Simon and Katie Tucker. 2012. 'A Contextual Study of the Medieval Hospital and Cemetery of St Mary Magdalen, Winchester, England', *International Journal of Paleopathology* 2(4): 170–180. https://doi.org/10.1016/j.ijpp.2012.09.018

Roksandic, Mirjana. 2002. 'Position of Skeletal Remains as a Key to Understanding Mortuary Behaviour'. In William D. Haglund and Marcella H. Sorg (eds.), *Advances in Forensic Taphonomy: Method, Theory and Archaeological Perspectives*, pp. 99–117. London: CRC Press.

Saunders, S.R., Herring, D.A. and Boyce, G. 1995. 'Can Skeletal Samples Accurately Represent the Living Populations They Come From? The St Thomas' Cemetery Site, Belleville'. In A.L. Grauer (ed.), *Bodies of Evidence: Reconstructing History Through Skeletal Analysis*, pp. 69–99. New York: Wiley-Liss.

Seik, Thomas. 2014. 'An Exploration of Tactile Interaction in Osteology and Material Culture', *Platforum* 14: 147–164.

Sofaer, Joanna. 2012. 'Touching the Body: The Living and the Dead. In Osteoarchaeology and the Performance Art of Marina Abramović', *Norwegian Archaeological Review* 45(2): 135–150. https://doi.org/10.1080/00293652.2012.703686

Waldron, Tony. 2009. *Palaeopathology*. Cambridge: Cambridge University Press.

Walker, Phillip L., Johnson, John R. and Lambert, Patricia M. 1988. 'Age and Sex Biases in the Preservation of Human Skeletal Remains', *American Journal of Anthropology* 76: 183–188. https://doi.org/10.1002/ajpa.1330760206

Welch, Christina. 2021. 'Religion, Touch and Death; Ritual and the Human Corpse'. In Amy Whitehead and Christina Welch (eds.). *Religion and Touch (Religion and the Senses* series), pp. 214–235. Sheffield: Equinox.

White, Tim D. and Folkens, Pieter. A. 2005. *The Human Bone Manual*. London: Academic Press.

Witcher, Robert. 2019. 'Editorial: Sutton Hoo at 80', *Antiquity* 93: 565–567. https://doi.org/10.15184/aqy.2019.86

Young, Andrew. 2014. 'Excavations in Advance of Redevelopment at 75 Sea Mills Lane, Bristol, 2013', *Bristol and Avon Archaeology* 25: 1–19.

**Heidi Dawson-Hobbis** is a Senior Lecturer in Biological Anthropology at the University of Winchester and an honorary research associate at the University of Bristol. She is a committee member of the Human Osteology Special Interest Group, Chartered Institute of Archaeologists. Her PhD research focused on the associations between health and burial status of medieval children, and she is currently working on several skeletal collections from nineteenth century Bristol.

Part Two

CULTURAL SENSES

Chapter 13

# Displaying the Dead with Decency: Practices at Funeral Homes and at BODY WORLDS

## LUCY JACKLIN AND CHRISTINA WELCH

In this chapter we combine the perspectives of two voices to explore the sense of decency in relation to the display of the dead. Both voices are of 'insiders' to the study of death. Lucy Jacklin started working in the UK funeral industry in 2016, and has seen many dead people in various conditions, from deaths through accidents where the body is not intact when it arrives at the funeral home, to natural deaths of people dying in their sleep; she has helped prepare many bodies for display to family and friends who wish to have a final goodbye to a loved one. She has visited several of the BODY WORLDS exhibitions. Although aware that both in a funeral home and in BODY WORLDS the bodies are artificially prepared for viewing, the private personalised viewings of still fleshy individuals soon to be buried or cremated seemed to her very different from the plastinated bodies stripped of their flesh and original identity, presented for public display; plastination is the process used to preserve bodies for display in BODY WORLDS (herein BWS) exhibitions (Pashaei 2010).

Christina Welch meanwhile is an academic. She has been teaching about death theory and socio-cultural and religious approaches to death, dying and bereavement since 2008. Her main research area in relation to death and religion has been the visual representation of dead bodies in the form of Northern European Renaissance-era cadaver sculptures which depict an emaciated naked body, and in Death and the Maiden imagery where a young woman is juxtaposed with a representation of Death in the form of a man. The subject of decency has been touched on in a number of her writings on these topics; cadaver sculptures can be found in many Northern European churches and cathedrals and depict naked high-status people, mostly men, who protect their groin with a strategically placed hand or fold of the burial shroud, and much Death and the Maiden imagery, a form of vanitas art, is explicitly sexual in nature.

In bringing together the academic and experiential when thinking about the sense of decency in relation to the display of the dead, we aim to highlight the role of flesh/skin in determining personhood/subjecthood and explore the general acceptability of exhibiting a deceased human in the West. We should note that by the West we mean contemporary cultures with their roots in Northern European Enlightenment Christianity; we are aware the West is a complex and problematic term and that this short-hand definition is overly simplistic, but unpacking it is beyond the scope of this chapter.

Before embarking on the chapter proper, it is important to note that decency is culturally contextual, with the propriety of any situation or interaction regulated by religious mores, legal prohibitions and personal perceptions of what is respectful. There has long been controversy over plastination, with issues raised over corpses obtained from a psychiatric hospital in Kyrgyzstan where legislation over the use of dead bodies is 'far looser than in Europe' (Stern 2003: 6), and with corpses obtained from China when confirmation could not be obtained that they were not executed prisoners (Harding 2004). Exploring decency around BWS's obtaining of corpses is beyond the scope of this chapter, which focuses on the sense of decency in the posing and display of dead human bodies.

It is also important to note that this chapter does not explore the topic of decency when a corpse is deliberately abused or disrespected, as such acts are almost universally considered indecent. This feeling is most notable when the dead body still has a sense of personhood (that is, when it is a recent fleshy corpse recognisable as a once alive human being). During the worst of the Covid-19 pandemic there was alarm over the trucks in New York brimming with the dead, and the need for mass graves on Hart Island (Hennigan 2020). In the UK, there was fury when it was discovered that Jimmy Savile, a well-known television personality and charity fund raiser, had sexually abused corpses in several hospital morgues (Halliday 2014), and outrage when it was reported that bacon-rashers had been placed on the corpse of a deceased Muslim that lay in a mortuary (Kirby 2003). Accusations of International War Crimes by Russian forces following their

February 2022 invasion of Ukraine include the desecration of Ukrainian corpses (Whatcott 2022). When it comes to acts such as these, there is a general consensus in contemporary wider society that the bounds of death and decency have been breached.

However, concern about abuse of the dead is not new. In Northern Europe from the 1500s onwards graverobbing to provide surgeons with bodies on which to learn anatomy was largely understood as disrespectful, and the use of corpses of the poor and criminalised in England for the same purpose led to the 1770 'Tyburn Riots Against Surgeons' (Fitzharris 2016). Further, during the Victorian era there are many reports of the dead in overcrowded urban English graveyards dug up to allow new burials, with disinterred bones and parts of still enfleshed bodies casually discarded (NHM 2017). There are then multiple personal and political, and even financial, reasons why dead human bodies might be treated with disrespect, but what is clear from the many examples of this practice, is that although culturally contextual, there is a sense that, in general, still fully enfleshed human corpses should be treated like a live human, and that this is different from the way one might treat dry bones. So, this chapter concerns the sense of decency as it applies to bodies that have a strong sense of personhood about them.

*Note: this chapter includes detailed information on the embalming process.

## BODY DISPLAY IN BODY WORLDS (BWS) AND FUNERAL HOMES

According to their website, the philosophy of BWS is 'preventative healthcare' with the exhibitions they put on aiming to educate about the 'inner workings of the human body and the effects of healthy and unhealthy lifestyles.' However, scholars such as Burns (2007: 12) have queried this, citing the entertainment factor of the exhibitions as a similarly predominant theme; a topic we will come to later. The BWS exhibitions contain whole human bodies as well as individual organs, sections of blood vessels and transparent slices through the body; as noted, we concern ourselves here only with the specific whole plastinated bodies. BWS claim that 87% of visitors felt they knew more about the human body after visiting an exhibition, 87% feeling a reverence for the human body after their visit and 68% stating they would pay more attention to their body after visiting a BWS exhibition (BWS 2022e). These statistics reinforce the educational remit of BWS and that their emphasis on health is also something visitors pick up on; as such it may seem strange considering bodies displayed in BWS against bodies displayed in funeral homes (given the latter do not have an educational or health remit). However, both locations pose dead bodies for viewing, and we believe that there are issues with the former in regard to decency.

One central difference between bodies displayed in funeral homes and in BWS exhibitions that affect a sense of decency is that the funeral home body is displayed only for a brief period of time, typically to the family and friends who choose to visit and say their goodbyes before the body is disposed of by burial or cremation. Sometimes the body is preserved through embalming, in a process that, as will be explained shortly, has similarities with the BWS plastination procedure. The plastinated body meanwhile is in itself a form of final disposal, according to the BWS creator Gunter von Hagens, who understands the process as a 'third choice' along with burial and cremation (in Walter 2004: 603). There have been/are many types of similar 'third choice' body disposal methods which like plastination mean the corpse does not naturally decay to bone and eventually turn to dust, nor is it cremated into ashes, with one well-known third choice being mummification of some kind. And in considering mummification and therefore the decency of third choice body display, there are numerous mummified corpses on public display in museums and typically there are relatively few concerns over this form of public display of a human corpse (see Kennedy 2008; EH 2009).

Of course, museum displayed mummies are typically ancient and are not deliberately posed by the museum for display, and this separates them from the plastinates which are placed in poses that are designed to highlight specific anatomical features when they are viewed in BWS. But it is important to note that a deliberately mummified corpse, such as an Egyptian mummy, was posed after death, although this posing is closer in terms of display to a funeral home body, which is deliberately posed in a coffin regardless of whether a viewing is expected or not. In Ancient Egypt bandages were used to cover the naked corpse instead of the clothing a corpse wears today, and a mummy would have their organs removed as a form of embalming, these being placed in canopic jars, whereas today if body parts are removed from a dead body this is either for organ donation purposes, or if a post-mortem is carried out (or the body is used as an educational specimen for medical training) the removed parts are later placed back inside the body; either way the invasive procedure is in some way disguised. But it is important to note that there are a variety of techniques (from non-invasive eyelid supports to invasive embalming) that mean a corpse today cannot be understood as totally unposed. As such, the posing of a body is as common to funeral homes as it is to BWS plastinates. We unpack this a little more for clarity.

It is normal practice, when a corpse is collected from the place of death and taken into the care of a funeral home, for a process to improve the appearance of the deceased to be carried out. Known as first offices, the corpse's eyes are closed, the mouth is shut, the corpse is washed, dressed, placed in a coffin and arranged to look like it is sleeping. This takes us to the nub of our issue: the subjectivity of the corpse, and the decency of the pose that the deceased is put into. Subjectivity or personhood is complicated. In a funeral home, the dead person is known to the visitors and as such has personhood. Indeed, so strong is the perception of personhood that should the clothes the corpse is dressed in be incorrect, or the make-up applied to the corpse make it look less like the dead person, those saying their last farewells may be distressed by the appearance of their loved one.

Personhood with museum exhibits, even for formally alive human beings, is highly complex (Jenkins 2010) but generally their placement in a museum takes them into the realm of objectification. Plastinated bodies too are objects. However, what differentiates these objectified humans from those on display in museums is that according to BWS, all bodies were donated with informed consent; this has not been obtained (nor is obtainable) in regard to ancient mummified corpses. However, we suggest that BWS plastinated bodies, by being posed, deliberately keep a sense of personhood that is generally not found in museum displayed mummies – there is a slightly different issue with museum displayed skeletons exhibited with grave goods which can provide some sense of identity and thus subjectivity, but this is beyond the remit of this chapter which focuses on embalmed and unembalmed bodies displayed in funeral homes, and plastinated bodies displayed in BWS.

Plastination is the process that von Hagens invented to extend the body preservation method of embalming almost indefinitely (BWS 2022a). It is a five-step process designed to preserve the body for educational and instructional purposes (BWS 2022b). John Troyer describes the result of this process as 'a timeless human corpse that resisted organic decomposition and visual degradation' (2020: 3). Although plastination and embalming involve different processes, they share a purpose of preserving the human body so it can be displayed. The processes of these preservation methods also share features. For example, out of the five steps in the plastination process three are also used in the embalming process typically employed in funeral homes. To provide the context required to expand the definition of decency, the similarities and differences between plastination and embalming are outlined below.

## PLASTINATION, EMBALMING AND DEALING WITH THE DEAD

The first step of the plastination process involves a method used in funeral home embalming where, 'Formaldehyde or other preservation solutions are pumped through the arteries to kill all bacteria and to prevent the decomposition of the tissues' (BWS 2022b). An artery is also selected for the input of embalming fluid, another formaldehyde-based solution, which is pumped into the body with an embalming machine, forcing the blood out of the body through the incision that the embalmer has made in a vein. The removal of body fat and water is the second step. In plastination, this is done by dissolving body fat and water in a bath of acetone which under freezing conditions ensures the acetone draws out all the water and replaces it inside the cells (BWS 2022b). In a funeral home fluid is also removed from the body but in a slightly different way. A trocar, which is a long, hollow pointed instrument, is used to puncture the abdomen and organs in order to drain fluid and release gas from the organs and body cavity. Once this has been done, more concentrated embalming fluid is passed through the trocar incisions and the abdomen puncture is then sealed to prevent leakage.

As noted, whilst the embalming process used in funeral homes slows the decomposition process enabling the body to be viewed before it is buried or cremated, '[p]lastinated specimens are expected to remain stable for at least four thousand years' (Walter 2004: 606). To create this long-term stability in the plastination process, forced impregnation is used (step three of the plastination process); this process is not used in funeral home embalming. Forced impregnation involves placing the specimen in a bath of liquid polymer. A vacuum is then created, causing the acetone in the cells to boil at a low temperature, drawing the liquid polymer into the cells, replacing the acetone which, as noted above, replaced the body fat and water (BWS 2022b). Step four of the plastination process involves positioning the body in the desired pose using wires, needles, clamps and foam blocks (BWS 2022b). Positioning is also needed in the context of funeral homes; however, it is achieved by placing the body in a coffin with padding under the head, such as a pillow, and padding under the elbows to elevate the hands which are then usually placed over one another on the abdomen to achieve the peacefully asleep aesthetic noted earlier. The fifth and final step in the plastination process is curing or hardening. This is done with gas, light or heat depending on the type of polymer that has been used. This process protects the plastinated specimen from decomposition (BWS 2022b).

Although it is necessary in the context of this exploration to discuss the realities of preserving dead bodies, funeral homes in Britain (and indeed elsewhere) provide little or no information about the physical process of embalming (Walter 2004: 612). In many funeral homes, any explanation of the process would focus on the aesthetic benefits of embalming, such as the slowed rate of decomposition and improved appearance of the deceased, rather than explaining the procedures described above; steps one and two, and the positioning. John Troyer has explored the secrecy around the embalming process in the funeral industry and the invisibility through which it functions, noting that the process and chemicals used by embalmers are hidden from public view (2020: 28). The reason for the clandestine nature of the embalming process relates to the invasive nature of the procedure. An in-depth explanation of the embalming process has the potential to cause the bereaved distress, and disclosing too much information about the process is typically actively discouraged for this reason.

However, embalming a dead body to display for living observers can do 'much more than suspend decomposition by altering the dead body's chemical physiology ... the concept of human death ... itself [can be] simultaneously altered' (Troyer 2020: 2). As the historian Philippe Ariès has observed, the concept of an embalmed body is ambiguous, with visitors on their farewell visitations, such as to a chapel of rest, coming without repugnance at viewing a corpse because, 'in reality they are not visiting a dead person ... but an almost-living one who, thanks to embalming, is still present, as if [they] were awaiting you to greet you or to take you off on a walk. The definitive nature of the rupture has been blurred' (1976: 101–102).

Due to the ambiguity created by the extensive processing of the dead, whether through plastination or embalming, displays of the dead in the context of a funeral home and in the BWS exhibitions do not represent the true nature of a dead body. Troyer points out that, 'as the previously unregulated post-mortem conditions of the dead body came under control ... through embalming, the living observer's embalmed vision effectively cocooned the corpse' (2020: 18). The cocooned vision of the embalmed, sleeping funeral home corpse and the plastinated anatomical corpse, both clinically engineered behind closed doors, does not grant the observer a realistic experience of being in the presence of a dead human body. The sights, sounds and smells associated with unprocessed death are not present in the company of an embalmed or plastinated body, and here they share commonalities with displayed corpses in museums. However, this is of no surprise as, 'if left unmediated, the dead [rotting] body is a shocking spectacle for those not accustomed to seeing physical decomposition' (Troyer 2020: 29).

There are, however, many cultures that have historically had a far closer relationship to a decomposing corpse (Hertz 2004 [1960]: 29–34), including those in the contemporary industrialised world before chemical embalming became a reality. Indeed, so recent is our lack of exposure to dead humans that relatively few people today know that the jaw of a corpse automatically opens as the muscles release the tension the body needed in life, and thus chin straps once held the mouth closed; evidence of this can be seen in an Early Modern sculpted stone cadaver of a now unknown male in the church of St Mary in Stalbridge, Dorset, England (Image 13.1). But altering the appearance of the dead to artificially shield the living from the aesthetics of decomposition is by no means a recent practice with, for instance, coins placed over the eyes of the dead being a once commonplace practice. However, these ancient processes to make the body socially decent were not invasive, whereas today, in much of the industrialised world, to make the dead visually decent for display to the living, they may have to endure the arguably indecent procedures described above.

Despite embalming and plastination serving the same purpose (to preserve the human body for display), Tony Walter employs the important distinction in regard to BWS, drawing on Robert Hertz's differentiation between a wet (fleshy) corpse and a dry corpse (skeletal remains or desiccated flesh). In the context of plastination Walter notes that 'in the Hertzian scheme, wet corpses are objects of mourning; dry remains are not. Plastination transforms a fresh corpse to be mourned into dry remains that may be exhibited as objects of curiosity and/or scientific education' (2004: 604). In response to this, we suggest that Walter is incorrect in assuming dry remains are not objects of mourning; even the long dead can still be mourned over (Chidester 1990), although we do agree with Walter when he observes, '... compared to other Europeans, the British are less aware of, and see less of, the dry dead...' (2004: 610); from the bone churches of Poland and the Czech Republic, to the ossuaries of Italy and Spain, much of Europe displays the dry dead in a way that Britain no longer does (Koudounaris 2011). However, ossuaries and bone churches are home to disarticulated skeletal human remains, and not plastinated human remains, which in BWS includes articulated bodies. In terms of the articulated BWS plastinates, it is important to note that these are typically devoid of skin; the bodies retain *in situ* their veins, arteries, nerves and muscles, all preserved through the process of plastination, but we argue, these are not the same as Hertz's dry remains.

**Image 13.1** Detail of the stone carved cadaver showing chin strap in the church of St Mary in Stalbridge, Dorset, England. © Welch 2015.

Certainly, they are not fleshy wet bodies, but neither are they the dry disarticulated bones or complete desiccated bodies of those people that the living firmly believe to be in the land of the ancestors. The plastinates occupy a liminal space between wet and dry where they remain in a type of suspended animation; objectified like a museum displayed mummy, yet posed in actions that give them subjectivity despite being skinless. With the plastinated bodies exhibited without their skin, there is a clear difference between them and the clothed fleshy corpses displayed in a funeral home. The next section therefore tries to make sense of the relationship between the dead in terms of skin and why the dead being naked might be understood as indecent, yet the dead without skin being exhibited in BWS rarely raises concerns over decency.

## THE DISPLAYED DEAD AND DECENCY

The dead in a funeral home if displayed naked would cause outrage. As noted above, these dead are, in the eyes of those saying their final fare-wells, to be treated as almost still alive. The visitors know the corpse is not sentient but all those involved in the care of the dead, from medical staff to undertakers and embalmers, treat the body with solemnity, and visit-ing family and friends expect this. The corpse is washed with dignity, it is dressed with care and posed in a respectful manner. The scene any visitor finds is one of decorum. This is of course because the deceased person is a named individual placed into their care, and the care of the deceased is as important to the funeral homes as is the care of the bereaved who are arranging the funeral. BWS exhibitions are different. The dead are unknown to the visitors, and that the corpses are more than naked is part of the attraction. The plastinates are not just unclothed and therefore nude, but largely fully defleshed. They are naked in the sense that they are exposed totally, they are stripped of the skin that holds their internal workings together, yet the form of their body remains, and they are easily identifiable as males with a penis, or females with breasts; as such they retain a subjectivity that an articulated skeleton does not have – few peo-ple beyond those trained to know the differences could spot a male from a female skeleton, or guess how old they may have been at death.

We now move to considering this subjectivity in more detail and look at some examples. The first example of BWS plastinates considered is a specimen displayed in the London BWS exhibition. Walter notes that of the 700 visitor comments in the BWS guest book he sampled in the late summer of 2002, most comments were positive. However, some visitors identified the poses that the plastinates were placed in as 'disturbing and distasteful' with the exhibition of babies considered questionable (2004: 621). The plastinate that could therefore be understood as one of the most controversial, and perhaps pushing at the boundaries of what is consid-ered decent, is the 'Reclining Pregnant Woman'; a woman pregnant with her eight-month foetus. She is displayed reclining with her eyes closed; her bent right arm takes the weight of her upper body, and her left arm is raised with her palm on the back of her head, ensuring both breasts (notably plastinated to be very pert) are fully visible. All her skin has been removed from her body bar her areola and nipples, which are erect. The retention of this area of skin is clearly intentional, and combined with the choice of pose, creates a sexualised look. Of course, nipples become erect in situations other than sexual arousal, but given this phenomenon is a result of the sympathetic nervous system sending messages to the nerves, all of which are inactive once the person is dead, the choice to show a plastinated woman with erect nipples is one that should at least raise questions. During pregnancy a woman's nipples do become more erect and can also start leaking fluid from 'as early as the fourth month'; however, the areola then becomes 'darkened noticeably' (Ford 2014: 201). As such, perhaps the choice to plastinate Reclining Pregnant Woman with erect nipples could be understandable, but only the first of these changes is evident and whilst leaking milk ducts would be almost impossible to show, the areola is very pale, almost milk white in appearance.

To add to the sexualisation aspect of this female plastinate, other BWS plastinated women are also displayed with erect nipples and pert breasts, for example 'Yoga Lady' from the 'Body Worlds and the Circle of Life' exhibition, who is posed preparing for 'the Wheel Pose' (Duffin 2015), and the plastinated woman on the 'All Anatomical Specimens, are Real' page of the BWS donations website (BWS 2022c). Posed men, meanwhile, despite having had nipples and areola in life, are plastinated without them (BWS 2022d); male plastinates just show the chest muscles almost as if they did not have nipples at all. Further, all plastinated men are posed with their skinned penis visible, but flaccid. It seems therefore that all female plastinates retain the one part of their skin that is often associated with sexuality, their areola and nipples, whereas male plastinates are displayed fully skinless.

Wade, on noting the sexualisation of the plastinated women, suggested that BWS deliberately show women as only 'good for two things: babies and sexual provocation'; a position she argues which is furthered by the non-active roles that women are posed in (Wade 2008). The active men and non-active women poses have changed slightly in recent years with, for example, a women shown on a trapeze (Glass undated: image 11). However, the skin of the areola and erect nipples remain. The sexualised poses of many of the female plastinates is redolent of wax anatomical models, colloquially known as Anatomical Venuses, which were once used to train male medical students in female anatomy, at a time when female cadavers were in short supply (Ebenstein 2016). Notably, all the Anatomical Venuses were moulded with pert breasts and erect nipples, and several had their right palm positioned under their head, much like 'Reclining Pregnant Woman'.

When thinking around the issue of decency in the display of corpses, it appears that 'Reclining Pregnant Woman' goes further than being overtly sexualised. BWS emphasises the medical aspect of their exhibitions, and any visitor will without doubt learn much about the human body from a visit. However, it is curious that the unborn child that 'Reclining Pregnant Woman' is carrying is not anatomised. The baby is fully fleshed, unlike the mother. The plastination of babies was one of the aspects that Walter noted in his study of visitor comments, but for a medical exhibition it seems somewhat strange that the baby is shown almost as if alive, where the mother is clearly dead. Here the borders between the medical and the show aspect seem to blur; 'Reclining Pregnant Woman' shows how a pregnant woman's body accommodates her child, but the baby's body does not show that both have the same organs, venal and nervous system etc. – albeit the baby's in miniature form. But there are other issues with this particular plastinate, there being controversy about how von Hagens obtained the specimen (Singh 2003). Rumours suggest she may have 'been the victim of an officially sanctioned execution' in Dalian, China who was pregnant by a married official (Anon [a] 2012); Dalian is an area from which von Hagens regularly obtains corpses. Von Hagens denied this claim and asked for a statement retraction; although it was not retracted, no court case has ensued (Anon [b] 2012). But regardless of where the woman's body was obtained from, it is unknown whether the non-anatomisation of the baby was her choice, or a decision taken by BWS. A further plastinate, 'Standing Pregnant Woman', is also displayed with her five-month foetus fully enfleshed. Both plastinates complicate the BWS claim that 'different stages of development' prior to birth are shown through these displays (Martinez 2012).

There are then, we argue, questions over the decency of the display of female plastinates in BWS. The overt sexualisation of females by retaining their areola and nipples when male plastinates have these removed is one. In funeral homes, care is taken to ensure no corpse is displayed with nipples on show, and female nipples would never undergo a treatment to ensure they stayed erect. The sexualisation of the dead is an anathema to funeral home professionals. Further, there is no information about why neonates are not anatomised especially when BWS claim that the plastination of pregnant women show the development of both bodies. Troyer asserts that 'the posing of dead bodies ... involves choices that confront Western attitudes about social decorum and institutional codes of conduct' (2020: 169), and it is clear to us that many of the BWS plastinates do this, particularly those including women. One BWS exhibit seems almost designed to push at the bounds of social decorum: the copulating couple that forms part of 'The Cycle of Life' BWS exhibition which opened in Berlin in 2009.

Acknowledging the sensitivity of the copulating couple display, the plastinates were shown in a separate room from the other specimens and were only accessible to those over the age of 16 years (Troyer 2020: 74–75). The display consists of two heterosexual couples engaged in vaginal intercourse. This is coupled on the wall behind, with a single slice of a plastinated couple posed having intercourse with his penis visible inside her vagina. They face each other in a sitting position and are displayed much like a painting or photograph in a frame on a wall behind the three-dimensional plastinates. This other couple, as is usual for BWS, shows a fully defleshed male, whilst the woman is defleshed bar her areola and erect nipples. They are set in the 'Reverse Cowgirl' position with the female astride the recumbent male, both of them facing the same direction.

About this display Troyer observes that showing the couple copulating '… transforms the human sex act, which is endowed with countless kinds of meanings, into a biologically inert, visual tableau' (2020: 85). This draws in part on Walter's argument that:

> undressing people to expose their skin is to sexualize them; but to undress them one step further, to take off their skin as well as their clothes, is to anatomize them. Sexuality is about the sight, the feel, the smell, of skin – utterly different from the smell-less sight of plasticized muscles and organs that we have here. (2004: 615)

To both Troyer and Walter therefore, we are presented with static scientific displays that medicalise the heterosexual act of procreation. However, as previously noted, the female plastinate retains her areola and nipples, whereas the male does not. Further, the female plastinate is not anatomically correct as she appears to have wings made of muscle that extend from her shoulders. Also, her abdomen is opened up with the left side seemingly held open by the male plastinate so her empty abdomen is fully visible. It appears her viscera have been removed to clearly show his erect penis inside her. There might perhaps be an argument to support this particular pose, as the act of vaginal penetration is clearly displayed. However, the sliced plastinates situated just behind this display do this job; his penis is shown inside her vagina. The three-dimensional display then is both anatomical and voyeuristic; there was no need to eviscerate the women to show the act of vaginal penetration. Indeed, she appears posed as a receptacle to show off her sexual partners' erection. In 2004, von Hagens was accused of sexism in his display which did not include female plastinates (Walter 2004: 483). Rather than rectify this by including female specimens fully defleshed and posed in similar ways to the male plastinates, BWS women in general appear overtly sexualised, this particular exhibit being a prime example.

Clearly no funeral home would display copulating couples so the issue of decency in this instance is moot; and as noted, nakedness is dealt with very differently in funeral homes. Of course, it could be argued, as Walter does, that the potential for indecency comes only with wet fleshy bodies, although a sense of decency is of course altered during certain life events such as at birth and giving birth, during sexual intercourse, and when dying. Yet by and large these are private affairs, or at least ones where public access is restricted and informed consent is given (if not by the actual person, then by family). Informed consent is a key issue and BWS asserts that this is given by those who are plastinated and displayed in their exhibitions; perhaps, even if consent is less than fully clear, the plastinates through anatomisation become 'objectified for study and internally exposed' (Cutler Shaw 1994: 37) and they are not the subjects, albeit dead ones, on show in funeral homes. Walter had noted that on the whole the public seem to support the transformation of a dead person to an anatomical object for consumption via the process of plastination (Walter 2004: 623) and it is clear from the lack of public push back, that visitors do not see the posed and displayed BWS bodies in the same way they would see a posed and displayed body in a funeral home; the former is an object and the latter a subject, although this is complicated by the issue of plastinated babies and some visitors did acknowledge a sense of discomfort with the posing of the now objectified people.

Rebecca Scott has explored this subject/object fluidity in relation to plastination and notes that the sense of reality for BWS visitors is confused and that '... positive visitor reactions suggest that either psychoanalytic thought cannot explain the experience of spectatorship, or that something powerful assuages the expected feelings and reactions' (2008: 6). The same could be said for visitors to funeral homes where a person's response to a dead human body would, '... shift from empathy to revulsion [if] it approached, but failed to attain, a lifelike appearance' (Mori et al. 2012: 98). This influences the level of acceptability and perception of decency in regard to exhibited BWS plastinates and funeral home corpses on display. Indeed, exploring the differences and similarities between embalmed Funeral Home bodies and plastinated specimens highlights the ambiguous nature of the displayed corpse and the need for a deeper analysis of the meaning of decency in this regard.

## CONCLUDING THOUGHTS

Both BWS plastinates and funeral home corpses are posed and displayed, yet being defleshed (or largely defleshed) sets the plastinates in the realm of scientific objects, whereas the fleshy funeral home body remains firmly a person. This distinction, however, is obfuscated by the overt sexualisation of the female plastinates who retain their areola and are plastinated with erect nipples, and by the evisceration of the female of the copulating couple in order for her partner's erect penis to be fully visible inside her empty abdomen. The plastinated babies inside their pregnant mothers also retain their subject status, and as such further complicate the subject/object divide when it comes to the display of women in BWS. If BWS is all about science and making the human into an anatomical specimen, then the male plastinates are objects, even those posed engaged in penetrative sex. But the plastinated women seem to occupy a different status; they are displayed as neither fully anatomical objects, nor fully subjects. Like the Anatomical Venuses, they are liminal creatures, almost confounding description. However, whether this makes them indecent is subjective; and there are certainly those who believe what BWS does is indecent (Geissinger and Geissinger 2008; Reuters 2009) or at least more showmanship than science (Singh 2003; Moore and McKenzie Brown 2008). It appears that whilst in funeral homes posed and displayed bodies (of any gender) are treated with respect and dignity, the sexualisation of female plastinates at BWS leans toward indecency.

## BIBLIOGRAPHY

Anon [a]. 2012. 'Body Worlds Exhibit Thought to Be Former Bo Mistress', *Goldsea.com* 19 August 2012. http://goldsea.com/Text/index.php?id=13468

Anon [b]. 2012. 'Plastination Firm Denies Displaying Bo Xilai Mistress', *Goldsea.com* 29 August 2012. http://goldsea.com/Text/index.php?id=13520

Ariès, Philippe. 1976. *Western Attitudes towards Death from the Middle Ages to the Present*. London: Marion Boyars.

Burns, Lawrence. 2007. 'Gunther von Hagens' BODY WORLDS: Selling Beautiful Education', *American Journal of Bioethics* 7(4): 12–23. https://doi.org/10.1080/15265160701220659

BWS. 2020. 'Gunther von Hagen's BODY WORLDS: The Happiness Project Amsterdam', *BODY WORLDS Amsterdam*. Retrieved from https://www.bodyworlds.nl/en/

BWS. 2022a. 'Body Worlds: FAQ', *BODY WORLDS*. https://bodyworlds.com/about/faq/

BWS. 2022b. 'Body Worlds: Plastination Technique', *BODY WORLDS*. https://bodyworlds.com/plastination/plastination-technique/

BWS. 2022c. 'Body Donation', *BODY WORLDS.* https://bodyworlds.com/plastination/bodydonation/

BWS. 2022d. 'Journey under the Skin', *BODY WORLDS.* https://bodyworlds.com/exhibitions/human/

BWS. 2022e. 'Philosophy', *BODY WORLDS.* https://bodyworlds.com/about/philosophy/

Chidester, David. 1990. *Patterns of Transcendence.* Belmont, CA: Wadsworth Pub. Co.

Cutler Shaw, Joyce. 1994. 'The Anatomy Lesson: The Body, Technology and Empathy', *Leonardo* 27(1): 29–38. https://doi.org/10.2307/1575946

Duffin, Erin. 2015. 'This Museum Hosted a Yoga Class with a Corpse', *doyou.com* 26 August 2015. https://www.doyou.com/this-museum-hosted-a-yoga-class-with-a-corpse/

Ebenstein, Joanna. 2016. *The Anatomical Venus: Wax, God, Death and the Ecstatic.* New York: D.A.P.

EH. 2009. 'Research into Issues Surrounding Human Bones in Museums', *English Heritage* 1 June 2009. https://historicengland.org.uk/content/docs/research/opinion-survey-results-pdf/

Fitzharris, Lindsey. 2016. 'The Battle over Bodies: A History of Criminal Dissection', *drlindseyfitzharris.com* 23 February 2016. https://drlindseyfitzharris.com/the-battle-over-bodies-a-history-of-criminal-dissection/

Ford, Claudia J. 2014. 'Pregnancy'. In Merril D. Smith (ed.), *Cultural Encyclopedia of the Breast*, pp. 200–210. Lanham: Rowman & Littlefield.

Geissinger, Steve and Geissinger, Michael. 2008. 'Lawmakers Call Body Exhibit "Freak Show"', *East Bay Times* 16 January 2008. https://www.eastbaytimes.com/2008/01/16/lawmaker-calls-body-exhibit-freak-show/#

Glass, Macy. Undated. 'Discover Denver: Gunter von Hagens tells the Story of the Heart', *Buckley Space Force Base.* https://www.buckley.spaceforce.mil/News/Article-Display/Article/323088/discover-denver-gunther-von-hagens-tells-the-story-of-the-heart/

Halliday, Josh. 2014. 'Savile Told Hospital Staff He Performed Sexual Acts in Corpses in Leeds Mortuary', *Guardian.com* 26 June 2014. https://www.theguardian.com/media/2014/jun/26/savile-bodies-sex-acts-corpses-glass-eyes-mortuary

Harding, Luke. 2004. 'Von Hagens Forced to Return Controversial Corpses to China', *The Guardian* 23 January 2004. https://www.theguardian.com/world/2004/jan/23/arts.china

Hennigan, W.J. 2020. 'Lost in the Pandemic: Inside New York City's Mass Graveyard on Hart Island', *Time.com* 18 November 2020. https://time.com/5913151/hart-island-covid/

Hertz, Robert. 2004 [1960]. *Death and the Right Hand.* London: Routledge.

Jenkins, Tiffany. 2010. *Contesting Human Remains in Museum Collections: The Crisis of Cultural Authority.* New York: Routledge.

Kennedy, Maev. 2008. 'The Great Mummy Cover-up', *Guardian* 23 May 2008. https://www.theguardian.com/artanddesign/artblog/2008/may/23/maevkennedyfriampic

Kirby, Terry. 2003. 'Three Arrested after Desecration of Muslim's Body with Bacon Strips', *Independent.com* 3 June 2003. https://www.independent.co.uk/news/uk/crime/three-arrested-after-desecration-of-muslim-woman-s-body-with-bacon-strips-107318.html

Koudounaris, Paul. 2011. *The Empire of Death: A Cultural History of Ossuaries and Charnel Houses*. London: Thames and Hudson.

Martinez, Britta. 2012. 'Body Worlds', *The Embyro Project Encyclopedia* 27 November 2012 https://embryo.asu.edu/pages/body-worlds

Moore, Charleen M. and Mackenzie Brown, C. 2008. 'Experiencing Body Worlds: Voyeurism, Education, or Enlightenment?', *The Journal of Medical Humanities* 28(4): 231–254. https://doi.org/10.1007/s10912-007-9042-0

Mori, Masahiro, MacDorman, Karl F. and Kageki, Norri. 2012. 'The Uncanny Valley [From the Field]', *IEEE Robotics & Automation Magazine* 19(2): 98–100. https://doi.org/10.1109/MRA.2012.2192811

NHM. 2017. 'Death, Corruption and Sanitation: London's Graveyards in the 19th Century', *Natural History Museum* 31 May 2017. https://naturalhistorymuseum.blog/2017/05/31/death-corruption-and-sanitation-londons-graveyards-in-the-19th-century-human-anthropology/

Pashaei, Shahyer. 2010. 'A Brief Review on the History, Methods and Applications of Plastination', *International Journal of Morphology* 28(4): 1075–1079. https://doi.org/10.4067/S0717-95022010000400014

Reuters. 2009. 'Copulating Corpses Spark Outrage in Berlin', *ABC News* 6 May 2009. https://www.abc.net.au/news/2009-05-07/copulating-corpses-spark-outrage-in-berlin/1675160

Scott, Rebecca. 2008. *Anatomy of Spectorship: Tracing the Body in Body Worlds, the Anatomical Exhibition of Real Human Bodies*. Master's thesis, Simon Fraser University. https://core.ac.uk/download/pdf/56373332.pdf

Singh, Debashis. 2003. 'Scientist or Showman?', *British Medical Journal* 326(7387): 468. https://www.ncbi.nlm.nih.gov/pmc/articles/PMC1125369/. https://doi.org/10.1136/bmj.326.7387.468

Stern, Megan. 2003. '"Body Worlds" and the Commodification of Health', *Radical Health Philosophy* 118: 1–6. https://www.radicalphilosophyarchive.com/issue-files/rp118_commentary_shinyhappypeople_stern.pdf

Troyer, John. 2020. *Technologies of the Human Corpse*. Cambridge, MA: The MIT Press.

Wade, Lisa. 2008. '"Your Body": Men Are People and Women Are Women', *The Society Pages: Sociological Images* 10 February 2008. https://thesocietypages.org/socimages/2008/02/10/your-body-men-are-people-and-women-are-women/

Walter, Tony. 2004. 'Plastination for Display: A New Way to Dispose of the Dead', *The Journal of the Royal Anthropological Institute* 10(3): 603–627. https://doi.org/10.1111/j.1467-9655.2004.00204.x

Whatcott, Elizabeth. 2022. 'Compilation of Countries' Statements Calling Russian Actions in Ukraine "Genocide"', *Just Security* 20 May 2022. https://www.justsecurity.org/81564/compilation-of-countries-statements-calling-russian-actions-in-ukraine-genocide/

**Lucy Jacklin** has a master's degree in Death, Religion and Culture from the University of Winchester, jointly winning the department of Philosophy, Religions & Liberal Arts master's graduation prize (2020/21). She has a professional and diverse background in the funeral industry and a special interest in environmentally conscious and alternative funerary practices.

**Christina Welch** is an interdisciplinary Religious Studies scholar. She led the master's degree in Death, Religion and Culture (formerly MA in Religion: The Rituals and Rhetoric of Death) at the University of Winchester from 2007 until 2021, and continues to teach on the programme. She has research interests around visual and material culture, particularly in relation to religion and/or death. She also works on issues around heritage, especially as they relate to religion and/or death in the Caribbean.

# Chapter 14

# Body Disposal, Decency and Dark Tourism: A Case Study Approach

## ALASDAIR RICHARDSON AND CHRISTINA WELCH

This chapter explores the sense of death and decency through two case studies. Firstly, it considers decency through the lens of a form of educational tourism, here Holocaust tourism. Concern over aspects of Holocaust tourism being in some way indecent is perhaps best outlined in the *Yolocaust* project. Here commemorative culture was explored through the lens of selfies with their online captions. One of these, the selfie which inspired the project, showed a young man jumping on the concrete slabs (Staele) of Berlin's Holocaust memorial (see Woolf undated); the caption read 'jumping on dead Jews @ Holocaust Memorial'. The young man has apologised, stating he didn't mean to cause any offence (Shapira 2017). Shapira went on to combine selfies taken at Holocaust memorial sites such as that in Berlin, with photographs taken in death camps such as Auschwitz, of emaciated Jews and piles of dead bodies. His project sought to raise the issue of appropriate behaviour at Holocaust sites, be they memorial sites such as in Berlin, or the actual sites of the Nazi mass murder of Jewish men, women and children (Gunter 2017); and it must be noted here that other peoples the regime deemed unacceptable were also murdered.

The need for appropriate behaviour at Holocaust sites is important for anyone, but perhaps no more so than for teachers leading school trips. On these trips, groups of young people, often away from home for the first time, visit sites such as Auschwitz-Birkenau to learn about the Holocaust.

The author Dr Richardson is a former teacher turned academic whose research focuses on the relationships between Religion Education (RE) and Holocaust Education in England. His experience of taking trainee teachers and young people to Auschwitz informs our first case study exploration into the sense of decency and death through a deep dive into educational tourism. Richardson's exploration of educational Holocaust tourism is furthered by Welch's consideration of 'dark tourism', a topic she covers when teaching about Death, Religion and Culture. After considering a lesser-known site of the murder of Jews during the Holocaust, she extends the topic of death and decency further through the second case study which explores the topic of death and decency in regard to burial sites in Brazil of enslaved Africans who died during the time of transatlantic chattel slavery.

*Note: this chapter contains information on mass murder that some people may find upsetting.

## CASE STUDY 1: AUSCHWITZ AND EDUCATIONAL TOURISM

Auschwitz is a place that was never meant to be visited – yet nearly 80 years after its liberation by Soviet Forces on 27 January 1945, visitor numbers run to over two million people per year (Bartyzel and Sawicki 2020). Most visitors to the Auschwitz-Birkenau State Museum come on organised tours and are guided by museum-regulated guides. While the museum discourages visitors under the age of 14 years,[1] it is obvious that many of the visitors each day are young people on educational visits. The museum that exists in 'the post camp space' (Bartyzel and Sawicki 2017: 23) is now a UNESCO World Heritage site,[2] and arguably has become the fulcrum of memory of the Holocaust (Benton 2010). Consequently, this place that was never intended to be visited, now serves many purposes – as a site of memory and witness, as a post-historic space, as a museum, as a tourist attraction, and (perhaps most obviously) as a graveyard and memorial site. The museum and its many visitors necessarily navigate this uneasy nexus; at best it is a solemn and educational place, at worst it risks becoming a contrived 'Auschwitzland' (Cole 2000: 110).

1  'Regulations for visitors and persons staying on the grounds of Auschwitz-Birkenau Museum and memorial (valid from 1.03.2021)', https://www.auschwitz.org/gfx/auschwitz/userfiles/_public/visit/30_en.pdf
2  'Auschwitz Bikenau German Nazi Concentration and Extermination Camp (1940–1945)', https://whc.unesco.org/en/list/31

Founded in 1947 by survivors of the Nazi camp, the museum's initial purpose was to serve as a monument to the Polish tragedy of the Second World War. Over the years, other layers of narrative have been added, particularly in the National Exhibits in the former Blocks 13–16, 18 and 20–21. Most recently, the 'Shoah' exhibition[3] has been installed in Block 27 by the museum in partnership with Yad Vashem, the World Holocaust Remembrance Center in Israel. Presenting the memory of the victims alongside their physical remains has always been problematic. While the exhibitions endeavour to show the traces of their lives, the geography of the site is evidently saturated with human remains (such as in the ash pits at the back of the site of Auschwitz II, Birkenau). Most visitors to the museum at Auschwitz I are guided through a particular path: from the museum entrance through the 'Arbeit Macht Frei Gate', then to Block 4 (housing an exhibition entitled 'Extermination'), Block 5 ('Evidence of Crimes'), Block 6 ('The Life of the Prisoner'), the courtyard of Block 11 (the so-called 'Execution Wall'), Block 27 ('Shoah'), the Appellplatz (roll-call square), then finally to the site of the Camp Commandant's house, and the gas chamber and crematorium. At Birkenau, they usually visit several reconstructed barracks which illustrate living conditions in the camp (see Image 14.1), before walking along the railway tracks to the unloading ramp, and finally the sites of the ruined gas chambers and crematoria towards the back of the camp. At various points in this itinerary, visitors encounter places where people were murdered – most obviously the gas chambers – but also at places such as the Appellplatz (where gallows are visible), or the so-called 'Execution Wall' (where prisoners were routinely shot). Some of these places are original (such as the crematoria at Birkenau), while others are reconstructed (such as the gas chamber at Auschwitz I, and the 'Execution Wall').

While human remains are implicit (buried) at many of these sites, the museum chooses to display human remains more explicitly at certain points. For example, in Block 4 visitors pass by a large, translucent urn of human ash, a symbolically anonymous assemblage, displayed simply and marked only '1940–1945' amongst information panels telling the history of the Holocaust. Upstairs in Block 4, the museum exhibits almost two tonnes of human hair from female former inmates. The passage of time has almost entirely drained the hair of its colour and the room is dimly lit, with the windows covered. It is one of the few places in the museum

---

3 'Shoah: the new permanent exhibition in Block 27 at the Auschwitz-Birkenau State Museum', https://www.yadvashem.org/yv/en/exhibitions/pavilion_auschwitz/index.asp

where flash photography is not allowed, primarily to protect the fragile remains from corrosive light. This provokes a sombre atmosphere in which reverence is unspoken but seems expected. When presented in this way – alongside exhibits of the victims' everyday 'things' (such as their shoes, suitcases, religious prayer shawls etc. – see Image 14.2) and panels of information and photographs – the remains can easily be viewed simply as part of the collection; 'things' to be seen, studied and reflected upon. At the places of mass extermination at the Birkenau site, however, 'commemorative stones' (taking the form of headstones) are inscribed with the words: 'To the memory of the men, woman and children who fell victim to the Nazi genocide. Here lie their ashes. May their souls rest in peace.'[4] Yet these stones and the sites are not on the standard guided route and consequently remain largely unvisited.

**Image 14.1** Reconstructed barracks at Birkenau.
https://pixabay.com/photos/poland-auschwitz-architecture-2299550/

4  'Memorial and Museum: information plaques', https://www.auschwitz.org/en/visiting/information-plaques/

**Image 14.2** Pile of suitcases and baskets on display at Auschwitz-Birkenau.
https://pixabay.com/photos/auschwitz-camp-poland-concentration-1137819/

Much of my research has focused on the experiences of English teenagers on organised educational visits to the museum (Richardson 2019, 2021). The museum exists self-awarely in the 'post camp space' (Bartyzel and Sawicki 2017: 23) – KL Auschwitz (the Nazi camp) is not there – yet the remains of its victims continue to be very much present (buried or displayed). Just as the museum 'presents and *re*presents history' (Richardson 2019: 3) as a narrative, it does the same with the victims (they are both present *and* represented here). How young people encounter these presentations and representations is complex. Much of what (they think) they know before their visit comes from school, the media and conversations in their homes (Richardson 2012). While the topic of the Holocaust has been compulsory in the National Curriculum in England for more than 25 years (Pearce 2017), pupils' exposure to the topic and their consequent understanding can be uneven, in an increasingly decentralised school system (Pettigrew et al. 2009; Foster 2013). Teenagers in England are more used to encountering victims of Nazi persecution as survivor speakers (Pettigrew et al. 2009); since the Holocaust did not happen on British soil there are no sites or mass graves here. Consequently, their understandings of the places where murder took place (and where the bodies are) come largely from secondary sources such as textbooks and 'in all the films and everything' (Richardson, 2023: 213) that they might encounter.

This brief case study draws from data collected from 72 teenagers on an organised, government-funded educational visit, who responded through online surveys (n=58) and face-to-face interviews (n=14) (Richardson 2023). When asked about their encounters with the various sites at the museum, they reported feeling emotionally moved by what they saw. At points of explicit murder, such as the 'Execution Wall' for example, their responses were often prompted by the presence of objects of memorialisation, such as flowers placed there by other visitors. This site was both 'tragic' and 'terrible' to them. Students referred to 'the dehumanisation process' of the former camp and 'the sheer size of the concentration camps' at Auschwitz I and Birkenau. Some were overwhelmed by the felt proximity of the victims; as one put it, 'everywhere we went and everything we saw was so filled with human imprint'. I have speculated before to what limited extent we enable 'reflective spaces' during these encounters (Richardson 2021:13), and the need for us as educators to do so to prevent our students from withdrawing into an academic or 'theoretical retreat' (Brina 2003: 524), or them merely performing 'superficial acts of commemorative pageantry' (Richardson 2021: 13). It is important, I feel, that educators (and educational spaces such as museums) enable visitors to encounter material and allusionary traces of the dead with the space to process and express their responses to it, such as grief or the need to perform a commemorative act.

Material objects are evidently key to these encounters for young visitors. The museum exhibits at the Auschwitz-Birkenau State Museum particularly foreground objects relating to the victims, such as the belongings they brought with them; most of which were plundered by the Nazis to financially benefit their war efforts. The objects on display are only a tiny specimen of the total haul taken by the perpetrators during the camp's operation. Many museums choose to display single objects (usually on loan from larger collections) but given the vast archive at the museum, objects are presented in piles here. Thus, in the tangled mesh of wire spectacles, the sea of pots and pans, and the mounds of shoes, visitors are almost overcome by the numbers of people implied by the display. Educationally, we tend to focus on the individuals who suffered and died, or suffered and survived the Holocaust, rather than attempting to explore the whole, for fear that young learners might be overwhelmed by the vast numbers. However, in my research I have consistently found that teenagers connect intimately with the piled objects shown in the Auschwitz-Birkenau State

Museum display. They act as 'gateway' objects (Richardson 2012: 72) that enable them to see the (imagined) individuals who once owned them. For example, in earlier research I found that these gateway objects prompted teenagers to try to 'imagine how many people could have been wearing those' things (Richardson 2012: 108). In my more recent study, it was evident that the text of the Holocaust had the potential to act as a 'tarnished mirror of history' (Stern Strom and Parsons 1982: 2) for the teenagers. Photographs of former inmates displayed in Block 6 made one student 'really ... think about myself more than anything', while another reflected on seeing the human hair in Block 5 wondering if 'this could have happened to me' (Richardson 2023: 217).

If museums are intended to be educational at all (and I think we can assume that they are), then clearly there is an educational power and value in these objects. But this raises questions about decency when some of these objects are human remains. As educators we have to accept that 'Auschwitz is a stage' (Nesfield 2015: 52). But in the same way that 'it is important visitors understand the difference between authenticity and reproduction' (Richardson 2023: 219), so too it is important they understand the difference between the *traces* of people and the *physical presence* of their bodily remains, and how they might appropriately react and respond to these different encounters with decency. Teachers are role-models, and part of their work at sites such as this has to be to authentically model these responses for their students and to enable the 'reflective space' their students need (Richardson 2021: 13). This must, surely, also be the responsibility of the museums. Museums 'represent ideal learning environments' (Hooper-Greenhill 2011: 171), in which their every presentational choice is imbued with interpretation by future visitors. Hein spoke of how:

> In the transition from object to museum object, things gain and lose dimensions of use and exchange value as well as other dimensions of meaning ... things are divested of those very properties that made them eligible for selection by the museum. What was one of many becomes unique; what was functional becomes idle; what was private becomes public. (2014: 55)

This is particularly germane to the display of human remains at Auschwitz, in that the display of human ash and hair arguably has the potential to invert Hein's thinking – where what was once 'unique' is forced to become 'one of many'. In attempting to highlight the individuals, they can be lost in the many. Williams notes how museum objects gain 'a "life"' (2007: 31) once on display, but I would argue that the reverse might be true in the exhibition of human remains; an individual life is here potentially reduced to the status of an object. However, what is evident from my research is that teenagers have a clear ability to retain sight of the *individual* and the 'life' in the profusion of inanimate and human objects they witness at the Auschwitz-Birkenau State Museum. What we (and museum curators) need to ensure as educators, is that the young people in our care understand the need to recognise the difference between these materially different types of 'objects' to ensure the fragments of the human being are truly *seen* and are accorded a decency beyond being reduced merely to museum objects.

As such educational tourism, especially to sites such as Auschwitz-Birkenau where, as the *Yolocaust* project has shown, there is an overlap between educational tourism and dark tourism, needs to be mindful not only of ensuring students treat the site with decency, but that the students themselves are respected and given the space they need to reflect on their own experiences, actions and reactions to the museum, memorial and wider site. This is particularly the case when outside the grounds of Auschwitz-Birkenau (on private land) is an ice-cream stand (Bartyzel in Gazeta Krakowska 2023) which has been described as, 'not only aesthetic tastelessness, but also a lack of respect for the special historical place located nearby'. This lack of respect, however, can also been seen in the reactions of some visitors, with a tourist in April 2023 posing on the train tracks; tracks which transported around 1.3 million people to Auschwitz-Birkenau – 1.1 million of them dying there. The photograph of the young woman light-heartedly reclining, along with others of people walking on the tracks as if they were balancing beams, have been widely condemned (Do Couto 2023). For young people on educational visits who are trying to negotiate their own feelings about the atrocities, whilst their teachers may set good examples, the actions of other adults around the site could prove highly confusing. Thus, providing a dedicated space for young people (or indeed, any visitor) to reflect deeply on what they see, hear and feel, seems increasingly important.

## DARK TOURISM AS A CONCEPT

Dark tourism (also known as thanatourism) is tourism to sites of death and/or tragedy, suffering and loss. As Richardson has noted above, tourism to Auschwitz-Birkenau is considerable. As well as educational visits by school pupils, relatives of those who died, relatives of survivors (and at the moment at least, survivors themselves) and other members of the public visit the site and, as noted above, not all of the last group treat the space with respect. There are of course, other locations associated with the mass deaths of Jewish people at the hands of the Nazis, including lesser-known *Shoah* sites. *Shoah* is in many ways a more appropriate term for Jewish murder at the hands of the Nazis, as it means catastrophe whereas a Holocaust is a burnt offering to God (see Lev 9:16–24). However, the term Holocaust is widely accepted with, for instance, Yad Vashem in Israel being 'Yad Vashem – the World Holocaust Remembrance Center',[5] and as such both are used in this chapter. One lesser-known site is Paneriai (Ponar in Yiddish) near Vilnius, Lithuania. Here as many as 70,000 Jews were murdered and their bodies dumped in pits (Image 14.3). What is particularly resonant about this site in comparison to Auschwitz-Birkenau, is that because Paneriai is a little-known Holocaust attraction, it is free from any tourist trappings; be they entry gates and curated displays, or ice-cream stands and Costa Coffee concessions; Richardson spotted one of these in the Auschwitz-Birkenau car park on his Spring 2023 visit to the site. Set in woodland, Paneriai is quiet with few information plaques, but many stones placed around the site to commemorate, in traditional Jewish post-mortem memorial style, those who were murdered there.

**Image 14.3** One of the burial pits in Paneriai. © Welch October 2015.

5 'Yad Vashem', https://www.yadvashem.org

Here, although there is no official spot to reflect, the visitor cannot help but do that. On the rural walk between local train station and the place where the Jews were executed, and at the leafy execution sites, quiet contemplation is almost impossible. The lack of much in the way of material culture and the general absence of visitors ensures the space is pregnant with significance for those who go. Paneriai is not a site one could happen upon, and visitors are almost pilgrims in that they deliberately journey there, although the same could be said of many dark tourism locations including Auschwitz-Birkenau. And it is this notion of pilgrimaging to places of death and destruction that are largely unconnected directly with the visitor, that interests academics (Sharpley and Stone 2009; Hooper and Lennon 2017; Lewis et al. 2021) and journalists alike (Sampson 2019; Kemp 2021).

Moving away from locations connected with the *Shoah*, perhaps the most notable dark tourism sites are other places of mass death. In America, the site of the World Trade Centre in New York following the 9/11 terrorist attack of 2001, where almost 3,000 people died, attracts around 6 million visitors annually (Shalomov 2018). The co-called Killing Fields in Cambodia where under the Khmer Rouge regime (1975–1979) between 2 and 3 million people, from subsistence farmers through to teachers and to Buddhist monks, were murdered, sees around 800 visitors a day during the high season (Pann 2017). The most well-known of the sites in terms of tourism is Choeung Ek where there is a genocide centre and a memorial containing the disarticulated bones and skulls of some nearly 9,000 of the victims (see Fleischman 2017). A small-scale study conducted by Bickford from late-2007 into early-2008 explored the reactions of visitors, most of whom were international. Although Bickford concluded that 'it is almost impossible to measure whether the site produces ... positive results directly', a number of tourists reported that visiting the site made them consider the effects of genocides more closely, and that the rawness of human remains and remnants of material culture from the period gave a visceral power to the experience (2009: 8–9).

Other dark tourism sites include disaster sites such as Pripyat in Ukraine, the site of the Chernobyl nuclear disaster in April 1986. As with Berlin's Holocaust memorial, there have been concerns raised about the number of people taking 'selfies and ... snapp[ing] artistically macabre shots of ruined relics' (Street 2019) at the site; a place where at least 30 people died (two from the explosion and a further 28 within two weeks from acute radiation syndrome, plus others whose later 'deaths cannot necessarily be attributed to radiation exposure') and thousands of men, women and children had to be resettled. Further, there are the long-lasting effects of the disaster in terms of land pollution, and physical and mental health conditions (WNA 2022). Yet this and similar places globally are noted as 'must-see' destinations with the dark-tourism.com website covering 116 countries, even having its own Darkometer which allows visitors to the sites to 'provide a quick and easy spot impression of how dark any particular place' is; Auschwitz is listed as 10, Choeung Ek has a score of 9 whilst at the time of writing Chernobyl is without a rating.

But smaller sites such as shrines and graveyards or other burial spots also fall under the category of dark tourism. As a death scholar, much of what Welch does for research would place her as a regular dark tourist; academic dark tourism is not explored in terms of ethical self-reflection in this piece though both Welch and Richardson are aware of the potential issues that this activity raises. But aside from scholarly or formal educational visits, the reasons that people visit dark tourism places vary. Tourist expert Hayley Stainton suggests they allow visitors to connect emotionally with historical events whilst also allowing space for real-world visitor education (Stainton 2022). Whilst in many instances this may be the case, as the *Yolocaust* project shows, a connection with the place may be less for emotionally connecting with historical sites of murder or disaster, and more for what is termed digital narcissism; a form of collecting 'ghoulish souvenirs' (Hodalska 2017), without having to pay for a postcard.

Dark tourism is not new: medieval and early modern public executions were a social event, with pilgrimages taken to sites of martyrdoms, and 'evidence ... [going] back to the Battle of Waterloo [in 1815] where people watched from their carriages the battles taking place' (John J. Lennon in Sampson 2019). The reasons for dark tourism, apart from the educational trips noted above, are beyond the scope of this chapter, but some forms of dark tourism raise ethical issues around the sense of decency of visitor behaviour and whether it is appropriate to be rating sites for how dark the tourism is. However, the second case study moves away from those who visit dark tourism sites, to the sites themselves and the lack of a decent burial given to the human dead considered Other.

## CASE STUDY 2: BURIAL SITES IN BRAZIL OF ENSLAVED AFRICANS

The second case study explores body disposal and the sense of decency as it relates to the burial sites of enslaved Africans during the time of transatlantic chattel slavery. Tourism to these sites does exist, but as most locations of bodies remain unknown, it is really only the excavated sites that have garnered the attention of both dark tourists and the descendants of the African people who come to pay their respects and honour their roots. This differentiation is important, just as categorising descendants of *Shoah* victims who visit sites of former Holocaust camps as 'tourists' could be deemed inappropriate. However, this form of visiting is often categorised as memory tourism which has been defined by Dephine Bechtel and Luba Jurgenson as visiting 'places with which one maintains a strong personal biographical relationship, these places are also those of past suffering, loss, or oppression experienced personally or by members of the group to which one belongs' (in Hertzog 2023).

This second case study focuses on the burial of enslaved Africans in Brazil. Brazil was colonised by the Portuguese and received the highest number of enslaved Africans. Klein and Luna in their book *Slavery in Brazil* estimate that '4.8 million Africans arrived on its shores' (2010: 36). Records in Brazil from the early-to-mid-1800s show that common graves were often used for enslaved Africans who had died; however, there were differences in terms of decency depending on where one died. In Olinda, Pernambuco, for instance, common graves mean side-by-side burials rather than internment in a mass grave pit. Enslaved people were buried separately from non-enslaved people, although both burial areas had registers (separate of course!). In the burial records for the enslaved people, the given name of the enslaved person was recorded alongside personal information such as their marital status, place of birth and cause of death; although the inclusion of the name of the person who claimed ownership over the interned individual ensured that the recorded death was clear in assigning Other status.

However, in Rio de Janeiro, Brazil's largest city, mass grave pits were commonplace and contemporary descriptions note the burial grounds for enslaved Africans were more like rubbish tips than cemeteries. In Rio de Janeiro, there was a specific cemetery for the city's poor and enslaved individuals. The Black Cemetery of Nossa Senhora da Misericórdia, the Mercy Hospital, was described in an 1825 report, as 'wretched and nasty'. The space was 80 square metres and thousands of bodies were buried there annually. The dead were largely brought naked to the site and thrown into ditches and pits. Because of the heat and the vermin, decomposition was fast, and it took little time before the pit was virtually empty and ready to be refilled. Any remaining bones and skulls were removed from the pit and piled up; the report notes that the skulls still had their hair (Eduardo

Theodoro Bösche in Conrad 1994: 148–49). And a similarly stark picture emerges from the Cemitério dos Pretos Novos (Cemetery of the New Blacks), Gamboa, in the port region of Rio, which operated from 1769 to 1830 and was excavated in 1996. It is believed that the cemetery contained the remains of 20,000 to 30,000 enslaved Africans, largely men aged '18–25 [years] who had died during the three-month sea journey [from Africa] to Brazil or soon after arriving' (Phillips 2005); although official records state smaller numbers (Deister 2022). Excavations found 'skulls on top of other skulls, bodies piled up on each other' (Phillips 2005) where bodies were dumped alongside general everyday garbage (Deister 2022). The site is now a memorial museum, and the focus of memory tourism in the city (Gonçalves, 2021).

Yet, whilst it appears that there is a stark difference between these two geographical areas in relation to the decent disposal of the enslaved dead, it is important to note that not all those who claimed ownership over enslaved African people ensured their bodies were buried decently. There are reports of slave masters across Brazil ridding themselves 'of [a] corpse in some secluded spot on the coast or outside [a] city' (Soares 2011: 159), and of the bodies of enslaved Africans buried in fields and forests (Conrad 1994: 63). Despite enforced baptisms into Christianity (in Brazil, Roman Catholicism), deceased enslaved Africans were routinely denied a dignified burial.

## CONCLUDING THOUGHTS

This chapter has explored death in relation to the sense of decency. Decency is a culturally-relative notion, and Welch's chapter in this work raises this in relation to the Wari' people and their change from post-mortem cannibalism to burial of their dead. However, some acts seem to be almost universally perceived as disrespectful, and this typically includes the desecration of dead bodies and the sites where the dead lie. Sites where large-scale deaths have taken place, where disasters have occurred, and where bodies are buried, have attracted and continue to attract the living in an activity now called dark tourism, and Richardson and Welch have here sought to explore this phenomenon. Richardson has focused on a form of dark tourism that is educational: the visits by English school students to Auschwitz-Birkenau and how the space does not currently allow for young people to fully reflect on what they experience, that is, what they see and feel. This is important as each of those who died there, or survived against the odds, were individual people; yet, as Richardson notes, they tend to become one of a mass within the context of the memorial site.

Not all actions in and around the site could be deemed decent; selfies and similar acts such as those the *Yolocaust* project focused on are a case in point here. In many ways Auschwitz-Birkenau contrasts with Paneriai. The former is well publicised, busy and explicitly designed for visitors to learn about the *Shoah*/Holocaust, whereas the latter is quiet and off the beaten-track, and a place without the pedagogical information boards that inform the visitor about events – at Paneriai one implicitly contemplates the hatred-fuelled mass-murder of Lithuanian Jews (people Othered by the Nazi regime); any teaching is done subconsciously. Exploring these sites opens up questions about dark tourism, which has a long history, and in some way speaks to a human need to connect.

The second case study shifts to explore those whose deaths are not marked but were still Other to the dominant culture; the mass burial of enslaved Africans trafficked to Brazil as chattels. Without grave markers, these men, women and children are examples of the millions of people who died throughout the New World as effective objects. Largely dehumanised in life, their bodies were not treated with respect at death. Not to diminish the victims of the chattel slave trade, this case study also stands as testimony to the many millions globally whose bodies are not marked today, and in many cases have never been marked: the poor, the dispossessed, the unknown, the Other/Othered – any visit to a graveyard or cemetery will only show markers for those wealthy enough to afford them. Just as in life, in death social status often comes to the fore. As with those who were murdered in the *Shoah*/Holocaust, or died enslaved, the sense of decency in regard to the dead remains as pertinent an issue as ever.

## BIBLIOGRAPHY

Bartyzel, Bartosz and Sawicki, Paweł (eds.). 2017. *Report 2016*. Wadowice, Poland: Państwowe Museum Auschwitz-Birkenau w Oświęcimiu.

Bartyzel, Bartosz and Sawicki, Paweł (eds.). 2020. *Report 2019*. Wadowice, Poland: Auschwitz Birkenau Memorial.

Benton, Tim. 2010. 'Heritage and Changes of Regime'. In Tim Benton (ed.), *Understanding Heritage and Memory*. Manchester: Manchester University Press.

Bickford, Louis. 2009. 'Transforming a Legacy of Genocide: Pedagogy and Tourism at the Killing Fields of Choeung Ek', *International Center for Transitional Justice*. https://www.ictj.org/sites/default/files/ICTJ-Cambodia-Legacy-Genocide-2009-English.pdf

Brina, Carolyn. 2003. 'Not Crying, But Laughing: The Ethics of Horrifying Students', *Teaching in Higher Education* 8(4): 517–528. https://doi.org/10.1080/135625103200 0117607

Cole, Tim. 2000. *Selling The Holocaust: From Auschwitz to Schindler. How History Is Bought, Packaged, and Sold.* New York: Routledge.

Conrad, Robert E. 1994. *Children of God's Fire: A Documentary History of Slavery in Brazil.* Pennsylvania State University.

Dark-tourism.com. https://www.dark-tourism.com/index.php

Deister, Jacqueline. 2022. 'Descoberta do Cemitéio dos Pretos Novos no Rio complete 26 Anos no Mê de Janeiro', *Brasil de Fato* 11 January 2022. https://www.brasildefato. com.br/2022/01/11/descoberta-do-cemiterio-dos-pretos-novos-no-rio-completa-26-anos-no-mes-de-janeiro

Do Couto, Sarah. 2023. 'Tourists Spark Outrage after Posing for Photos on Auschwitz Train Tracks', *Global News* 17 April 2023. https://globalnews.ca/news/9629329/auschwitz-train-tracks-photos-woman-outrage/

Fleischman, Julie M. 2017. *Remains of Khmer Rouge Violence: The Materiality of Bones as Scientific Evidence and Affective Agents of Memory.* PhD dissertation, Michigan State University. https://d.lib.msu.edu/etd/6679

Foster, Stuart. 2013. 'Teaching About the Holocaust in English Schools: Challenges and Possibilities', *Intercultural Education* 24(1–2): 133–148. https://doi.org/10.1080/14675986.2013.772323

Gazeta, Krakowska. 2023. 'Auschwitz Criticises "Tasteless" Ice Cream Stand Set up on Land Outside "Death Gate"', *Sky News* 13 May 2023. https://news.sky.com/story/auschwitz-criticises-tasteless-ice-cream-stand-set-up-on-land-outside-death-gate-12879788?fbclid=IwAR3nTmvr6dQUAeIe2aUHiOjX DUI_YxygIjp5hS_to1atvVJd_Dnh29H1xW8

Gonçalves, Renata de Sá. 2021. 'Walking through Rio de Janeiro's "Little Africa": Places and Contested Borders', *Vibrant: Virtual Brazilian Anthropology* 18: e18601; https://www.redalyc.org/journal/4069/406969792008/html/.      https://doi.org/10.1590/1809-43412021v18d601

Gunter, Joel. 2017. '"Yolocaust": How should you behave at a Holocaust memorial?', *BBC News* 20 January 2017. https://www.bbc.co.uk/news/world-europe-38675835

Hein, Hilde S. 2014. *The Museum in Transition: A Philosophical Perspective.* Washington, DC: Smithsonian Institution Press.

Hertzog, Anne. 2023. 'Tourism and Places of Memory: Exploring the Political Side of Tourism and the Spatial Dimension of Memory', *European Memories* 22 April 2023. https://europeanmemories.net/magazine/tourism-and-places-of-memory-exploring-the-political-side-of-tourism-and-the-spatial-dimension-of-memory/

Hodalska, Magdalena. 2017. 'Selfies at Horror Sites: Dark Tourism, Ghoulish Souvenirs and Digital Narcissism', *Zeszyty Prasoznawcze* 60(2): 405–423. https://doi.org/10.4467-22996362PZ.17.026.7306

Hooper, Glenn and Lennon, John J. (eds.). 2017. *Dark Tourism: Practice and Interpretation.* New York: Routledge.

Hooper-Greenhill, Eilean. 2011. *Museums and Their Visitors.* Abingdon, Oxon: Routledge.

Kemp, Sam. 2021. 'Walking amongst Shadows: An Introduction to Dark Tourism', *Far Out* 29 October 2021. https://faroutmagazine.co.uk/an-introduction-to-dark-tourism/

Klein, Herbert S. and Luna, Francisco V. 2010. *Slavery in Brazil*. Cambridge: Cambridge University Press.

Lewis, Heather, Schrier, Thomas and Xu, Shangyu. 2021. 'Dark Tourism: Motivations and Visit Intentions of Tourists', *International Hospitality Review* 36(1): 107–123. https://doi.org/10.1108/IHR-01-2021-0004

Nesfield, Victoria L. 2015. 'Keeping Holocaust Education Relevant in a Changing Landscape: Seventy Years on', *Research in Education* 94: 44–54. https://doi.org/10.7227/RIE.0020

Pann, Molyny. 2017. 'Too Many Tourists a Concern in Cambodian "Killing Fields"', *VOAnews* 1 April 2017. https://www.voanews.com/a/cambodia-killing-fields-tourists/3790526.html

Pearce, Andy. 2017. 'The Holocaust in the National Curriculum after 25 Years', *Holocaust Studies* 23(3): 231–262. https://doi.org/10.1080/17504902.2017.1296068

Pettigrew, Alice, Foster, Stuart J., Howson, Jonathan, Salmons, Paul, Lenga, Ruth-Anne and Andrews, Kay. 2009. *Teaching about the Holocaust in English Secondary Schools: An Empirical Study of National Trends, Perspectives and Practice*. London: Institute of Education, University of London.

Phillips, Tom. 2005. 'Slaves' Mass Grave is Grim Reminder of Brazil's Racist Legacy', *The Guardian* 30 December 2005. https://www.theguardian.com/world/2005/dec/30/brazil.mainsection

Richardson, Alasdair. 2012. *Holocaust Education: An Investigation into the Types of Learning that Take Place when Students Encounter the Holocaust*. Brunel University. https://bura.brunel.ac.uk/handle/2438/6595

Richardson, Alasdair. 2019. 'Site-Seeing: Reflections on Visiting the Auschwitz-Birkenau State Museum with Teenagers', *Holocaust Studies* 27(1): 77–90. https://doi.org/10.1080/17504902.2019.1625121

Richardson, Alasdair. 2021. 'Lighting Candles in the Darkness: An Exploration of Commemorative Acts with British Teenagers at the Auschwitz-Birkenau State Museum', *Religions* 12: 29. https://doi.org/10.3390/rel2010029

Richardson, Alasdair. 2023. '"Did You Have a Good Trip?" Young People's Reflections on Visiting the Auschwitz Birkenau State Museum and the Town of Oświęcim'. In Diana I. Popescu (ed.), *Visitor Experiences at Holocaust Memorials and Museums*, pp. 210–223. Abingdon, Oxon: Routledge.

Sampson, Hannah. 2019. 'Dark Tourism, Explained: Why Visitors Flock to Sites of Tragedy', *Washington Post* 13 November 2019. https://www.washingtonpost.com/graphics/2019/travel/dark-tourism-explainer/

Shalomov, Yulia. 2018. 'Reflecting on 2018: See the 9/11 Memorial & Museum's Year in Review', *911memorial blog*. https://www.911memorial.org/connect/blog/reflecting-2018-see-911-memorial-museums-year-review

Shapira, Shahak. 2017. *Yolocaust.de*. https://yolocaust.de

Sharpley, Richard and Stone, Philip R. (eds.). 2009. *The Darker Side of Travel: The Theory and Practice of Dark Tourism*. Buffalo: Channel View Publications.

Soares, Mariza de C. 2011. *People of Faith: Slavery and African Catholics in Eighteenth-century Rio de Janeiro*. Trans. Jerry D. Metz. Durham, NC: Duke University Press.

Stainton, Hayley. 2022. 'What Is Dark Tourism and Why Is It So Popular?' 24 May 2022. https://tourismteacher.com/dark-tourism/

Stern Strom, Margot and Parsons, William S. 1982. *Facing History and Ourselves: Holocaust and Human Behaviour*. Watertown: International Educations Inc. https://www.facinghistory.org/resource-library/holocaust-human-behavior?utm_term=holocaust%20and%20human%20behavior&utm_campaign=NEW_Holocaust&utm_source=adwords&utm_medium=ppc

Street, Francesca. 2019. 'Chernobyl and the Dangerous Ground of "Dark Tourism"', *CNN* 25 June 2019. https://edition.cnn.com/travel/article/dark-tourism-chernobyl/index.html

Williams, Paul. 2007. *Memorial Museums: The Global Rush to Commemorate Atrocities*. Oxford: Berg Publisher.

WNA. 2022. 'Chernobyl Accident 1986'. World Nuclear Association. https://world-nuclear.org/information-library/safety-and-security/safety-of-plants/chernobyl-accident.aspx

Woolf. Undated. https://www.woolfinterior.com/journal/berlin-holocaust-memorial

**Alasdair Richardson** is a Reader in Education with a research specialism in Holocaust education. He recently explored the emotional labour involved in taking school children to Holocaust sites such Auschwitz (2021, 2023) and how best school children can engage with commemoration at Holocaust sites (2019). His monograph on *The Salesian Martyrs of Auschwitz* was published in 2021.

**Christina Welch** is an interdisciplinary Religious Studies scholar. She led the master's degree in Death, Religion and Culture (formerly MA in Religion: The Rituals and Rhetoric of Death) at the University of Winchester from 2007 until 2021, and continues to teach on the programme. She has research interests around visual and material culture, particularly in relation to religion and/or death. She also works on issues around heritage, especially as they relate to religion and/or death in the Caribbean.

Chapter 15

# Satire in the Time of a Pandemic: An Interview with Cold War Steve

## LAURA HUBNER

This chapter examines, via an interview format, the role of satire during a global pandemic (specifically Coronavirus, or Covid-19, which began to gain force in the UK in March 2020), concentrating on the work of contemporary British satirist and digital collagist, Christopher Spencer, known as 'Cold War Steve'.[1] While Spencer began creating digital collages on Twitter in 2016, the discussion focuses on his artwork during the peak of the pandemic, as rising and multiple deaths across the UK cast a spectral presence.

The British government's response to Covid-19 has been strongly, and often compellingly, criticised. Lisa Montel, Anuj Kapilashrami, Michel P. Coleman and Claudia Allemani found a failure to protect vulnerable groups adequately in the UK both from a public health perspective and with respect to 'the right to health' as defined under international human rights law, concluding: 'The COVID-19 pandemic has caused many deaths that could have been avoided had we been better prepared with strong rights-based provisions' (2020: 238). Critique of the British government's hypocrisy, greed and inadequate handling of the pandemic lies at the

---

1 The name originates from the early days in 2016 when Spencer used the @Coldwar_Steve account to post amusing images of the actor Steve McFadden (Phil Mitchell from British television soap opera *EastEnders*) against backdrops of cold-war imagery, as an 'everyman' or disapproving onlooker.

emotional core of Cold War Steve's satirical humour. In some respects, this is in keeping with a long tradition of British satire, comparable, for example, with prose satire during the plague-ridden Elizabethan era, which began to illuminate inequalities in the system, intensified by exploitative aristocratic or middle-class avarice.[2]

However, notable nuances are evident in Spencer's generous approach to dissemination and communication, that are key to exploring the shifting roles of artist and satirist today. His vast volume of work emanates from the images he regularly posts on Twitter (now X), sometimes more than once a day, via the Twitter feed @coldwarsteve, where audiences share their laughter, comment on his work, read meanings from it, draw attention to key parts, crop to zoom in on close-ups, re-edit or add animations, retweet in new contexts, or post their own artworks in response. Added to this is the sheer artistic quality and comedic talent underlining Cold War Steve's idiosyncratic dystopian landscapes and surreal visions populated by politicians and celebrities. In just a few years, his work has been widely acclaimed, leading to an impressive range of public outputs and events, including solo exhibitions, books, commissions for the National Galleries of Scotland and Whitworth (Manchester), Birmingham Museum and Gallery, and magazine covers including *TIME* (17 June 2019), plus a giant billboard installation (2019) and guest interview (2022) at Glastonbury Festival. The Sky Arts documentary, *Cold War Steve Meets The Outside World* (Evans 2020), featuring Spencer as he constructed four huge outdoor artworks in Medway, Liverpool, Coventry and Bournemouth, was shortlisted for the 2021 Grierson Documentary Awards and the exhibition was nominated for the 2021 South Bank Awards, adding to numerous prior indicators of esteem.[3] However, the Twitter posts remain integral to Spencer's daily working life and faithful relations with his audiences – a key part of his genuine, constant persona (as modest 'everyman' and trusted observer from Birmingham, England). They offer a lifeline to many struggling to digest rising moral injustices during these troubled times, suggesting that contemporary satire has the capacity to act as cultural educator, or speak more directly to the fears of the people.

---

2  See, for example, William Kerwin, 'Writing the Plague in English Prose Satire', focusing on the work of William Bullein and Thomas Dekker (Kerwin 2010: 37–54).

3  For example, Spencer's jigsaw *Hellscape* was shortlisted in 2020 for the Design Museum's Design of the Year Award and his book *A Prat's Progress* (2019) was nominated for The Deutsche Börse Photography Foundation Prize.

Spencer has said he found the Brexit results in 2016, following the UK's European Union (EU) Referendum, extremely distressing, deciding to channel his reactions into his art, so it slowly became 'more satirical and political' (Spencer, cited in Jonze 2018). He has stated that being able to make and post these satirical collages has kept him 'sane' (Sherwood 2019). It has also helped his followers: 'I know from my Twitter audience they are completely dismayed by what's happening – not just Brexit, but Trump, the rise of the far right, the increase in hate crimes. But there's something quite powerful about laughing at these people, flaying them alive with humour and sarcasm' (Spencer, cited in Sherwood 2019). In the Introduction to *Cold War Steve: Journal of the Plague Year*, Spencer writes that once Britain had left the EU (31 January 2020), there was anticipation over whether his output might slow down. At this point there was little sense of the scale of the pandemic to come. Even when the enormity became clear, it was not immediately apparent that such a tragedy could be conducive to any kind of humour:

> From mid-February and into March, as the coronavirus extended its tentacles around the globe, I wasn't certain whether I should be satirizing something that was so foreboding. Our plucky prime PM saw no reason to attend five Cobra meetings on this emerging pandemic, but people were scared. People were dying .... (Spencer 2021: 5, Thursday 29 July 2021)

When we spoke on the telephone (20 September 2022), Spencer elaborated on the genesis of his work and the targeting of its humour (and rage) during these 'foreboding' times.

*Laura Hubner: What initially got you making satirical collages and who was the artwork intended for?*

Christopher Spencer (Cold War Steve): Initially, right when it started, they weren't satirical. I'd done collage-making before many years ago at art college but then I didn't carry it on .... I did art periodically as a hobby, but I'd found myself rolling along some 20 years doing crap jobs, just getting by. My mental health wasn't great. I had a really bad patch. And coming out of that, I started to mess around on my phone (because you can get these cheap cut-and-paste apps) and I'd spend hours making little pictures, putting different people's heads on – just as a kind of therapy. Then I started to share them on Twitter. And they weren't satirical really. But it got picked up and people seemed to enjoy it. And I loved the feedback because you're meeting people with a similar mindset. And then as I was doing this the political landscape in this country deteriorated. More and more. Primarily following the referendum. When Brexit won as people voted to leave the EU it was devastating. Normally my means of coping would have been to get drunk and rant, but now with this mechanism I had in place I was able to channel some of that into making these pictures: as an outlet to express what I was thinking. It all grew from that. And the political landscape grew increasingly worse with Brexit approaching. When we eventually left, it was the question of what's going to happen now.

Along comes Covid. With the complete ineptitude of the government in place again. I was able to channel my angers and fears throughout that period as well. It's ongoing. It doesn't seem to end does it! [Laughs] Good for business, I guess! For what I do. But not good for the soul. With Brexit it was like: 'What have we done?!' And that was something that linked across, bridging the gap between the Brexit pieces I was doing and the Covid pieces, as you've got the same people really that are responsible for hoodwinking the public into voting us out. These people are now in charge of the reaction to this global pandemic. The lies and incompetence continued. And now it was people's lives that were in their hands. My wife's a carer. She was becoming devastated because they were releasing people from hospital straight into care homes without having tested them or anything. Of course, the virus then ravages everyone. And then there was just death every day. And Matt Hancock[4] was bragging about the 'protective ring' that he'd put around the care home. I was reading that fuming. I wasn't sure how to approach it at first. How do you satirise a global pandemic? But eventually the anger got so much. Every day there was something new that was happening or wasn't happening. It got to the point I had to do something.

*During the pandemic a lot of people drew comfort from seeing their anger at the government's incompetence and their fear of death communicated in your work. Did you sense at the time that your comedy could help people feel they are not alone?*

That's the key point. I put the pieces out there, not sure how it would go down. But then people were getting in touch, through the comments on Twitter. It's like a meeting room almost of people, and they're saying 'Yes – We see this. This is what's happening. We're not reading about this

---

4  Matt Hancock served as Secretary of State for Health and Social Care from 9 July 2018 until his resignation, 26 June 2021.

anywhere else.' None of the press were talking about what was happening. It wasn't on the television, but here I was holding the mirror up to it and people were getting some comfort I think, and I was as well, in that shared distress. Although it is distressing, it is also about being able to laugh at the incompetence. Initially I feared it might be disrespectful at the time to make fun of something like that, but on reflection it seemed to bring the point home better, I think. Which is the only way I know how to do it really. Other than rant or release a written piece on Twitter, which no one's going to spot or care about it. But if an *image* suddenly comes up it grabs people.

*Exactly, we find that so often with satire: the value of the visual over the written form for gaining audiences' attention quickly. And with your work, the responses you get are immediate, which is something relatively new in the history of print or cartoonist satire.*

Yes. That's the key. It's the immediacy.

*And your followers continue to rise at a phenomenal rate.[5] It is not uncommon for each new image to receive over 20,000 likes, thousands of retweets, plus hundreds of comments and 'quote tweets' within just a few hours.*

It still hasn't properly sunk in yet to be honest. It brings its own issues in a way. Because whereas to start with I would put something out without thinking too much, now I'm a bit more considered about what I'm doing. And the pieces themselves can take days sometimes. But although it's changed a lot, the essence of it is still the same. It's still reacting to events as quickly as I can. It's about not waiting. A traditional cartoonist in the old sense – the Georgian ones – would have to do the etching, and then it would be printed, and it would take some time. Even with the modern cartoonists it's still going to be the next day before anyone sees it. But with Twitter it can be on the news and an hour later I can whack something out. It's got that immediacy and I think that's what helps.

*Satire has traditionally been studied for its capacity to ridicule, humiliate, shame and criticise. Your work is very much aimed at the policy makers. And it's not just targeting incompetence; it's hypocrisy – plus other vices. It's not targeted at the people...*

---

5  There are 417.4 K followers (30 October 2022).

No – that's the key point. Someone said as long as you punch up, then I think it's fine. It is always aimed at the decision makers. The hypocrisy, the greed, the corruption.

*I was thinking about this, because with this process you can respond directly. With Twitter you can tag someone who's just said or done something. You have tagged Boris Johnson for example.*[6]

Yes!

*Presumably you've never had a reply from someone saying they now see the error of their ways or might change what they do!*

[Laughs] I never used to tag them, but I've started to do that. Because they'll say something that's so ridiculously untrue or hypocritical and I'll attach a little picture on it. No, they've never got back .... A couple of politicians have blocked me. But others don't. I do wonder sometimes if say Johnson has seen or heard about a particular tweet I've done, or someone's shown it to him. I know what I do isn't going to change their opinion, but it gives a sense of satisfaction at least to think they'd see it ... and maybe think about what they've done. They're surrounded by sycophants, so no one is ever telling them what they are doing is corrupt. You hope these little things maybe get through and chip away slowly.

But the main thing they do is to help people feel they are not alone, and they are able to at least laugh at what's happening. I don't know about any change or anything.

*The concept of 'chipping away' is powerful.*

Well, I can't claim to have been the person that brought down Johnson! [Laughs] But someone once said if Johnson goes it could be my doing because the party visuals [following 'partygate'] were so visceral.[7] That was a shock. Not only was all that happening but they were partying as well! I ramped up these visceral grotesque party scenes that were getting lots of views and likes.

6  Alexander Boris de Pfeffel Johnson served as British Prime Minister and Leader of the Conservative Party from 24 July 2019 until his resignation, 6 September 2022.

7  The gatherings and parties of the British government and Conservative Party staff held in 2020 and 2021 during the COVID-19 pandemic, when public health restrictions prohibited most gatherings, have been referred to as 'partygate'.

*Sometimes you've retweeted an artwork when it's happening all over again. Sometimes the original had a prophetic quality, or retweeting means it gains a new significance in light of recent change.*

Haha! 'Yeah, this is happening again!' Then I don't need to do another piece, just roll out that one again! Still relevant.

*Could we move on to discuss some specific artworks? (See Image 15.1.) The image of Dominic Cummings playing chess with Death, drawing inspiration from the iconic scene of the knight playing chess with Death in Ingmar Bergman's* The Seventh Seal *(1957), the Swedish film set during the medieval plague – an apposite image during these unstable times ...*

**Image 15.1** Collage by Christopher Spencer, originally posted 13 September 2020.

I don't know the ins and outs of *The Seventh Seal*. But I love it. That image of Death in the film is great. The figure appears in some great shots, so that's one reason to use it. But also, whereas the knight in *The Seventh Seal* is playing chess to prolong his life – the longer he is playing chess he can ward off death and carry out a meaningful deed ... here 'Our Knight' (Cummings) – because Cummings at that point was seen to be the one who was pulling all the strings ... he was an unelected bureaucrat basically. He'd been instrumental in Brexit, in getting Johnson in, and during all these press conferences you'd always see him lurking in the shadows watching and he seemed to be the one that was in control – And so here he is playing Death at chess to try and ward off the pandemic that was at this time just getting worse and worse. It is exasperating to watch, it's like oh my god … it is not going well. And just by his armrest (you can barely make it out but) there's a *Chess for Dummies* guidebook stuffed down there, which is saying that he doesn't even know how to play chess and yet we are expected to believe that he can. What hope is there!

*Yes, and Johnson stands at the podium in the background …*

Looking at his master! Because Cummings was at that point! He got the proroguing of parliament when things were going badly, and someone referred to him as Rasputin almost. This mad, malevolent force that was controlling everyone and everything in Downing Street.

*Another image that uses the same figure of Death in a different pose is the one as he appears in the road before Johnson. (See Image 15.2.) Can you speak about this? Is there any shame in Johnson's face as he catches sight of the ghosts of dead figures (representing all the people who died in care homes) in the rear-view mirror? Or is his expression simply empty – no recognition?*

**Image 15.2** Collage by Christopher Spencer, originally posted 26 May 2021.

Yes, that's it – I mean, he's never going to be remorseful is he! The image refers to something he'd said when Keir Starmer opened Prime Minister's Questions asking him if he agreed with what his 'former closest adviser' said: 'When the public needed us most, the Government failed.' Johnson had replied that everything would be reviewed in a public inquiry, stating, 'I notice he is fixated, as ever, on the rear-view mirror.' But the point being made here to Johnson is that if you do look in the mirror, you'll see you're responsible for thousands of miserable deaths. And so, Cummings actually *is* Death in this one!

*Yes, it can take a little while to notice that's Cummings as Death. How are you seeing this figure of Death here – as killer, as warning, as barrier, for example?*

There is Death Cummings ahead in the road – predominantly as an ominous being approaching. I don't know whether it is as killer, warning or barrier – all of those, I think. A lot of the images I do, I leave open for interpretation. That's why I never put any title or my own commentary on. I just put the image out. I let people find their own meanings. Their comments are great because people pick up different elements ... and that's a perfect example. The mirror, the ghosts, the figure of Death. There's debate about what they signify.

*As you have spoken about before, this is a difficult, sensitive subject area for humour. Are you careful not to show death in real terms? You would not show people on ventilators, for example, or suffering. How death is presented is so important.*

Yes, I didn't use hospital patients or people who have actually died. There are lots of images of elderly people walking, depicted from behind, the majority from the 1970s or 1980s. So, they are not recognisable.

*The diverse representations of death across your collages are striking, each with their own emotional punch. The ghostly figures return quite frequently. Could you say a few words on their use in the image with Cummings sat at the desk in the bluebell wood?* (See Image 15.3.)

Yes, they feature quite a lot. That was the first time they featured, the Bluebell Wood one. It was just after Cummings' press conference in Downing Street rose garden after his long journey from London up to Durham during the lockdown. He broke his own lockdown rules – that was obvious to everyone. All the contempt that he showed for everyone in the country. Saying he'd then gone for a daytrip to test out his eyes, and walking through a bluebell wood, and all the rest. And so, he's depicted in there with these ghosts. And there is the crashed car with Johnson and Hancock, along with renowned serial killer Harold Shipman looking out the passenger window. Again, it raises the issue of sensitivity to subject matter. I mean there are thousands of Shipman's victims, and I was aware of that. And I was worried, thinking whether it is right that I put him in. But he's responsible for killing thousands of elderly patients, he is accountable for multiple deaths, and so are these people that are in the picture with him. And it's that juxtaposition really: He's 'Doctor Death' – so are you – and so are you. That's what I'm trying to say anyway. These people should equally be vilified.

**Image 15.3** Collage by Christopher Spencer, originally posted 25 May 2020.

*Some of the images of death at that time are particularly hard-hitting: the body bags in the rose garden for instance.* (See Image 15.4.)

The wedding one, yes. When Johnson had his 'secret wedding'. Those body bags and the plague cart at the back with the bodies on – I've not really thought about it before but there's a lot of death in my work. It is quite stark. But again, they are clearly props – in this case from an Italian horror film, I think. They're not actually 'real'. Again, the key to it is the contrast. The wedding day … but don't forget about what else you've been responsible for.

**Image 15.4** Collage by Christopher Spencer, originally posted 30 May 2021.

*Would you see some subject matter as beyond satire? The war in Ukraine, for example?*

Yes. Again, I have satirised the reaction. So, I have reminded people about what Nigel Farage has said about Vladimir Putin being the greatest leader in the world.[8] And his cosy relationship with Donald Trump who is now full-on fascist. The war in Ukraine is too tragic – you can't do pictures of that. Because it is just too much. It's more the people like Farage that I'll try and get to.

You draw on a broad range of contemporary cultural references, including those from popular culture (films and TV shows), which help universalise your work. And populating your work with British celebrities, like Steve McFadden or Cilla Black, brings identification from more local audiences. But your work is inspired by a more historical reach as well. With respect to direct influences on your pieces as artworks, particularly in the more complex narrative arrangements you do, you often take inspiration from the expansive and imaginative landscape traditions of painters like Pieter Bruegel and Hieronymus Bosch. And people have likened your satire to eighteenth century satirists like William Hogarth.

8 Nigel Farage was Leader of the UK Independence Party (2006–2009 and 2010–2016) and the Brexit Party (2019–2021).

Bruegel and Bosch have been an influence from the beginning really, even for the composition itself. I love the big grand ones, like *The Triumph of Death* by Bruegel and *The Garden of Earthly Delights* by Bosch. I like to have the different scenarios within the piece. The one corner is saying something, another corner is saying something else. There's a narrative running throughout the piece. It is difficult to release something with such detail that people are going to see on a phone, because in some ways it would be better if it was on a huge billboard or canvas. But at least with the phone you can zoom in to see everything and actively follow different themes around it. Their influence really is in the composition and moral tales that they put in their work. And then obviously with a figure like Hogarth, my aims are similar – with his comment on social issues at the time. But it is a mixture with each piece I do. I want it to be three things really. I want it to stand out, and make people laugh probably. I want it to make people think also, about what it says – the message. But then also to be a work of quality just as a composition in itself – aesthetically, I want it to be a standalone piece. So, a lot of thought goes into the composition. I don't want it to look like it's just a throwaway meme! I want each image to be something that could feature in a book or that someone might want a print of at some point.

*Yes, I noticed this for instance with the most recent image you have posted – the queue of people waiting to see Queen Elizabeth II lying in state (posted 18 September 2022). It is a beautiful composition. Many of the Twitter comments pick up on the humour targeted at celebrities (David Beckham or Philip Schofield, for example), but one follower has commended the use of lighting. The artistic quality here is very much apparent, aesthetically.*

It's always good to receive comments like that (because that's not often said actually). Again, in terms of the meaning here, there is the jarring of the rough sleepers (the homeless people all year round) and the queue of people (given free blankets). So, there are a lot of different things being said.

*Do you think satire/comedy defuses the horror or intensifies it?*

It's a good question. And it's a tightrope walk between trying to communicate a serious message and me being ousted off Twitter forever. Putting a foot wrong. But then to say it with some humour in there. It does defuse it, I think. Especially with Covid. It was such a horrific time, and everyone was being kept apart – it did defuse it. And then for people to be able to comment at a time when they couldn't meet people. But they could talk to each other on social media. They could share the horror and also laugh at it. That really helps to defuse it as well. But it can also – if the target is Boris Johnson, or Dominic Cummings breaking his own Lockdown rules – then the humour can intensify it. I think it can bring it home.

*How have the different ways of exhibiting your work – on Twitter, in public places, exhibitions and books – created different effects? What have been the benefits and limitations of different viewing contexts and interactions?*

I've done a few different exhibitions. I always love the outdoor ones like those for the Sky Arts Film. That was during the pandemic – the first lockdown, I think. To get out and see the pieces, big and as they should be, is always amazing. We visited various places with the film, and everywhere we displayed we had issues with the council. We presume that when the council had agreed to having my work displayed, they had no idea who I was. Because when they discovered who I was, they all tried to stop me doing it. In Bournemouth, we had to cover half of it in black plastic. Everywhere we went we were having that problem. But then the public by and large were totally supportive. And even if they didn't necessarily agree with some of the political stance, they still agreed there should be no issue in expressing ideas. You shouldn't censor art. It's not a healthy democracy if you start censoring art and artists. So, I think they did like them. And *Benny's Babbies* (in Birmingham Museum) is one of the rare ones I've done that isn't negative! It's a celebration of Birmingham and its people. It's popular and that's amazing because it's a piece that's done with love and fondness. Rather than most of the pieces that I've done through kind of gritted teeth! To do one like that was brilliant – such a nice relief. To be able to come home. It was just before Covid. That between Brexit and Covid period of calm, tranquillity and positivity. And then it kind of started again. So, it's not all death and misery! But yes, my bread-and-butter work will remain that way.

*Over time, I imagine, images you have posted on Twitter in the past begin to adopt new meanings, as hypocrisies, such as 'partygate', come to light.*

There's the one that I did when Queen Elizabeth was mourning, sitting on her own at (her husband) Philip's funeral. And later we found out that the night before that there were parties in Downing Street. And I did the picture of them all at the back there partying. Any time after this, when Johnson shared a tweet about Her Majesty (this was before she died) like on the Jubilee, I would retweet it, as if to say, 'What do you mean in sending that? This is what you actually thought. You've got no respect or honour for her.' I keep reminding them of that. But that is one where you either laugh or cry. You laugh at the absurdity of it. But there is a deep sadness. I'm a republican (I don't like what the monarchy stands for at all), but you can't help but feel sadness – when all that was going on. It's wrong on every level.

*Thinking about how your satire relates to time: there are the live, fresh interactions that come with Twitter, but then there's a different relationship with the more recently collated online archive on the website www.coldwarsteve.com. I imagine the archive helps keep the satire viewable in the longer term. Would you say it offers a different way of providing context – a timeline of your work?*

Yes, the archive is brilliant. And I use it quite a lot. If I'm looking for an appropriate image to retweet, I can't scroll through my own stuff. I think about when I did it. Then, I go and look at the archive – it saves a lot of time!

*It is interesting to reflect on the different spaces for exhibiting your satire. Your book,* Journal of the Plague Year, *offers a space for humour shared at home with friends and family, perhaps, and for re-viewing the artwork as a collection – for processing events of that difficult year. But Twitter is the space where the creative energy is born and rejuvenated – where new ideas can be shared. That must be invaluable for you as an artist?*

I try and make a point of reading and responding to each comment, which is impossible now because there are so many, but I do try to go through them all, because if people have taken the time to comment on it then I think the least I can do is acknowledge that. A lot of the comments and thoughts are brilliant – I think they're better than anything I could write! That's why I don't write anything myself underneath it because the discussions that people have are fundamental.[9] The piece is always taken better as a whole – with the comments there as well. I think they bring a lot more to it.

---

9  The archive has direct links through to Twitter next to each image.

## AFTERWORD: CONCLUDING THOUGHTS

Death and grief are treated with a sustained sensitivity and compassion in Cold War Steve's collages; fundamental to the artwork's satirical humour is bringing to account poor governmental handling of the pandemic, at a time when societal fears of death, alongside paradoxical fears of spreading the virus and separation from loved ones, was becoming a daily concern. Moreover, the process of disseminating the artwork actively encourages audience engagement, which forms a crucial part of the communication process, reconceptualising orthodox relationships between art, artists and audiences and bridging gaps between traditional concepts of 'high' and 'popular' culture. The artworks are often displayed with dizzying speed seconds after (and sometimes prophetically before) actions take place in parliament, and meanings continue to be deciphered and reformulated as soon as and long after the artwork has been posted. In these ways, Cold War Steve's artwork allows for a satirical comedy that inspires trust and a means of communication whereby the collective expression of fears acts as a healing or empowering process – by negotiating or critiquing ethical quandaries, governmental decisions and actions, for example, or by confronting fears of death.

## BIBLIOGRAPHY

Bergman, Ingmar (dir.). 1957. *The Seventh Seal*.

*Cold War Steve Presents ... A Prat's Progress*. London: Thames & Hudson, 2019.

*EastEnders*. British television series, BBC One, February 1985–.

Evans, Kieran (dir.). 2020. *Cold War Steve Meets the Outside World*.

Jonze, Tim. 2018. 'In the Bleak Mid-Brexit: A Christmas Gift from Coldwar Steve', *The Guardian* 23 December 2018. https://www.theguardian.com/politics/2018/dec/23/bleak-mid-brexit-christmas-gift-coldwar-steve-twitter-boris-johnson

Kerwin, William. 2010. 'Writing the Plague in English Prose Satire'. In Rebecca Totaro and Ernest B. Gilman (eds.), *Representing the Plague in Early Modern England*, pp. 37–54. New York: Routledge.

Montel, Lisa, Kapilashrami, Anuj, Coleman, Michel P. and Allemani, Claudia. 2020. 'The Right to Health in Times of Pandemic', Special Section: Big Data, Technology, Artificial Intelligence and the Right to Health, *Health and Human Rights* 22(2) December: 227–242. https://www.hhrjournal.org/2020/11/the-right-to-health-in-times-of-pandemic-what-can-we-learn-from-the-uks-response-to-the-covid-19-outbreak/

Spencer, Christopher. 2021. *Cold War Steve: Journal of the Plague Year*. London: Thames and Hudson Ltd.

Sherwood, Harriet. 2019. 'Cold War Steve: Satire is my Antidote to a Scary World', *The Guardian* 15 June 2019. https://www.theguardian.com/artanddesign/2019/jun/15/cold-war-steve-satire-is-my-antidote-to-a-scary-world-interview

**Laura Hubner** is Professor of Film and Media at the University of Winchester, UK. She is author of *Fairytale and Gothic Horror: Uncanny Transformations in Film* (Palgrave Macmillan, 2018) and *The Films of Ingmar Bergman: Illusions of Light and Darkness* (Palgrave Macmillan, 2007), co-editor of *The Zombie Renaissance in Popular Culture* (Palgrave Macmillan, 2014) and *Framing Film: Cinema and the Visual Arts* (Intellect, 2012), and editor of *Valuing Films: Shifting Perceptions of Worth* (Palgrave Macmillan, 2011). Her next monograph launches the book series she is editing, *Iconic Movie Images* (Winchester University Press).

# Chapter 16

# 'It's Not Funny Is It?': Humour as a Coping Strategy against Death by Funeral Workers in the UK

## ANGIE MCLACHLAN

Over the past thirty plus years that I have spent working in the funeral business and with funeral professionals, it has been apparent that self-care and coping strategies are some of the most important skills for all funeral staff to learn; alongside, of course, the many practical techniques of death care, communication skills and event management. Daily, we may use a combination of compassionate listening, understanding, logistical acumen, plus specialisms of art and science while preparing a funeral for a person and serving the needs of their loved ones (some of this is noted in the chapter by Jacklin and Welch). Self-care for funeral workers is vital, especially necessary when working with people following a sudden death, or perhaps one that has occurred through medical complexities or accidental circumstances. Humour can be the difference between coping and not coping with one's work.

With over three decades of involvement and working with death within UK funeral teams of many kinds, this chapter has been written generally, but also from an insider's perspective. I have been hands-on in 'worst-case scenarios', and been privileged to facilitate the best outcome possible for the deceased, funeral director and family. Therefore, my knowledge of what funeral workers in the UK have to deal with daily, is first-hand, embedded and deeply embodied; in saying this I mean that I too have personally experienced most aspects of UK funeral work, not just as an academic or casual observer but from an informed position. I am able to interpret and look at funeral workers' coping strategies through experiential knowledge alongside a variety of academic texts, particularly Berger (1997), Freud (1928), Clack (2002) and Davies (2002), scholars who informed my 2010 Death, Religion and Culture MA dissertation on *Coping Strategies of Cemetery and Crematorium Workers.*

This chapter includes aspects about insider funeral humour gleaned from years of professional experience and personal observation, plus incidences of funeral humour that colleagues have gifted me, to use anonymously. These examples will effectively illustrate the different types of humour being used by funeral workers who find themselves in unusual and sometimes unlikely situations, many of which would be spoken about only within their immediate team, or with other 'funeral insiders'.

*Note: this chapter may contain some information that readers may find upsetting.

## WHY FUNERAL WORKERS MIGHT NEED TO 'COPE WITH DEATH'

Our daily work can be an assault on all our senses as well as a drain on our emotions. Yet funeral workers are expected to, and do, 'just get on with it', usually without recourse to support or professional/psychological work-related after-care. For the most part, the difficult, distressing and unpleasant aspects that funeral workers may have to cope with during working hours remain invisible, and often unspoken outside work. Our days may be filled with situations not fully understood or imagined by those outside the funeral business. The media, especially in the genre of film or soap-opera drama, may only convey certain recognisable features of death and funerals, often sanitised and foreshortened for public consumption, or to fit in with the plotline. In reality, funeral workers need to deal with whatever their work demands, coping with experiences that may sometimes be shared along with other frontline emergency services, coroner's officers, pathology technicians and medics. We usually try to keep these extreme experiences 'in-house', knowing they are considered as 'too sensitive' or 'too much information' for people who don't experience what we do day after day. The particularly gruesome aspects of our work are often hard to discuss, even with other 'funeral insiders'; impossible with the recently bereaved or the general public. Shouldering and managing the difficulties that surround working with death and multiple deaths on a daily basis, therefore, needs careful processing.

Further, the compounded effect of witnessing multiple cases of second-hand grief (seeing and even feeling the grief of other people), from multiple funerals, has an impact on funeral workers. Each worker tries to serve their clients as if each one, each circumstance, each family's funeral, is the only one on their mind at the time of the family's need, when in fact the worker might be supporting numerous families in that period. Significantly, through working with death(s) daily, funeral workers may be perceived as having to embrace feelings and emotions more profound, weightier, than could merely be expressed in words. According to Hertz, 'we all believe we know what death is because it is a familiar event and one that arouses intense emotion. It seems both ridiculous and sacrilegious to question the value of that intimate knowledge and to wish to apply reason to a subject where only the heart is competent' (1960 [1907]: 27).

Funeral work is complex, nuanced and highly situational. How it is perceived and coped with by the funeral workforce may also be influenced by the individual's personal situation; home-life, gender identity, sexuality, age, culture or religion, and professional experience may all come into play and potentially trigger the need to 'cope' in a variety of ways. Funeral staff usually work within a diverse environment. They may oversee, observe or be practically involved in different, even singular, pieces of the funeral jigsaw. This jigsaw could include witnessing intense grief of the bereaved and/or the ravages of illness or bodily trauma of the deceased. Collecting people who have died from mortuaries, nursing-homes, private homes and hospices is commonplace. If on 'Coroners Call' (being part of a team charged with collecting a deceased person on behalf of His Majesty's Coroner), a funeral worker may also be required to recover a body from an unforeseen, unusual or unexpected circumstance, often stepping into 'frontline response', working at the location of death, alongside police and other appropriate emergency services. These workers witness deaths by suicide, accident and/or drug overdose, as well as dealing with decomposed bodies or bodies that are in parts rather than whole. These permutations of the intense aspects of death commonly make up the worker's day-to-day experience. Research has found that when all the stages or processes in the jigsaw are added up from the collective team effort, a single funeral may take 72 hours of work to arrange and accomplish (NAFD 2019: 16). Consequently, amongst the grimness and visceral nature of death, funerals and death surely aren't funny, are they?

## DARK HUMOUR IN THE FUNERAL SERVICE

It must be emphasised at this point, that this is a discussion about how funeral workers cope through using humour, which in my experience was never done detrimentally against the deceased or their mourners. In fact, this chapter explores how humour is used as a method of fending off the worst scenarios of death; the peculiar, strange, uncomfortable, traumatic and, sometimes, the embarrassing – when things 'go wrong' at a funeral (and of course on rare occasions they do go wrong!). How else might one cope with the cumulative effect of hours of combing through undergrowth on a railway track for human remains, or the hours spent transporting a large person for hundreds of miles, who having died several weeks ago has turned blue and has the penetrating aroma of a large stilton cheese even through three layers of body bag? We cope in various ways, by offloading with fellow team-mates, crying privately later, by drinking a stiff shot of our chosen spirit, going for a run or walk in nature or by hugging our own loved ones mindfully on our return home. We may take recourse to religious faith or spirituality. Alternatively, more often than not, we might just 'laugh off' the situation, because anything else might still let the horror and sadness of the situation permeate – much like the persistent smells of death; to affect us and infiltrate our memory, our mood or our dreams.

Coping is not a singular process. Workers combine a variety of strategies; the power of humour is that it allows funeral workers an outlet through which to process or transcend the seriousness of being immersed in death. In the face of trauma, humour powerfully transforms the situation into a useful immanent experience. Whatever the specifics within the event experienced, coping needs to be both effective and powerful to avoid the chance of residual trauma now widely recognised as Post Traumatic Stress Disorder (PTSD). This technique of using coping strategies to handle the experience of death and second-hand grief helps workers to rise above death and achieve 'experiential transcendence' (Chidester 1990: 40). This may be done by working through the event to the best of one's ability, and afterwards finding ways to manage the stress of what one has experienced or witnessed.

Clack also speaks of the usefulness of engaging completely with being human and reaching a non-religious immanence, through experiencing a 'this-world spirituality' (2002: 8–9). Thus, in the context of this chapter, funeral workers can be seen to achieve immanence as described in the writings of Chidester (1990) and Clack (2002). It may then be argued that if it is possible to rise above death, to transcend it, humour could be a valuable tool that's used as part of achieving the experiential and embodied immanence. Having a sense of humour at work enables funeral staff to engage with their death-work safely, in all its aspects, and within the breadth of their personal human emotion, situation and experience.

Funeral workers use two distinct types of humour – situational or situated humour, and gallows humour.

### Situational or Situated Humour

Situational humour is mirth created as a result of an incident that happens, or has happened, during working hours. Situational humour is considered to be a moderate humour, enjoyed during a re-telling of an unforeseen or accidental event. It may also be situated, shared at the time, directly as the scenario unfolds. This 'on the spot humour' is usually conveyed as an insider-coded response between co-workers. A slightly raised eyebrow, or quiet expletive delivered imperceptibly *sotto voce* is ample to share a joke within a tightly disciplined team, a well-timed action against death. Douglas Davies coined the phrase 'words against death' (2002: 1), as a description of how human beings use a wide range of ritual and rhetoric in the face of death, to lessen the impact of its reality and therefore to triumph over the effect or event of death. In labelling this as a defensive activity against something shared and significant, Davies cautions that whilst the term is a generalisation, he hopes it can be seen as 'beyond the superficial' (2002: 3). Thus, when funeral workers react with humour as a team, the context is anything but superficial. In these circumstances, their behaviour could well be described as 'working against death' in the way in which Davies purports 'words against death'.

Being an 'insider' is crucial to the way in which funeral workers locate, use and share humour in order to deal with their work. They can find themselves in many physically restrained or emotionally restricted environments, such as church or crematorium funerals, visits to client's homes, care homes, hospital/hospice/public mortuaries, or even on shift for His Majesty's Coroner, and the workplace then becomes an unknown destination where a sudden or unexpected death has occurred. In these circumstances, work may be disorientating as well as unsettling. It is here that humour allows death-workers to gain perspective, reinforce team relationships and, above all, remain grounded and situated. It grounds workers to their familiar internal landscape where they can calm the emotional agitation of the unexpected or unknown experience. Critchley states that 'humour puts us back in place, whether the latter is our neighbourhood, region or nation' (2002: 73–74). Thus, when in the context of 'working against death' in a distinctive (and often sacred) location, death-workers may be 'placed', relieved and united by the humour that they experience and share as 'words against death' (Davies 2002: 1).

Situational humour is therefore perfect as a strategy, for example when the vicar falls into the grave, or a group of mourners start a fist fight at the cemetery gates (yes, these have happened). It may also come into play unexpectedly if the tension gets a little too much to bear, or if the situation seems beyond ridiculous. Situational humour gets workers through difficult or unusual circumstances. For example, humour worked when once the vehicle we used to pick up the deceased, a large black estate car, lost its silencer in the middle of the night on New Year's Eve; it sounded like a rocket – hardly subtle. Humour eased the nerves of the three live occupants as a police car followed along behind us for several miles before 'pulling the vehicle and team over for a chat'. The police knew that we had probably been out to collect a deceased person, the private registration plates and style of vehicle gave us away. The driver of our car, himself a retired policeman, got out to talk to the officers who had been following us; one worker stayed seated in the front passenger seat. However, those police in pursuit were never aware that behind the tinted back windows of our vehicle, the whole back bench-type seat was laid completely flat, without provision for a seated passenger. There was, unbeknown to the police, another worker, lying down (hiding to avoid the fine for riding without a seat belt) in the back of the car, alongside the deceased person who was strapped securely onto a stretcher; those were the days before most estate cars were fitted with split rear seats. Who was the quieter of the two passengers in the back? On that occasion I was the live one lying next to the stretcher trying very hard to supress gales of laughter until we were waved on our way by the police. Despite being in the midst of the gravity of death, it made for a memorable night being out at midnight and working on that New Year's Eve. That evening, we served the needs of a family and had an unexpected adventure. We would hope that had the person on the stretcher been able to speak, they too would have had a laugh about their penultimate journey.

Clearly, this type of situational humour can be (and was), relayed, amplified, enjoyed and, importantly, processed in full voice, when the team returned to base. It is these stories that form the argot (an insider language or vocabulary used by close-knit teams or groups) of the funeral world. For the team involved, the relief of enjoying this type of humour is palpable, whether in pulling the vicar out of the mud, or in the case of the previous story, fending off the teasing from the midnight police escort who, as it happened, didn't know the other half of the story.

Situational humour can also be both poignant and subversive. One crematorium authority put forward a ruling that banned people from being dressed in their own clothes in their coffin – only 'gowns' or very light cotton clothes were deemed acceptable (from a smoke emission point of view). After one cremation service, the funeral director was standing in the 'Flower Court' watching the mourners chat and admire the tributes. The cremator attendant sidled up to the funeral director and discreetly opened his hand to reveal several distinctive rivets and metal buttons from a pair of jeans. Clearly the youngster's 'own clothes' had been used for their funeral the day before. They had not been dressed in the 'crematorium friendly', but horribly unfashionable, gown. 'Yesterday!' the attendant said tersely. Without a moment's hesitation the pinstriped professional replied, 'They should never have eaten those ... no wonder they died, poor thing.' Both then turned on their polished heels and busied themselves with 'their family of the day'.

### Gallows Humour

The second kind of humour funeral workers use is gallows or dark humour; often instantaneous, reactive and explosive. Gallows humour is potentially more precarious and if witnessed outside the close-knit argot of the team or work-based unit, can be misconstrued. This type of 'fending off' humour tends to be in response to a particularly difficult situation, event or emotion. For example:

> I had just spent hours embalming and re-building a youngster who died from suicide just prior to their graduation. It had been difficult and exacting work, a backbreaking session that included hours of micro-suturing and facial reconstruction. I had to use a lot of wax and makeup in order to camouflage the worst of what had been considerable damage. It was a physically and emotionally shattering day at work, shattering for me and also for the funeral director who had spent many hours supporting the grieving family. God knows what they must have been going through ....
>
> After I finished, the funeral director and I carefully dressed the youngster in their graduation outfit prior to putting them safely in their coffin ready for their family to visit. As the funeral director walked out of the embalming

theatre, they stooped down to retrieve a small makeup stick that had fallen out of my kit. They held it up and squinted at the label, reading it aloud: 'Hide-a-Blemish ... Oh my God, that's a bit of a steep understatement!' We looked at each other and instantly burst out laughing – because it really was the most ridiculous understatement in the circumstances. Then we cried, both of us. The intensity and overwhelming nature of our day at work was enormous; but that joke just helped. Somehow, after laughing and crying, we felt better – it was all such an impossible situation. (Embalmer 'M', 20+ years' experience)

As seen above, humour helps to 'moderate the intensity of negative life events' (DeSpelder and Strickland 2002: 16). Not only is humour effectively 'words against death' (Davies 2002: 1), but it works to redeem a situation. Berger (1997) posits a theory on the transcendent effect of 'Redeeming Laughter'; and it was Freud (1928) who developed the concept of 'gallows humour', in which he discussed the phenomenon of dark humour found to be a coping mechanism for people in difficult situations where they have little or no control. The recourse to humour and having a sense of humour can also be understood as having a transcendent aspect (Berger 1997: 205).

It is recognised, therefore, that humour allows funeral workers to engage with the realities and difficulties within a restrained work environment and, at the same time, safely feel the benefit of their emotional release. Humour offers funeral workers a transcendent, curative technique through which they are able to distance themselves from the trauma and rise above the situation. Additionally, shared humour acts to re-bond a work team during an unsettling incident, or afterwards, in its re-telling. In addition to it being shared humour, gallows humour may also be internalised and deeply embodied; a more personal way of responding to aspects of work through the way we look at life. As two members of the funeral workforce informed me:

My life changed during a training session at a mortuary when I witnessed my first full post mortem examination. I was standing next to the pathologist, watching; without warning, they just handed me the person's brain seconds after removing it. I was standing there, holding a person's whole brain in my cupped hands – it felt like an incredible honour, however, the inner me thought 'oh my god! – what if I dropped it ... what do I do with it now? I still laugh when I recall my feelings of honour but how shocking it all was. (Funeral worker 'A', 15 years' experience)

I don't know about you, but I walk down a street, or look at a crowd of people out and about and I can't help just knowing what size coffin they would fit

> into ... and when a motorbike roars past, overtaking when I'm driving, my instant thought is 6'2" × 22" – I don't say anything, but I just can't help think it! (Funeral director 'S', 10 years' experience)

While in theory, it may be understood that both modes of humour (situational and dark) could be satisfactory and transformative as coping methods for funeral workers, in practice, using humour safely necessitates a personal awareness and disciplined self-management as to its 'appropriate' (discreet, veiled or undetectable) use. Furthermore, the funeral workforce requires a competent manager who can perceive when there is need to assist staff who may be struggling to cope, and to detect and deflect the over-use of ribaldry.

Experiences at work may be confronting and it is difficult to be emotionally prepared all the time. One can be caught off-guard. On one visit to a hospital mortuary under very difficult and tragic circumstances, a funeral worker was told that it would not be possible to get a coffin size for the deceased who had died in an accident. The worker asked why and was told wryly that 'the size could be anything they chose, from 4 feet to half a mile as the body was in tiny bits'. This situation was clearly shocking, heartrending, appalling and beyond the usual acceptable source of humour; however, confronted by the horrible facts, both people concerned understood each other and shared a 'laugh' of intense discomfort as they imagined a half mile long coffin. In conjunction with this episode, there were privately shed tears in the 'removal vehicle' on the way back to the funeral premises, shared 'off-loading', conversations within the team when back at work and a few stiff drinks on return home in the evening. In using these strategies, staff were able to release emotions whilst a semblance of 'normality' was maintained. The coffin chosen was of a normal size and only the professional teams involved, and the closest relative, actually knew the real extent of the injuries to the person whose funeral was being arranged.

Furthermore, when funeral workers use humour, it temporarily suspends the rules of ordinary life. In the face of death, humour can make the situation seem better, by creating a 'transcendence in a lower key', a 'redeeming laughter' (Berger 1997: 205). Through humour, death is not embodied, but rather transcended away from the ritual performance of work. It's effectively bypassed in the re-telling of a mishap, or a joke about the seemingly inappropriate choice of music such as 'Burn Baby Burn' (1976, by The Trammps) at the crematorium, or the floral tribute teddy-bear left propped up in church that leaves a puddle (akin to it having had a wee) under the coffin. These gentle jokes as described by Berger are seen as the kind that have the effect of suspending the rules of ordinary life. They temporarily make the situation seem better. However, although the humour is situated in the world of experience, Berger also suggests that there are parallels between the power of the joke and religious experience; the power of humour creates a reality that 'has redeeming qualities that are not temporary at all, but rather that point to that other world that has always been the object of religious attitude' (Berger 1997: 206). Hence, humour is a long-lasting coping mechanism. Additionally, Berger discusses how the characteristics of humour enable those who share a joke to be transported to other times outside reality (as experienced in an intense religious transcendence), as though they are experiencing a threshold that can be passed over and then be crossed back again; revisited to soothe as necessary (1997: 206).

Furthermore, Berger also suggests that 'this transcendence need not only be understood in religious terms', that the level of transcendence may 'pass from lower to higher key', in which the comedy 'presents a world without pain' (1997: 210). Through this form of transcendence, even the most painful realities dealt with in black humour are neutralised when translated into terms of comedy. There is a period of suspension, an escape from reality provided by humour (Berger 1997: 210). As such, gallows humour in particular fits in with both transcendent and immanent aspects of coping. While not being religious in its transcendent effect, gallows humour can fulfil potentially the criteria of Chidester's 'experiential transcendence' (1990: 40). Funeral workers incorporate death into their lives, by thinking about it and by experiencing it while working daily. Essentially by fully immersing in death (through engaging in the concentrated act of funeral work), they engage with immanence and move through it, and experience an uplifting transcendence of death. Immersion in death in this instance is an action which, Chidester asserts, helps the person to rise above death, or go beyond 'painful realities' (1990: 40) and, as Berger states, to 'neutralize' them (1997: 210). Importantly, Berger further affirms that this transcending aspect of humour has redeeming qualities that are not temporary; these give the performer or recipient of the humour a lasting transformative experience, a feature parallel to that of religious transcendence (1997: 205). It is evident therefore that the suspension of reality through humour works. Rather than just a reactive momentary or fleeting event, it is undoubtedly a useful, curative and long-lasting coping strategy for funeral workers.

Nevertheless, it is important to note that in the twenty-first century, we in the UK, live in a society with increasingly strong notions of what is deemed suitable or unsuitable to share or speak about openly. Further, when coupled with the public expectation of the highest ethical standards in all funeral businesses, this means that the general attitude to anyone using humour within such a complex workplace as a funeral home may be particularly challenging. It must be noted, however, that a focus on ethics and respect has always had a considerable place in the approach and behaviour of professional funeral providers, and rightly so. With current culture in mind, it might be advantageous to hypothesise that the general public may not consider funeral humour as a totally acceptable workplace coping strategy. Nonetheless, and especially in the throes of a global Coronavirus pandemic where funeral workers have often been pushed beyond their physical and emotional limits, dealing with (in some cases) a hugely increased number of deaths and funerals, covert, transformative humour as argot within their work teams might be more important than ever. Although potentially wearing thin now, being confronted by offers of a 'Corona Beer' after work may go into the annals of funeral history for the years 2020–2022, the name of the beer being close enough to the pandemic of Covid-19, a strain of pathogen within the large family of Coronavirus.

## CONCLUDING WORDS

This chapter has shown that in the context of daily death-work, humour as a coping strategy firmly sits within Davies' concept of 'words against death' (2002: 1). This is especially pertinent in the context of formalised ritual, precise rhetoric, associated grief and the need for staff to maintain an aura of professional excellence. It is evident that humour within the funeral workplace and workforce is a powerful and lasting strategy for 'working against death'. I have contended that humour, as a coping strategy, may have enduring spiritual and redemptive benefits for funeral workers, supported by Clack's 'this-world spirituality' (2002: 8–9) and the work on humour by Berger (1997), and most specifically Freud's 'Dark Humour' (1928), which this chapter suggests is a key form of humour used by funeral workers to ward off the effect of death.

This chapter has also suggested that for funeral workers, humour is being used as a flexible and important coping mechanism. More than this, while literally staring into the face of death daily at work, humour is a coping strategy that acts to transcend that presence of death, both of ourselves and others, along with the ritual and rhetoric of multiple funerals. Humour allows us to cope, by literally blowing death away with the power of the joke, acting to raise spirits, change the atmosphere and soften it so that employees do not carry the emotional rigour of their work outside their allotted shifts. Further to this, humour also acts to help funeral workers rise above the cumulative effect of being in the presence of second-hand grief, or for long hours in constrained or extreme environs where it is vital to act and appear calm and professional at all times.

The curative powers of laughter against death and the wide use of gallows humour as a coping mechanism allow a deep contrast between the usually sombre performative ritual at the public funeral, or at 'removal' (collection of the deceased from the place of death, home or hospital – using a removal vehicle or private ambulance), where participants have to 'restrain' or 'inhibit' personal inclinations and tendencies (Blumer 1969: 11). These coping mechanisms are not aired in public; they are resorted to in private areas 'back-stage', within a tightly-knit working team, as argot (language or slang particular to work-team); or through personal processing at home.

Through the understanding of carefully used humour and the benefits of restorative immanence gained through sharing a laugh with fellow insider funeral staff, it is possible to realise that humour, even of the darkest nature, can be an effective and positive coping tool. Humour may be used while remaining professional and immersed in all the realities and variables of funeral work. Death may be transformed and even transcended by shared humour or when privately used by workers. With respect to the scholars cited and through actual examples of the use of humour from funeral insiders, this chapter demonstrates that it is also possible to enjoy death-work within the breadth of human emotion and experience.

Appropriate use of humour is a powerful rebuttal of the difficulties and stress of 'working against death' especially in extreme circumstances. Personal death and grief are not funny in themselves. However, the logistics of funeral work can easily catch funeral workers unaware, and laughter is often the immediate and natural result. As a final reiteration, managing the use of humour by funeral workers is the key to its effectiveness. Building, maintaining and managing close-knit working teams with emotional intelligence as well as competence of hands and hearts could make even the most subversive or dark humour a useful way of 'Working against Death'.

# BIBLIOGRAPHY

Berger, Peter L. 1997. *Redeeming Laughter: The Comic Dimension of Human Experience*. Berlin and New York: Walter De Gruyter.

Blumer, Herbert. 1969. *Symbolic Interactionism: Perspective and Method*. Los Angeles: University of California Press.

Breton, André. 1997, *Anthology of Black Humor*. Trans. Mark Polizzotti. San Francisco: City Light Books.

Chidester, David. 1990. *Patterns of Transcendence: Religion, Death, and Dying*. Belmont: Wadsworth Publishing Company.

Clack, Beverley. 2002. *Sex and Death: A Reappraisal of Human Mortality*. Cambridge: Polity Press.

Critchley, Simon. 2002. *On Humour*. London and New York: Routledge.

Davies, Douglas J. 2002. *Death, Ritual and Belief*, 2nd edition. London and New York: Continuum.

DeSpelder, Lynne Ann and Strickland, Albert Lee. 2002. *The Last Dance: Encountering Death and Dying*, 6th edition. Boston: McGraw-Hill Higher Education.

Freud, Sigmund. 1928. 'Humour', *The International Journal of Psychoanalysis* 9(1): 1–6.

Hertz, Robert. 1960 [1907]. *Death and the Right Hand*. Trans. R. Needham and C. Needham. London: Cohen West.

NAFD. 2019. 'How Many Hours Does It Take to Arrange a Funeral in 2019', *Funeral Director Monthly* (November): 16–20. https://www.nafd.org.uk/wp-content/uploads/2021/06/How-many-hours-does-it-take-to-arrange-a-funeral-in-2019-November-2019.pdf

**Angie McLachlan** has over 30 years of experience on death care and provides resources guidance and care of the body training to specialist organisations, and to individuals. She is a member of the British Institute of Embalmers and was recognised in 2015 for her funeral work as one of five finalists in the 'Major Contribution to the Understanding of Death' by the Good Funeral Awards. She holds a BA (Hons) in Death Loss and Palliative Care, and an MA (with Distinction) in Religion: The Rhetoric and Rituals of Death from the University of Winchester.

Chapter 17

# When Glaciers Die: Mourning and Memorialisation in Ecological Devastation

## JONATAN SPEJLBORG JUELSBO

On 18 August 2019, around a hundred people gathered by the foot of a mountain in the western part of Iceland. The crowd was a mix of 'scientists, activists, dignitaries, farmers, politicians, journalists, and children' (Johnson 2019) and the occasion for this gathering was the mounting of a memorial plaque on top of the mountain commemorating the death of the glacier called Ok (short for Okjökull) – a glacier that had diminished so much in recent years that it had now been declared dead.

The memorial event was initiated by researchers Cymene Howe and Dominic Boyer from Rice University, Texas, USA, after a period of researching how Icelanders perceived and related to the consequences of climate change such as glaciers melting, and after having produced a movie about Ok's passing called *Not Ok* (Howe and Boyer 2018). In a press release Boyer says, 'In the same spirit as the film, we wanted to create a lasting memorial to Ok, a small glacier that has a big story to tell' (in McCaig 2019) and Howe continued, 'with this memorial, we want to underscore that it is up to us, the living, to collectively respond to the rapid loss of glaciers and the ongoing impacts of climate change' (in McCaig 2019).

When the planned event was shared on social media it gathered significant attention from both local and international media and thus, on the day of the event, around a hundred people showed up to walk to the top of the mountain together, and mounted the plaque with the text stating:

A letter to the future
Ok is the first Icelandic glacier to lose its status as a glacier. In the next 200
years all our glaciers are expected to follow the same path. This monument
is to acknowledge that we know what is happening and what needs to be
done. Only you will know if we did it.
August 2019
415 ppm CO2

In this chapter, the Okjökull memorial serves as a backdrop to an exploration of what it can mean to experience a sense of loss in relation to
significant changes in the natural environment and the death and disappearance of entities such as glaciers in times of rapid climate change and
mass extinction. While I will not pursue an analysis of this particular event
but merely offer it as an example of memorial practices relating to climate
change, this chapter will focus on the concept of ecological grief, developed as an articulation of the ways in which environmental change affects
mental and emotional well-being, and I will argue that emerging, contemporary practices of memorialisation can be seen as ways of 'remembering
for the future' (Campbell 2014: 135) – ways of remembering that aspire
to be faithful to the past in order to create liveable futures. I will argue
that these practices are complex assemblages of acts of mourning, ontological positioning, political statement and activist practice while also
being ambiguous practices that expose the quality and history of relations
between humans and non-human entities.

Many of the theories of grief and mourning that I will be drawing upon
have been developed in the context of mourning other human lives, and in
most cases mourning a loss for which the mourner is not (directly) responsible. But losses associated with climate change differ in that they involve
the loss of other-than-human beings, and we, as humans, are intimately
involved with causing this loss. This can complicate both the affective
response and the process of grieving (Menning 2017: 40). The term 'other-than-human' will be employed throughout this chapter and includes a
wide range of non-discrete entities such as microbes and bacteria, plant
and animal species as well as entire ecosystems. The term functions in this
case both to de-centre the human from ecological and ethical thought and
to highlight the interconnectedness and mutual vulnerability between the
human and other entities.

Furthermore, the significant change to environments and ecosystems
caused by human practices as well as the effects including rising temperatures and ocean acidification are felt more severely (and directly) in
some places and by some people than others. Such differential exposure

and vulnerability is influenced by several factors including race, gender, culture and poverty as well as geographical location – for example, arctic communities (Thomas et al. 2019). To go more into depth about this uneven distribution is outside the scope of this chapter but needs to be taken into consideration when exploring practices of memorialisation emerging in the context of climate change. Thus, the term ecological grief is, in this chapter, intended to embrace a broad range of experiences and affects that might differ significantly both within and between people and cultures.

## ECOLOGICAL GRIEF

In her essay on ecological loss, 'Environmental Mourning and the Religious Imagination', Nancy Menning concludes, 'grieving starts with loss .... Loss points us back to connection. We grieve what we love, those entities with which we have relationships that are partly constitutive of our identities' (2017: 58). Grieving is a response to a loss of something that matters, something with which we are deeply related and connected.

Under the umbrella of ecological grief, this loss can relate to the diminishing (bio)diversity of life when plants and animals go extinct, it can relate to the losses of places we care about, it can relate to the loss of certain ways of life that become impossible as they depend on conditions that no longer exist. But ecological grief can also be seen as not just reflecting losses that have occurred, but equally the anticipation of future loss – further decline in biodiversity, more extinctions to come, tipping points being crossed and large-scale alterations to the conditions of living – and thus be understood as a form of anticipatory grief (Cunsolo 2012).

If grieving starts with loss, it also starts with love. Grief is not distributed evenly to all things that are lost but is reserved for the loss of that which we love; that which matters to us. Following Judith Butler, we can take this to mean that things that we do not care about cannot be experienced as being lost in a way that provokes grieving. Such 'hierarchy of grief' (Butler 2004: 32) means that we grieve the loss of some things and beings, while other things and beings merely disappear.

Some lives, Judith Butler notes, are grievable, and others are not; the differential allocation of grievability that decides what kind of subject is and must be grieved, and which kind of subject must not, operates to produce and maintain certain exclusionary conceptions of who is normatively human: what counts as a liveable life and a grievable death? (2014: xiv). Butler's analysis reveals how the discrimination of which lives count as grievable simultaneously creates categories of lives which are not considered lives at all – 'the matter is not a simple one, for, if a life is not grievable, it is not quite a life' (2004: 34). Cunsolo builds on Butler to suggest that also the lives of other-than-human beings are lives that have not been deemed grievable:

> There are, tragically, bodies that do not matter in the public sphere, or bodies that have been disproportionately derealized from ethical and political consideration in global discourse: women, racial minorities, sexual minorities, peoples of different religions, certain ethnic groups, economically and politically marginalized groups, Indigenous peoples, and those living with HIV/AIDs, to name but a few. To this list of derealized bodies, I would also add non-human bodies – animal, vegetal, and mineral. (Consolo 2012: 139)

While Butler and Cunsolo clearly articulate the violence at the heart of practices that deem certain lives and bodies ungrievable, there is another layer of violence at play simultaneously. If certain deaths are not grievable, then experiencing grief in relation to those deaths becomes somewhat unintelligible or marginalised. This can be seen as an additional marginalisation both of the affective response and of those who experience this affect. As Lisa Kretz states, 'People who wish to give voice to the harms to the Earth through mourning are often emotionally oppressed. The systematic denial of this attempt at emotional expression is disempowering' (2017: 263). Through the concept of 'outlaw emotions' (emotions that are 'conventionally unacceptable'), Kretz argues that the marginalisation of certain emotions in relation to climate change is entangled with histories of relegating emotions 'to the domain of the irrational' (2017: 261, 269). She explains how discrimination against certain affects works against both those that experience those affects and the epistemic quality of emotions in general: 'when power differentials work against the emotional uptake of members of certain groups we are faced with systematic epistemic denial' (Kretz 2017: 269). According to Kretz, the denial of emotional uptake, the impossibility of being met and acknowledged with your emotions, is partly constitutive of an environment in which complicated affect such as ecological grief might turn into despair and depression. This also means that nurturing spaces, discourses and practices that allow for emotional uptake is not a solitary endeavour – emotional uptake, the acknowledgment by others of your emotional experience, is a collective, social practice.

In this light we can see the development and usage of a term such as ecological grief as performing several functions. It is a way of reorienting our understanding of the other-than-human as something that both requires and deserves to be mourned. And simultaneously it can be seen as a way of carving out space for emotional uptake and acknowledgement of complex affective responses in relation to climate change while also recognising those people who experience and share these affects.

When Kretz equates the refusal of emotional uptake with epistemic denial she tells us that there is something to be learned from engaging with emotions; that the way we feel about something is a way of knowing something, and that the kind of knowing that an attention to affect offers can help us navigate the situations we find ourselves in. What we can learn and know from recognising grief associated with climate change and ecological devastation is, according to Burton-Christie, that we, as humans, are not separate from the environment around us, that we are indeed part of the natural world and as such are embedded in relationships of care and responsibility: 'grief and mourning can be seen not simply as an expression of private and personal loss, but as part of a restorative spiritual practice that can rekindle an awareness of the bonds that connect all life-forms to one another and to the larger ecological whole' (2011: 30).

Burton-Christie draws on traditions of ecological ethics and Christian monastic practices to argue that grieving for the natural world is both a way to come to recognise an ecological awareness and a critical practice for continuously nurturing this awareness. The epistemic denial of grief as a source of knowing the world is accompanied by a moral deficit as our inability to recognise our responsibility towards the natural world and our role in its current degradation:

> To know must include not only an acknowledgement of the deep and binding claim that the familiar and the dear have upon our moral imaginations .... It must also include a recognition of how pervasive is our habit of *evading knowing*, of refusing to see and take responsibility for our complicity in the destruction of the world. Our inability to mourn, seen from this perspective, is an expression – one of the most telling – of the profound moral emptiness that afflicts us. (Burton-Christie 2011: 43)

For Burton-Christie, there is a 'haunting silence' (2011: 41) when it comes to recognising that the current ecological devastation is a result of our inability to deal with such destruction, and particularly our own involvement in it. We deflect our responsibility and resist the call to grieve. But as long as we resist this call, we will not be able to respond in any meaningful way: 'if we hope to arrive at a deep and authentic response to this crisis, we will have to find a way to speak honestly about all we are losing and what this loss means to us. This is why the work of mourning is so important' (Burton-Christie 2011: 42).

Grieving the natural world matters because in this grief lies the possibility to recognise our entanglement with the other-than-human. The process of grieving exposes our shared vulnerability and calls forth a responsibility to care. Grief transforms us. And so, we must first be open to be transformed by it. Therein lies the work of mourning that Cunsolo, Burton-Christie and Butler all point towards. The ongoing work of allowing ourselves to be transformed by grief and to act from a recognition of a shared vulnerability. Butler articulates the relation between mourning and the openness to be transformed in unpredictable ways in the following passage:

> Perhaps, rather, one mourns when one accepts that by the loss one undergoes one will be changed, possibly for ever. Perhaps mourning has to do with agreeing to undergo a transformation (perhaps one should say *submitting* to a transformation) the full result of which one cannot know in advance. There is losing, as we know, but there is also the transformative effect of loss, and this latter cannot be charted or planned. One can try to choose it, but it may be that this experience of transformation deconstitutes choice at some level. (Butler 2004: 21)

## RESISTANT MOURNING

In their writings on mourning as political, ethical and transformative practice, both Cunsolo and Butler build on a theoretical ground established by Jacques Derrida as part of his life-long engagement, and struggle, with psychoanalysis and his extensive writing on the occasions of the deaths of his friends.

Derrida did not agree with how mourning had been theorised by Freud (see Kirkby 2006). In *Mourning and Melancholia*, Freud (1973 [1917]) presents the process of mourning as a response to the experience of loss in which the mourner goes through a period of intense emotional pain, a loss of interest in the surrounding world and an inability to take part in activities that are not somehow connected to (the memory of) the one who has been lost. This period is one of recognising that the other is ultimately gone, leading to a slow detachment of the libidinal ties and thus regaining the ability to form new relationships, in some sense replacing the one who has been lost. Mourning, in this sense, is the healthy response to loss whereas melancholia is the pathological version in which the loss cannot be overcome, the libidinal ties are never severed, and the other is kept artificially alive as a narcissistic project, incorporated into the self, constituting an 'attempt to keep the dead alive within, sealed up in a kind of psychic crypt' (Kirkby 2006: 466).

Derrida was not satisfied with these options of either abandoning the friend who had died by severing emotional ties and moving on, or incorporating the friend into oneself in a mummified state. For Derrida, the responsibility towards the other meant maintaining their otherness, both in life and in death, and both options were for him ways to deny that exact otherness. To remain faithful to the responsibility one has to the other Derrida instead suggested that mourning involves a partial incorporation of the other into oneself – partial, meaning an incorporation which does not engulf the other, but where the other remains Other in oneself (Derrida 2001). Mourning, in a Derridean sense, is not a process that is ever concluded, but rather an ongoing conversation with the Other as they exist in oneself. Mourning is in some sense a failure to move on, which does not mean a failure to engage with the world after loss. A loss which is both total and impossible of an Other who is both completely gone and never gone at the same time.

The path that Derrida suggests for mourning is strangely close to the descriptions of melancholia offered by Freud. While, for Freud, melancholia was a pathological state in which there was a refusal to let go of the other, for Derrida such a refusal is essential for mourning. For Derrida, mourning has a melancholic dimension in the sense that it is something we carry with us forever, not as pathology but as part of our responsibility to the other, the irreplaceable other who is no longer here, but who lingers on in us, as a ghost in our memories of the future. This mourning is future-oriented in the sense that the new relation to the other after death is ongoing, while for Freud, mourning was the process of foreclosing on the idea of any future relation with the dead (Secret 2015: 144).

If we consider this refusal to let go in relation to ecological grief it becomes clear how an insistence on remembering can, in certain contexts, hold a specifically political and ethical dimension. Building on work by Spargo (2004) and Rae (2007), Barr elaborates on the development of 'resistant mourning' as a response to the enormity of death and destruction in Europe in the first half of the 20th century:

> [A]s the cataclysm of the First World War and then the incomprehensible horrors of the Spanish Civil War and the Second World War unfolded, many writers, activists, and artists began to realize that, when confronted with

the traumatizing, unjust, and uncountable losses of the wars, the idea of resolvable and consolatory mourning was not only impossible, it was also unethical .... The comfort provided by conventional mourning and its artistic representations could lull people into passive forgetfulness, which could result in history repeating itself. Thus an insistence on remembering, on dwelling in the pain of unjust loss, was deemed necessary by politically engaged artists as a sort of ethical insurance that such losses would never be allowed to happen again. (Barr 2017: 192)

To Barr, this means that 'a psychoanalytic model of compensatory, resolvable mourning is 'inadequate for comprehending or commemorating the horrors of the twentieth century's wars, mass deaths, myriad other atrocious injustices, and ecological catastrophes' (2017: 193).

While Derrida offered the perspective that the death of the other is unbearable and thus cannot be resolved, Barr adds that the death of the other is, in some cases, also unjust – which emphasises the unethical nature of forgetting. Resistant mourning offers an alternative model for grief in times of ecological devastation and mass extinctions. It offers a model for mourning which insists that remembering collectively is necessary for preventing future loss, and it insists that questions of responsibility are a part of this remembering. The demand to resist forgetting and resist consolation can be seen as a melancholic necessity, a kind of melancholia much aligned with the unbearable nature of loss proposed by Derrida. For Barr, melancholia offers the necessary recognition of injustice and implies a call to act:

To be clear, this melancholic focus on death is not meant to be morbidly paralyzing – it is meant to energize and galvanize the survivors; in a sense, it is actually hopeful, driven by the vision of a future in which these wrongs have been righted .... This ethical imperative links modernist responses to the horrors of war to contemporary political and aesthetic forms of engagement with social injustice and looming environmental catastrophe. (Barr 2017: 197)

Considering ecological grief through the lens of resistant mourning offers a strategy for noticing the political and activist practice involved in grief responses in relation to climate change. It frames grieving as a future-oriented practice that insists on the need to not forget, the need to not repeat, and the need to engage with questions of responsibility and complicity.

## MEMORY AND MEMORIALISATION

Considering this need articulated above, to not forget, I will turn slightly to the field of memory studies and memorialisation to articulate the role of memory in practices of responsibility and relationality and to explore some threads between memorialisation and ecological grief.

In her book *Our Faithfulness to the Past* (2014) Campbell suggests that it is through sharing memories that we form both identities and relations with others. She states,

> Sharing memory is how we learn to remember, how we come to reconceive our pasts in memory, how we come to form a sense of self, and one of the primary ways in which we come to know others and form relationships with them, reforming our sense of self as we come repeatedly under the influence not only of our own pasts as understood by others but of the pasts of others. (Campbell 2014: 2)

Here Campbell articulates remembering as a performative act that is not primarily understood as implying meaning, and thus interpreted not as a text but instead, she argues, as an enactment of relationships which implies responsibility.

Campbell's work with contexts in which memories and memory practices of certain groups have been oppressed also gives us insight into how the enforcement of certain memories and certain ways of remembering can be an act of violence. In the case of the 'Indian Residential School Truth and Reconciliation Committee' in Canada, Campbell argues for the importance of not just listening to indigenous perspectives on experiences of the Indian Residential Schools, but also being conscious of how such a listening is staged so that the memories can be shared in ways that will not (again) violate how memories were traditionally shared in indigenous communities (2014: 178–203). In this sense, it is not just the memories in themselves that matter, or that they are shared, but also how they are shared. This again, points to the performative aspect of remembering collectively as a situated, embodied practice. Restorative memory work thus involves more than listening to memories of oppression, it involves a collective practice of developing spaces for such memories to even be remembered as such; a practice similar to developing spaces for emotional uptake for certain feelings to be felt and recognised. Memory, understood as collective practice, is not stored in the individual and recalled from this storage but must be understood as existing within a relational fabric.

Another important aspect that Campbell addresses, and which Shotwell has been further articulating, is the importance of identifying with past wrongs, rather than attempting to disidentify from them, when pursuing relations of solidarity (Campbell 2014; Shotwell 2016). For example, while I may wholeheartedly disagree with past and present practices of violence and discrimination, it is only by recognising the ways in which my own position (and life) is shaped by these histories that I can begin to act responsibly. Campbell asserts that:

> if we yearn for solidarity with others, taking responsibility for who we are now requires us to take responsibility for the way that history has shaped our relationships. Making ourselves accountable for this history is to identify with those in it ... through resisting the distinction between answering for oneself and for those others. (2014: 132)

Such identification with people and practices in history which we disagree with is not easy work, but necessary for supporting other kinds of relational patterns, for 'in entering worlds of memory in which we are not at ease, we can nevertheless engage with values, give weight to fragile cultural imaginaries, support identities, and undertake new relationships that I will characterise as relationships of solidarity' (Campbell 2014: 82).

To both Campbell and Shotwell memory is social and relational, it is embodied, situated and performative, and the act of remembering is to be considered through the lens of responsibility; responsibility for the future implies responsible memory practices. Practices that acknowledge the histories that have shaped our relations and practices that nurture relations of solidarity. The theoretical lens offered by Campbell and Shotwell invites a perspective on memorialisation practices that takes into consideration not only the meaning(s) (in a semantic sense) of such practices, but also how the performative aspects are constituting certain relational patterns and engaging with bodily, habitual aspects of how we remember and what that means for potential futures. This seems particularly relevant in the context of climate change in which memorialisation must deal with the complexity of historical complicity in what has disappeared, what is disappearing and what will disappear. Memory practices are not places to search for purity, but places to recognise our own complicity in contemporary harm (Shotwell 2016).

I find much resonance between these theories offered by Campbell. and Shotwell and the theoretical lens offered by Young (1992) in his articulation of the counter-monument. In his study of memorialisation practices in Germany in the generations following World War II, Young argues that

Germany is faced with the question of how to ethically engage with the memories of the Holocaust, memories of themselves as perpetrators: 'How does a state incorporate its crimes against others into its national memorial landscape? How does a state recite, much less commemorate, the litany of its misdeeds, making them part of its reason for being? Under what memorial aegis, whose rules, does a nation remember its own barbarity?' (Young 1992: 270). Young argues that the erection of monuments has traditionally been integral to the affirmation of 'the righteousness of a nation's birth, even its divine election. The matrix of a nation's monuments traditionally employs the story of ennobling events, of triumphs over barbarism, and recalls the martyrdom of those who gave their lives in the struggle for national existence' (1992: 270). Furthermore, Young articulates that traditionally monuments, rather than ensuring that remembrance will be an ongoing practice, can be seen as a way to confine memories to specific places and objects and to offer a kind of forced resolution to complex and ambiguous pasts. Monuments can, in this sense, allow forgetting rather than promote remembering. And they can be seen as a result of wanting to forget under the guise of wanting to remember. As a response to these tendencies in traditional practices of memorialisation, several German artists developed what Young calls counter-monuments: 'brazen, painfully self-conscious memorial spaces conceived to challenge the very premises of their being' (1992: 271). These monuments, rather than resolving the past, emphasise the impossibility of such resolution. Rather than legitimise they problematise. And rather than impose a past, they question it. To Young, these are not just other monuments, but another kind of monument whose:

> aim is not to console but to provoke; not to remain fixed but to change; not to be everlasting but to disappear; not to be ignored by its passersby but to demand interaction; not to remain pristine but to invite its own violation and desecration; not to accept graciously the burden of memory but to throw it back at the town's feet. (1992: 277)

A counter-memorial 'mocks the traditional monument's certainty of history' (Young 1992: 295) and instead offers itself as a mirror that forces viewers to continuously engage with practices of complicated and uncomfortable remembering.

Considered in relation to climate change the counter-monument offers a theoretical frame that is aligned and related to the concept of resistant mourning and to Derrida's call for the necessity to not consider mourning as a process that seeks resolution or conclusion. Counter-memorials can be seen as attempts to engage with Campbell's call for responsibility in practices of remembering and as noticing how remembrance shapes past, present and future relations. Furthermore, counter-memorials offer a problematisation of the past that involves elements of complicity in producing both past and present harms and thus engages us ethically as rememberers.

## RETURNING TO OK

By bringing attention to a felt sense of loss in relation to climate change and by creating frames for meeting around this loss, the Ok memorial manifests a clear intention to work with the extension of grievability to the other-than-human, at the same time creating conditions for securing emotional uptake by inviting people into a social, collective ritual where the expression of certain affects can be understood as meaningful. Later, in O'Dowd (2019 [online]), Howe asserts that:

> by memorializing a fallen glacier, we want to emphasize what is being lost or what is dying ... [a]nd we also want to draw attention to the fact that climate change is also something that humans have accomplished, if you will, although it's not something that we should be particularly proud of.

There is an insistence to remember that this death has been caused by human action and thus a resistance to forgetting either the death itself or its causes. This accomplishment needs to be remembered, yet not as an expression of human exceptionalism but as a call to recognise both historical and present responsibility for this death and the future death of all the world's glaciers – and the consequences thereof.

By seeing the event in relation to the aspects of ecological grief described in this chapter we can begin to notice how some of the affective, activist and political dimensions of grief, mourning and remembering are woven together in memorial practice. The memorialisation of Ok can be seen as being an attempt at what several writers on climate grief have been articulating and calling for, namely at extending grievability, at representing non-human victims of slow violence, at realising some of the transformative potential of grieving and at remembering responsibly.

## CONCLUDING WORDS

This chapter has attempted an articulation of climate change through the lens of grief in relation to current ecological devastation. While 'grief' as a term does not necessarily cover the complexity of affective responses to climate change, this approach has highlighted the way in which theories on grief and mourning offer practices for extending grievability to the other-than-human, for nurturing spaces for emotional uptake, for transforming our relationships to the natural world and for recognising the necessity to resist both emotional resolution and forgetfulness and instead insist on collective remembering and justice. Furthermore, it has explored the significance of memories and practices of remembering for how we form relations and identities. Memorialisation is therefore more than just valuing certain things in the past through recollection. It is a site- and time-specific practice of developing and performing emotional relations, and a practice of responsibility. The memorial event that was carried out on the death of Okjökull is offered as an example of emerging practices of responding to ecological grief, understood here as a sense of loss associated with climate change – a sense of loss that calls for ethical and political responsibility.

## BIBLIOGRAPHY

Barr, Jessica M. 2017. 'Auguries of Elegy: The Arts and Ethics of Ecological Grieving'. In Ashlee Cunsolo and Karen Landman (eds.), *Mourning Nature – Hope at the Heart of Ecological Grief and Loss*, pp. 190–226. Montreal: McGill-Queen's University Press.

Burton-Christie, Douglas. 2011. 'The Gift of Tears – Loss, Mourning and the Work of Ecological Restoration', *Worldviews* 15(1): 29–46.

Butler, Judith. 2004. *Precarious life – The Powers of Mourning and Violence*. London: Verso Books.

Campbell, Sue. 2014. *Our Faithfulness to the Past*. Oxford: Oxford University Press.

Cunsolo, Ashlee. 2012. 'Climate Change as the Work of Mourning', *Ethics and the Environment* 17(2): 137–64. https://doi.org/10.2979/ethicsenviro.17.2.137

Derrida, Jacques. 2001. *The Work of Mourning*. Chicago: University of Chicago Press.

Freud, Sigmund. 1973 (1917). *Mourning and Melancholia* in Vol. 14 of *The Standard Edition of the Complete Psychological Works of Sigmund Freud*, pp. 237–259. Trans. and ed. James Strachey. London: Hogarth.

Howe, Cymene and Boyer, Dominic. 2018. *Not OK – A Little Movie about a Small Glacier at the End of the World*. https://www.imdb.com/title/tt8879642/

Johnson, Lacy M. 2019. 'How to Mourn a Glacier', *The New Yorker* 20 October 2019. Retrieved from https://www.newyorker.com/news/dispatch/how-to-mourn-a-glacier

Kirkby, James. 2006. 'Remembrance of the Future: Derrida on Mourning', *Social Semiotics* 16(3): 461–472. https://doi.org/10.1080/10350330600824383

Kretz, Lisa. 2017. 'Emotional Solidarity – Ecological Emotional Outlaws Mourning Environmental Loss and Empowering Positive Change'. In Ashlee Cunsolo and Karen Landman (eds.), *Mourning Nature – Hope at the Heart of Ecological Grief and Loss*, pp. 258–291. Montreal: McGill-Queen's University Press.

McCaig, Amy. 2019. 'Lost Glacier to be Honored with Memorial Monument', *Rice University News Release* 18 July 2019. Retrieved from https://news2.rice.edu/2019/07/18/lost-glacier-to-be-honored-with-memorial-monument/

Menning, Nancy. 2017. 'Environmental Mourning and the Religious Imagination'. In Ashlee Cunsolo and Karen Landman (eds.), *Mourning Nature – Hope at the Heart of Ecological Grief and Loss*, pp. 39–63. Montreal: McGill-Queen's University Press.

O'Dowd, Peter. 2019. 'Researchers Memorialise First Major Icelandic Glacier Lost to Climate Change', *wbur.org* 16 August 2019. Retrieved from https://www.wbur.org/hereandnow/2019/08/16/dead-icelandic-glacier-lost-to-climate-change

Rae, Patrivia (ed.). 2007. *Modernism and Mourning*. Lewisburg: Bucknell University Press.

Secret, Timothy. 2015. *The Politics and Pedagogy of Mourning – On Responsibility in Eulogy*. London: Bloomsbury.

Shotwell, Alexis. 2016. *Against Purity – Living Ethically in Compromised Times*. Minneapolis: University of Minnesota Press.

Spargo, R. Clifton. 2004. *The Ethics of Mourning: Grief and Responsibility in Elegiac Literature*. Baltimore: Johns Hopkins University Press.

Thomas, Kimberly, Hardy, R. Dean, Lazrus, Heather, Mendez, Michael, Orlove, Ben, Rivera-Collazo, Isabel, Roberts, J. Timmons, Rockman, Marcy, Warner, Benjamin P. and Winthrop, Robert. 2019. 'Explaining Differential Vulnerability to Climate Change: A Social Science Review', *WIREs Climate Change* 10(2): e565. https://doi.org/10.1002/wcc.565

Young, James E. 1992. 'The Counter-Monument: Memory against Itself in Germany Today', *Critical Inquiry* 18(2): 267–296. https://doi.org/10.1086/448632

**Jonatan Spejlborg Juelsbo** is an artist, educator and co-founder of the LungA School in Seyðisfjörður, Iceland. He has a master's degree in Death, Religion and Culture from the University of Winchester. His practice-based research is concerned with creating social structures in which cultures, languages, ideas and beliefs become apparent, so as to understand them better, as well as creating spaces for imagining and living in other ways, stories, practices and ideals that nurture the relational web comprised of both human and non-human beings.

# Chapter 18

# Grave Goods as Continuing Bonds

## KYM SWAN

This chapter has two themes. Firstly, it is about the relationships between people and how these evolve through the process of death. Secondly, it is about the use of objects, which survivors' gift to the deceased, as an expression of the bond they shared and will continue to share even though death has separated them. The importance of this topic extends beyond those who dig up, display and/or write about items placed deliberately into graves, to those who, like me, work as funeral arrangers. The bereaved in England (where I work) freely ask me about flowers or donations in lieu of flowers, but when it comes to requesting that an object be placed in a coffin, their demeanour often changes; they become hesitant, even nervous. They often assume, incorrectly, they are making an unusual request. Of course, if the body is to be cremated there are certain items that, for health and safety or emissions reasons, cannot be burned (and indeed some items from a person's body, such as pace-makers, need to be removed), but the inclusion of 'grave goods' into a coffin today is not unusual. I hope this chapter may provide comfort to those seeking to continue their bond with a loved one beyond the grave, by understanding that such an act (placing goods in a grave) has a long tradition.

## GRAVE GOODS IN HISTORY: MYTH AND RITUAL

Archaeologists have evidenced that placing material objects with the deceased is a practice which has occurred since Palaeolithic times, where evidence of ritual disposal of the deceased has been uncovered, dated between 90,000 years and 10,000 years ago (Spellman 2014: 22; Härke 2014: 41). There appear to be no specific date ranges given for when the modern or recent period begins (Mytum 2017: 154; Hovers and Belfer-Cohen 2013: 631). Yet researchers clearly state that modern humans relate mortuary ritual to religious, spiritual and social practices, and that the inclusion of gifted objects was associated with these processes (Hovers and Belfer-Cohen 2013: 631). This gifting of items to the deceased appears to have been part of a larger ritual process, not merely an act of 'the disposal of the dead' (Price 2014: 186). Ritual also incorporated the role of myth, as the ritual surrounding mortuary practices served to give, for those with a belief in a deity, 'unhindered passage to God in the next world' (Davies 2017: 112).

Perhaps the most succinct explanation for myth comes from Segal, who determined that myth arises to fulfil a need (2010: 372). Belief in particular myths may have generated payoffs to the believers, stimulating an ongoing conviction for future generations. Segal considers the core meaning of ritual to be 'action' (2010: 387). Yet the action of ritual and belief are entwined; for Segal, 'action has come to be regarded as the *expression* of belief and even the *instillment* of belief' (2010: 387). Considering the two main classical theories regarding ritual, this view of ritual being 'fundamentally a matter of *belief* is one. The other links ritual to feelings: importantly, the use of ritual can either create feelings in the participants, or release them (Segal 2010: 387). For Grimes, the use of the term ritual depends on many factors and the use of a rigid definition is almost harmful, as the way ritual is defined depends greatly upon *who* is using the definition (2014: 187). 'Ritual is like any other key term. Tailored to fit "us" it may look ill-fitting on "them"' (Grimes 2014: 187). For Grimes, we should not be attempting to answer the question, What is ritual? Rather, we ought to be considering how we use the term in any given circumstance (2014: 188). Yet Grimes does offer a definition, that ritual is 'embodied, condensed, and prescribed enactment'; there is a deliberate simplicity to this definition, inviting the reader to question and evolve it further (2014: 195). Like the belief in myth, according to Davies, ritual practice also has its own payoffs, and costs, in an emotional sense (2015: 105). In times of crisis and transition, the use of ritual 'serve(s) to regulate and refine human feelings' (Davies 2015: 117).

Ritual occurs in a wide variety of human activities and in a mortuary context, it helps to realise myth in a practical and physical sense, providing benefits to survivors and generating a cohesive community with shared behaviours and emotions (Davies 2000: 97). Some theorists suggest that using ritual and gifted objects could control the potential danger and disorder which accompanied the unknown, they could be a form of hope to the survivors, wherein the deceased secures peace, and they are able to integrate with their society anew; ritual provides a framework for rationalising experiences outside of human understanding (Hackett 2010: 166; Davies 2017: 112; Douglas 2002: 119). These 'developing sequences of ritual actions' evolved and grew depending on the needs of the society (Price 2014: 186). The use of death rituals acts as a form of agreement between human beings, that 'they will not let each other die': the memory of them will endure, and while death may break the bonds, ritual re-establishes the relationships once more, post-mortem (Chidester 2002: 17).

## MORTUARY PRACTICE AND SPIRITUALITY

Spirituality has been a part of changing cultural trends in modern society, sparking alternative forms of ritual and bonding that cross the boundaries between the living and the dead (King 2011: 323). While families who have identified themselves to the funeral director as non religious continue to form rituals around the departure of a loved one, these rituals have an increased focus on the life of that individual, as opposed to being predominantly religious in content (Spellman 2014: 198). Both King and McClure consider spirituality to be linked with human imagination (McClure 2013: 729; King 2011: 21). McClure believes it is the human's capacity for 'seeing beyond oneself toward what transcends human existence' (2013: 729). For King, there is a greater holistic definition which encompasses, not only imagination, but also 'humans' creativity and resourcefulness … [and] relationships, whether with oneself, others or a transcendent reality, often called the Divine, God or Spirit' (2011: 21). This leads King to the use of a plural form, spiritualities, which encompasses the varying degrees within which spirituality takes place, defined as the 'ideas, practices and commitments that nurture, sustain and shape the fabric of human lives, whether as individual persons or communities' (2011: 21). The use of objects has often facilitated the rituals and rites of funerary services, and for some, the belief in the ability to transcend to a realm other than our current one (Chidester 2002: 18, 36; Turner 1969: 94).

Chidester's work has been criticised for lacking clarity on the term 'transcendence'; Davies considers that he refers to the term simply as a 'coping device' (Davies 2017: 30). However, for Chidester, 'transcendence' is humankinds' ability to transcend death and the various ways that people have 'found to deal with the fact of death' (2002: x). His work is important for several reasons. He outlines four patterns to transcendence that his research has shown features across all religious traditions. The four forms are: ancestral transcendence, experiential transcendence, cultural transcendence and mythic transcendence (Chidester 2002: xi).

The primary two forms considered in respect of this chapter are cultural and ancestral transcendence. Cultural transcendence results directly from the 'social event of death' (Chidester 2002: 16). This form of transcendence focuses on social connections and bonds, including 'obligations, and exchanges that cannot be broken by death' (2002: xi). Ancestral transcendence also refers to bonds between the living and the dead, but from the perspective of family relationships and the bonds that continue to live on down the family line (2002: xi). While ancestral transcendence can be thought of as the biological being transcending, and biological continuity through surviving family members, cultural transcendence is, to Chidester, about 'collective memory and commemoration that keep persons alive as social persons' (2002: 16). Understanding the patterns of both cultural and ancestral transcendence may increase understanding of the effects of death myths and rituals, and the influences these may have upon the actions of societal members and individuals when a person dies. Responses, and resulting actions and effects, could potentially determine which gifted objects are used and how, or not at all.

It is important to note that death and dying have distinctive differences; death is considered as a 'biological transition', while dying is a 'social act' (Allan Kellehear in Robb 2013: 6). Robb explores the implications for the 'agency of the dead', where he describes the term 'agency' as 'acting in such a way as to affect the flow of events' (Robb 2013: 9). Even when a person dies, they still exert an influence over those they have left behind. Robb explains a view which is believed to descend from the work of Phillippe Ariès, noting that 'social process looks to accomplish multiple things, making sense of biological acts, doing the right thing by the person, transforming them into a new kind of being, arranging matters such as succession and allowing the expression of emotions' (Robb 2013: 6).

Ariès wrote about five variations of death from a European perspective, which occur in a sequential timeframe from the early Middle Ages through to the present day. The tame death begins, followed by the death of the self (late-Middle Ages), remote and imminent death (late-sixteenth to late-eighteenth centuries), death of the other (nineteenth to early-twentieth centuries) and climaxing with the invisible death of the mid-twentieth century to present day (Ariès 1991: 603–611). Of the five, the tame death is most attributed to funerary ritual involving community. In the late Middle Ages, for Ariès, death was primarily about the family and extended community, rather than just the dying individual (1991: 603). Ariès considered death ritual as a way of society protecting itself from the ferocity of nature (1991: 603–604).

It is vital to consider that conjecture may be prevalent when considering mortuary practice theories; material objects located with the deceased may not be representative of the wider culture, therefore caution is required (Spellman 2014: 22–24; Harper 2012: 45; Härke 2014: 54). Material objects found with the deceased were often termed as grave goods, yet this can be misleading, and interchangeable names have also generated confusion; material culture, artefacts, sacred items, ritual items, material objects and burial offerings are all names given to the material items found placed with the deceased (Ekengren 2013: 2; Prown 1982: 2). In this chapter, the term gifting has been applied to the deliberate placing of material objects with the deceased post-mortem, regardless of the bodily disposal method used. Gifting objects to the deceased can be seen as evidence of continued bonding, yet there are a variety of reasons attributed to this behaviour: emotional bond building, protection for the living, life after death and controlling the immediate environment are all reasons cited in an attempt to understand, and define, why our ancestors placed emphasis on the use of material objects within death rituals (Spellman 2014: 23).

## GRAVE GOODS AND SOCIETY THEN AND NOW

Historically, grave goods were assumed to belong to the deceased, yet research has shown this is not always the case. The fragmentary nature of what remains may be part of a larger verbal and non-verbal communication system, therefore may not be a true reflection of the wider society and culture (Parker Pearson 2007: 100; Harris et al. 2017: 201; Harper 2012: 45; Ucko 1969: 270; Spellman 2014: 22). Historical archaeological research has rarely directed focus onto the question of *why* items were placed with the deceased, considering the objects as purely functional to the context in which they were historically found (Ekengren 2013: 2). Objects were often placed with the deceased, regardless of the method of bodily disposal, for example, by burial (inhumation) or cremation (where items are placed with the cremated remains, referred to as cremains or cremation burials) (Taylor et al. 2009: 18.45; Parker Pearson 2010: 8). Because material culture is created, or modified, by humans, Prown argues that it gives an insight into the functions of both the individual and the society it was generated from (1982: 5–6).

Set-aside items used as part of mortuary ritual take on a special role (Davies 2015: 117) as they are removed from the world of the living and take on a liminal status alongside of the deceased. Riley defined 'things set aside and protected in any given society' as sacred (2008, 274). These sacred objects are by their ritual and mythic uses in death rituals, imbued with a quality that removes them from the realm of the ordinary. Early archaeologists sought to create a classification system to both categorise, and attempt to understand, the various groupings of gifted items (Prown 1982: 2; Härke 2014: 44). Prominent researcher and archaeologist, Härke refined the classification of gifted items which he suggests includes 'all possible meanings' both past and present (2014: 44). Briefly, the major categories of gifted items, according to Härke, and further added to by other theorists, are: gifts for the afterlife (both the journey to it, and for use upon arrival within it), inalienable property (items bound up in the deceased's identity), potlatch (in the form of goods hoarding and deposition), status and rank, metaphor (the provision of material reminders of life events of the individual), gift giving, gift to deity (God/Goddess), feasting, forgetting, remembrance, the removal of items to prevent polluting effects to the remaining society and, finally, protection of the living (Härke 2014: 45–52; Taylor et al. 2009, 22.09, 22.37, 22.47; Crawford 2004: 89; Parker Pearson 2007: 99; Parker Pearson 2010: 11, 24; Brownlee 2020: 2.26; MacDougal 2018: 272).

There is a minimal amount of literature on the use of gifted items in the twenty-first century, particularly as a form of continuing bonds postmortem, and a lack of attributable meaning or classification as per Härke (Harper 2012: 43). Primarily the focus has been on 'linking objects', those objects retained by the living (Lau et al. 2018: 157). These linking objects are so called due to the ability they have in linking the living with the dead through memory, but they are kept by the living rather than gifted to the deceased (Lau et al. 2018: 157; Foster et al. 2011: 423–424). Linking objects can include a lock of hair, a piece of jewellery, clothing and/or other personal belongings kept as remembrance (Lau et al. 2018: 157). Härke has argued that for some bereaved people, it can be difficult to cope with grief if they have too many material possessions lingering after that person's death (2014: 52). However, this chapter relates to the gifting of objects to the dead post-mortem, not to linking objects that the bereaved hold as mementos of the deceased.

Termed as 'modern day grave goods', these refer to objects gifted to the deceased and take the form of letters, photos, jewellery, poems, soft toys and sports paraphernalia (Taylor et al. 2009: 21.15). Inalienable property is used to describe items that are so bound up in the identity of the individual, that they cannot be parted with them (Taylor et al. 2009: 22.31). These inseparable possessions are 'considered part of the body, not the person' and are likely to include items such as spectacles (Brownlee 2020: 12.47). Gibson reflects that photographs are often connections with key points in time and space and are an intrinsic part of 'memory formation' (2005: 82). Items such as photographs and poems that were important to the deceased or act as reminders to the bereaved of the deceased, are items sometimes gifted post-mortem, suggesting they form part of a continued bond between the living and the dead, allowing the living to express their loss (Foster et al. 2011: 423–424; Harper 2012: 52). The changes seen in contemporary gifting may reflect the way families communicate their wishes for funeral services, regardless of being religious, spiritual or otherwise. Objects may have become more about the individual and their identity. Assisting in forming attachments and bonds between the deceased and the living, as opposed to preparing the deceased individual for what lies beyond.

Commonly seen in contemporary funeral homes are families that wish to incorporate religious elements, such as symbols of faith in the form of jewellery, though they do not consider the deceased as having practised a faith (author's personal observation). The range of gifted objects for these individuals is broad; items included are letters, cards, flowers, teddies, photographs and jewellery (Harper 2012: 52; pers. obs.). Common objects gifted to the deceased may consist of items of identity, such as glasses, photographs, jewellery (that which was always worn everyday), letters, cards, soft toys and flowers (pers. obs.; Taylor et al. 2009: 23.31). Jewellery items might be depictions of deities, for those who consider themselves spiritual, such as Anubis from Egyptian mythology, Pentagrams/Pentacles in rings or as pendants, and necklaces made from precious stones, and these objects would qualify as inalienable property (pers. obs.). Härke notes that metaphor may provide those grieving with a pathway towards aligning their internal world with the outside one (2014: 48) which, Guthke writes, can give 'shape to the shapeless by approximating it to the familiar, therefore endowing it with meaning' (1999: 8). Items such as photographs may have been placed with the deceased to serve as physical representations of the individuals' achievements (Härke 2014: 48). Often items gifted to the deceased are for the benefit of the families who remain, rather than the benefit of the person who has passed away, providing a framework for grieving and processing loss.

## GRAVE GOODS AND BONDS WITH THE DEAD

Bonds and ties to the deceased can be classed as 'a close connection between two separate objects or two objects glued as if inseparable' (Jonsson and Walter 2017: 407). The term 'continuing bonds' was first explored by Klass, Silverman and Nickman, and refers to the evolving relationship between the deceased and the living, and the observation that an attachment does not evaporate when one person dies (Silverman and Klass 1996: 3; Bell et al. 2015: 376; Parkes and Prigerson 2010: 68). As Foster et al. note, 'A growing body of literature has described various expressions of continuing bonds and suggested that maintaining connections with deceased loved ones is an integral component of adaptation to bereavement' (2011: 421).

Indeed, Parkes and Prigerson believe that continuing bonds may assist in 'mitigating the pain of grieving' (2010: 64, 73), while for Silverman and Klass and for Guthke, continuing bonds are understood as a way of reconstructing our world in the face of death (Silverman and Klass 1996: 20; Guthke 1999: 8). The early models for coping with grief were designed to work through overburdening emotions via a series of tasks and expressed a strong emphasis on the severance of ties on the occurrence of death (Root and Exline 2014: 2; Stroebe et al. 1996: 32). Often the continued attachment of the living to the dead was viewed as a 'maladaptive loss reaction' (Root and Exline 2014: 2). As further research has been undertaken, however, mourning, grief and attachment are increasingly seen as forms of adaptation to, and a natural part of, the loss experienced through death (Root and Exline 2014: 1; Silverman and Klass 1996: 14).

A person's death may create a discrepancy in the mind of a survivor, between their internal model of the world which incorporates the deceased, and the real world in which the deceased is no longer present (Härke 2014: 48). This concept originates from the 'attachment theory' which was developed by John Bowlby and Mary Ainsworth over sixty years ago (Gullestad 2001: 3). Bowlby writes about the 'making and breaking of affectional bonds', a concept they first explored in 1977:

> Attachment theory is a way of conceptualizing the propensity of human beings to make strong affectional bonds to particular others and of explaining the many forms of emotional distress and personality disturbance, including anxiety, anger, depression, and emotional detachment, to which unwilling separation and loss give rise. (Bowlby 2005: 151)

Harlow acknowledges that Bowlby's work has been controversial, and theories developed from it have been contested (2021: 79). Yet the principles have been deepened and developed and are now being applied in contemporary social care settings (Harlow 2021: 79). After the death of an individual, attachments may re-form once the community has redefined itself, and survivors form new ties with the deceased, allowing them to live on in an altered state of being (Chidester 2002: 16).

## CONCLUDING THOUGHTS

The role of myth has been considered within a mortuary framework, where it may have been applied to the areas of life that were unknowable and unexplainable. Ritual is a method of communicating to the community; myth and ritual are intimately entwined, ritual realising myth in physical form. The practice of ritual, and engagement with myth, cements critical life values and bonds people together in the face of chaos (Davies 2017: 168; Hackett 2010: 166; Metcalf and Huntingdon 1991: 25). While historically the use of gifted objects was thought to assist the deceased in the afterlife, modern-day use appears to be primarily about relationships between the deceased and those left behind. The most significant category in the 21st century appears to be inalienable property, as part of recognising the identity of the individual, and as a formation of bonds between the deceased and the survivors. The other category which appears dominant within modern rituals is that of metaphor: meaning-making and identifying key periods of the individual's life using objects gifted to the deceased. The role of attachment theories and continuing bonds, and the practice of utilising gifted objects, can fulfil important psychological needs for the survivor, yet they form but a part of the complex whole, where ritual and even myth act as vehicles for individuals to process loss and reintegrate back into society (Hunter 2018: 198; Harlow 2021: 79).

# BIBLIOGRAPHY

Ariès, Phillipe. 1991. *The Hour of Our Death*. London: Oxford University Press.

Bell, Jo, Bailey, Louis and Kennedy, David. 2015. '"We Do It to Keep Him Alive": Bereaved Individuals' Experiences of Online Suicide Memorials and Continuing Bonds', *Mortality* 20(4): 375–389. https://doi.org/10.1080/13576275.2015.1083693

Bowlby, John. 2005. *The Making and Breaking of Affectional Bonds*. Oxford: Routledge.

Brownlee, Emma C. 2020. '3.1 Archaeology of Early Medieval Europe: Grave Goods, Identities and Personhood', *Foreign Countries*. https://www.youtube.com/watch?v=FHpn1eS8Xqg

Chidester, David. 2002. *Patterns of Transcendence: Religion, Death, and Dying*, 2nd edition. London: Wadsworth.

Crawford, Sally. 2004. 'Votive Deposition, Religion and the Anglo-Saxon Furnished Burial Ritual', *World Archaeology* 36(1): 87–102. https://doi.org/10.1080/0043824042000192641

Davies, Douglas. 2000. 'Robert Hertz: The Social Triumph Over Death', *Mortality* 5(1): 97–102. https://doi.org/10.1080/713685991

Davies, Douglas. 2015. *Mors Britannica: Life Style & Death Style in Britain Today*. Oxford: Oxford University Press.

Davies, Douglas. 2017. *Death, Ritual and Belief: The Rhetoric of Funerary Rites*, 3rd edition. London: Bloomsbury.

Douglas, Mary. 2002. *Purity and Danger: An Analysis of Concepts of Pollution and Taboo*, 7th edition. London: Routledge.

Ekengren, Fredrick. 2013. Contextualizing Grave Goods: Theoretical Perspectives and Methodological Implications. In Liv Nilsson Stutz and Sarah Tarlow (eds.), *The Oxford Handbook of the Archaeology of Death and Burial*, pp. 173–194. Oxford: Oxford University Press.

Foster, Terrah, Gilmer, Mary Jo, Davies, Betty, Dietrich, Mary S., Barrera, Maru, Fairclough, Diane L., Vannatta, Kathryn and Gerhardt, Cynthia A. 2011. 'Comparison of Continuing Bonds Reported by Parents and Siblings after a Child's Death from Cancer', *Death Studies* 35: 420–440. https://doi.org/10.1080/07481187.2011.553308

Gibson, Margaret. 2005. *Objects of the Dead; Mourning and Memory in Everyday Life*. Victoria: Melbourne University Press.

Grimes, Ronald L. 2014. *The Craft of Ritual Studies*. Oxford: Oxford University Press.

Gullestad, Siri Erika. 2001. 'Attachment Theory and Psychoanalysis: Controversial Issues', *The Scandinavian Psychoanalytic Review* 24: 3–16. https://doi.org/10.1080/01062301.2001.10592610

Guthke, Karl S. 1999. *The Gender of Death: A Cultural History in Art and Literature*. Cambridge: Cambridge University Press.

Hackett, Rosalind I.J. 2010. 'Anthropology of Religion'. In John Hinnells (ed.), *The Routledge Companion to The Study of Religion*, pp. 165–185. London: Routledge.

Härke, Heinrich. 2014. 'Grave Goods in Early Medieval Burials: Messages and Meanings', *Mortality* 19(1): 41–60. https://doi.org/10.1080/13576275.2013.870544

Harlow, Elizabeth. 2021. 'Attachment Theory: Developments, Debates and Recent Applications in Social Work, Social Care and Education', *Journal of Social Work in Practice* 35(1): 79–91. https://doi.org/10.1080/02650533.2019.1700493

Harper, Sheila. 2012. 'I'm glad she had her glasses on. That really makes the difference': Grave Goods in English and American Death Rituals, *Journal of Material Culture* 17(1): 43–59. https://doi.org/10.1177/1359183511432987

Harris, Oliver J.T., Cobb, Hannah, Batey, Colleen E., Montgomery, Janet, Beaumont, Julia, Gray, Héléna, Murtagh, Paul and Richardson, Phil. 2017. 'Assembling Places and Persons: A Tenth-Century Viking Boat Burial from Swordle Bay in the Ardnamurchan Peninsula, Western Scotland', *Antiquity* 91(35): 191–206. https://doi.org/10.15184/aqy.2016.222

Hovers, Erella and Belfer-Cohen, Anna. 2013. 'Insights into Early Mortuary Practices of Homo'. In Liv Nilsson Stutz and Sarah Tarlow (eds.), *The Oxford Handbook of the Archaeology of Death and Burial*, pp. 631–642. Oxford: Oxford University Press.

Hunter, Jack. 2018. 'Ontological Flooding and Continuing Bonds'. In Dennis Klass and Edith M. Steffan (eds.), *Continuing Bonds in Bereavement: New Directions for Research and Practice*, pp. 191–200. London: Routledge.

Jonsson, Annika and Walter, Tony. 2017. 'Continuing Bonds and Place', *Death Studies* 41(7): 406–415. https://doi.org/10.1080/07481187.2017.1286412

Kellehear, Allan. 2007. *A Social History of Dying*. Cambridge: Cambridge University Press.

King, Ursula. 2011. 'Can Spirituality Transform Our World?' *Journal for the Study of Spirituality* 1(1): 17–34. https://doi.org/10.1558/jss.v1i1.17

Lau, Bobo H.P., Fong, Candy H.C. and Chan, Celia H.Y. 2018. 'Reaching the Unspoken Grief'. In Dennis Klass and Edith M. Steffan (eds.), *Continuing Bonds in Bereavement: New Directions for Research and Practice*, pp. 150–160. London: Routledge.

MacDougal, Renata. 2018. 'Ancient Mesopotamian Remembrance and the Family Dead'. In Dennis Klass and Edith M. Steffan (eds.), *Continuing Bonds in Bereavement: New Directions for Research and Practice*, pp. 262–275. London: Routledge.

McClure, Barbara. J. 2013. 'Divining the Sacred in the Modern World: Ritual and Relational Embodiment of Spirit', *Pastoral Psychology* 62: 727–742. https://doi.org/10.1007/s11089-013-0515-y

Metcalf, Peter and Huntington, Richard. 1991. *Celebrations of Death: The Anthropology of Mortuary Ritual*. Cambridge: Cambridge University Press.

Mytum, Harold. 2017. 'Mortuary Culture'. In Catherine Richardson, Tara Hamling and David Gaimster (eds.), *The Routledge Handbook of Material Culture in Early Modern Europe*, pp. 154–167. Farnham: Routledge.

Parker Pearson, Mike. 2007. 'Mortuary Practices, Society and Ideology: An Ethnoarchaeological Study'. In Ian Hodder (ed.), *Symbolic and Structural Archaeology*, pp. 99–113. Cambridge: Cambridge University Press.

Parker Pearson, Mike. 2010. *The Archaeology of Death and Burial*. Gloucestershire: The History Press.

Parkes, Colin Murray and Prigerson, Holly G. 2010. *Bereavement: Studies of Grief in Adult Life*, 4th edition. London: Routledge.

Price, Neil. 2014. 'Nine Paces from Hel: Time and Motion in Old Norse Ritual Performance', *World Archaeology* 46(2): 178–191. https://doi.org/10.1080/00438243.2014.883938

Prown, Jules David. 1982. 'Mind in Matter: An Introduction to Material Culture Theory and Method', *Winterthur Portfolio* 17(1): 1–19. https://doi.org/10.1086/496065

Riley, Alexander T. 2008. 'Renegade Durkheimianism and the Transgressive Left Sacred'. In Jeffrey C. Alexander and Phillip Smith (eds.), *The Cambridge Companion to Durkheim*, pp. 274–304. Cambridge: Cambridge University Press.

Robb, John. 2013. 'Creating Death'. In Liv Nilsson Stutz and Sarah Tarlow (eds.), *The Oxford Handbook of the Archaeology of Death and Burial*, pp. 441–458. Oxford: Oxford University Press.

Root, Briana L. and Exline, Julie J. 2014. 'The Role of Continuing Bonds in Coping with Grief: Overview and Future Directions', *Death Studies* 38(1): 1–8. https://doi.org/10.1080/07481187.2012.712608

Segal, Robert A. 2010. 'Myth and Ritual'. In John Hinnells (ed.), *The Routledge Companion to The Study of Religion*, pp. 372–396. London: Routledge.

Silverman, Phyllis R. and Klass, Dennis. 1996. 'Introduction: What's the Problem?' In Dennis Klass, Phyllis R. Silverman and Steven L. Nickman (eds.), *Continuing Bonds: New Understandings of Grief*, pp. 3–27. London: Routledge.

Spellman, William M. 2014. *A Brief History of Death*. London: Reaktion Books.

Stroebe, Margaret, Gergen, Mary, Gergen, Kenneth and Stroebe, Wolfgang. 1996. 'Broken Hearts or Broken Bonds?' In Dennis Klass, Phyllis R. Silverman and Steven L. Nickman (eds.), *Continuing Bonds: New Understandings of Grief*, 31–44. London: Routledge.

Taylor, Laurie, Harper, Sheila and Sayer, Duncan. 2009. 'Thinking Allowed: Modern Day Grave Goods. *BBC Radio 4* 14 October 2009.

Turner, Victor. 1969. *The Ritual Process: Structure and Anti-Structure*. New York: Aldine De Gruyter.

Ucko, Peter John. 1969. 'Ethnography and Archaeological Interpretation of Funerary Remains', *World Archaeology* 1(2): 262–280. https://doi.org/10.1080/00438243.1969.9979444

**Kym Swan** is an experienced Funeral Arranger within a national company, and a trained celebrant, whose interests embrace the complex fields of material culture within death rituals, and the impact of death on the environment. Passionate about raising awareness of death and the impacts it brings, Kym gives talks at events to both professionals and the public, allowing them to understand and develop a healthy relationship with death. She has an MA in Death, Religion and Culture and her thesis focused on the scantily studied area of gifting material objects to the deceased, a subject of importance to understanding the relationships and bonds sustained after death.

# Afterword

## GRAHAM HARVEY

Death is a thoroughly sensual matter. Bodies (of humans and other animals as well as of plants, planets and all other existences) die and decay in ways that involve visual, auditory, tactile, olfactive, gustatory and/or other senses. Similarly, and quite obviously, bereavement and grief are thoroughly sensual. These banal facts might conflict with *some* ways in which 'religion' is imagined or defined. They might also conflict with *some* ways in which dying, bereavement and grief are sanitised or otherwise separated from everyday life. Christina Welch and Jasmine Hazel Shadrack's *Religion, Death and the Senses* takes a justified place in the Equinox *Religion and the Senses* series. It evidences the sensuality of death, dying, bereavement and grief in a fascinating range of cultures and communities. It also enables a greater sensitivity to the sensuality of religion. Thus, it precisely matches the point of this series: to sharpen a focus on lived religion by beginning with sensuality rather than rhetorics and transcendence. Religion does not exist prior to or apart from sensual bodily acts but only as people 'do religion' (always as bodies).

Even for those religionists and clinicians who would like death to be transcended and/or isolated, the sensuality of bodily processes including dying, bereavement and grief provide challenging tests. If religion is not sensual, how do its ideas and practices, its traditions and ambitions, deal with bodies dying and decaying? If medicine is about preventing death, how do practitioners manage 'failures'? In reality, the sheer physicality of death, dying, bereavement and grief necessarily and inescapably engages people with their sensuality. When confronted by these processes, people's rhetorics and performances are assessed and possibly adjusted, adapted or abandoned. In these and other ways, death, dying, bereavement and grief are engines for the evolution of religion (and wider culture) and of the study of religions.

The well-selected community of contributors to *Religion, Death and the Senses* make a major contribution to the *Religion and the Senses* series by engaging us with the ordinary-and-exceptional ways in which death, dying, bereavement and grief are experienced, engaged and examined. In addition to including work by scholars from different disciplinary backgrounds, around a quarter of the contributors are not academics but death- and/or grief-related practitioners. This range of expertise and engagement is immensely valuable both for the generation and presentation of information and for the enriching of methodological reflection. On a more personal note, I'm pleased to see that some authors are graduates of the University of Winchester's MA programme, Death, Religion and Culture, in an earlier incarnation of which I had a role.

As in other volumes in this series, the editors and contributors do not attempt to say everything, they do not pretend that this is the last word. Indeed, the point of the book and the series is the opposite: to broaden and deepen conversations and debates. Thus, this book offers exemplary contexts and cases through which to consider varied sensualities and activities. Whether our attention and/or interest is practically or theoretically motivated – whether we are death-related practitioners (funeral directors, counsellors and so on) or scholars concerned with understanding and debating religions, cultures and communities – this book invites and inspires us to take matters further. We might consider what each chapter presents to us in relation to our existing knowledge and/or interests. We might take up the challenge of applying or assessing particular approaches or arguments in other arenas. We might seek to apply the methodological lessons braided in case studies and theorising.

To that end, my opening sentence might have given you pause to think, to question, to challenge. Or it might have been passed by quickly as the paragraph continued. Is death – or, for that matter, dying, bereavement and grief – really a thoroughly sensual matter? It is not too difficult to list examples of religious understandings of death – for the person or being who dies – as the cessation of senses. Or, perhaps put more carefully, religious teachers and texts often hold that the senses are transcended, transmogrified, or otherwise transformed.

The three thousand year old *Epic of Gilgamesh*'s evocation of a gloomy partial existence (hardly an afterlife) for all humans (including priests, kings and heroes) is not diminished by its message that lasting memories are made by the building of great walls and the telling of epic tales and biographies (Helle 2021). Similarly, king Gilgamesh learns that crushing grief cannot be assuaged by trying to preserve loved bodies – as, before long, in the case of Enkidu, 'maggots fell from his nose'. Enkidu is gone. Gilgamesh will die. All humans will die (unless deities transform them). While the real and virtual river of life flows on, humans are like the 'mayfly drifting down the river, its face turned toward the sun, but even then seeing nothing' (Helle 2021: 184). Death is not a character in this poetic epic – but dying and grief are threaded throughout, even in silences between the stanzas of speeches about mortality. Here, dying is the cessation of senses without a certainty of desirable sensual continuity and mourning is a burdensome sensuality. Remembered stories might last forever (if, as in the case of the *Epic of Gilgamesh*, archaeologists find them) but even if that realisation is wise, it is no great comfort.

In religious communities that encourage a hope of continuing life – whether 'eternal' or in new incarnations – there are still insensate bodies and debilitating griefs to deal with. Some of the most widely recognisable religious arts enable the sensuality of bereavement and loss, and perhaps express the sensuality of death and dying. Death and dying are made visible in paintings and statuary – for example, the Danse Macabre series that (as in *Gilgamesh*) insists on the democracy of death: all will die. Similarly, even those who anticipate that their deceased loved ones will either reincarnate or achieve liberation from *saṃsāra*, all will mourn (as representations in the *Ramayana* of Dasharatha's funeral show). Whether or not we find the intended message of relevant musical and visual arts (for example) meaningful, it is hard not to be moved, to find senses of loss and sorrow welling up. Perhaps senses of hope are also enlivened. But sometimes such cultural acts are intended precisely to dampen down the emotions, curtail those senses that might maintain relationships, and teach some kind of detachment – both from those who have died and from one's own sensuality. Indeed, for some, religion might be definitively imagined as sets of ideas ('beliefs' or 'worldviews') and practices ('rituals') in and through which sensual bodies are or should be restrained, restricted or even removed from attention. Many, but not all, death related beliefs and rites seem to privilege such moves.

Those are just sketches of two poles involved in facing and undergoing death, dying, bereavement and grief. There are others, as the chapters in *Religion, Death and the Senses* have shown. It is not only in religions that we can encounter such matters. But this is a series focused on religion – and seeking to find out how focusing attention on sensuality might improve the study of lived religion (the only kind there is).

As the editors note in their introduction,

> The bulk of this book ... explores the dead and the living; from those still alive but in the dying process to those the dead leave behind who, through ritual, find ways to connect with/to, and honour, their dearly departed. It also explores, through the academic study of death, the myths and rituals connected with death and grief, and the material and visual culture that remind the living of the finality of death as a concept and/or remind them of individuals who have died.

After the editors' introduction, this book expertly introduced us to aspects of death in which many senses play together – and are played on. Then we were treated to reflections on each of the so-called 'five senses' of sight, smell, sound, taste and touch. Then the 'cultural' senses of decency, humour and loss were explored. Each of us will have responded differently as we read. We will have paused at different points to consider what the authors presented to us. We might have gone online – or to other books – to follow up some ideas or to seek answers to new (to us) questions. This is, after all, not the last word about these sensual interactions with death, dying, bereavement and grief. If this book and the rest of the series work, we will have more to read, more to write, more to discuss, and importantly, more to sense and do. For some readers (like some authors here) the 'doing' is the crucial thing. Resources for contemplation and practice can weave interestingly with those usable in research and teaching. None of us are immune to death, dying, bereavement and grief – and should never succeed in definitively supressing emotional responses to what we read. If that is a form of objectivity, it is a deadly one that objectifies and de-animates us. Emotion and intellect are never separate, nor is the latter any less sensual than the former. That being so, there is radical edge to a book that invites or even requires a fuller range of responses than one that we might imagine to only engage 'minds'.

Another thing that I threw into my opening words (after the assertion that death is thoroughly sensual) was that the death of planets is thoroughly sensual. It is likely that this thought fermented after considering the death of glaciers. I paused to wonder how the death of planets might be tasted or smelled. It is not difficult to think about the sight, sound and feel of planetary – or stellar – deaths. We can even experience a sense of loss when astronomers show us exploding or collapsing stars. Perhaps the still growing knowledge that once there was almost certainly life on or in

Mars causes a similar sense of loss. But when I stopped thinking of stars and planets in general and returned to those glaciers and other Earth-lives threated with extinction, I found myself pondering not only how our planet Earth smells and tastes, but also about the sense of (in)decency in our 'Anthrobscene' era (Parikka 2015). The increasing acidity of oceans and the increasing methane levels in the air change the Earth's sensorium as clearly as increased radiation levels, plastic-fused rocks and chicken bones mark this destructive age (Caputi 2020: 11–12 citing Carrington 2016). Earth's sensorium has been changed and our senses are challenged. Our senses change precisely because we have them – or are them – because the Earth is sensual (to paraphrase the crucial message of David Abram's *The Spell of the Sensuous* 1997). It is not only our 'five senses' that are changed. Knowledge of mass extinction, death on a vast scale, often causes senses of loss, despair and outrage. Sometimes resistance and activism are inspired by senses of belonging – perhaps braided with the immediacy of senses of joy, recognition and engagement in being in familiar, 'at-home' ecologies. Sometimes, too, senses of hope and/or urgency outweigh a sense of futility.

Death, dying, bereavement and grief are permanent features of life and relationality. Even when faced with the current and expected scale of planetary death and grief, there are responses and resources in religious and other cultural lives that support ongoing life. I hope that you have found *Religion, Death and the Senses* inspirational of further thoughts and acts – whether for scholarly learning or for caring practice in relation to the dying and bereaved. It takes its place in the *Religion and the Senses* series as a further incitement to treat religion and religions as thoroughly sensual activities in everyday as well as exceptional circumstances.

## BIBLIOGRAPHY

Abram, David. 1997. *The Spell of the Sensuous: Perception and Language in a More-than-Human World*. New York: Vintage.

Caputi, Jane. 2020. *Call your 'Mutha': A Deliberately Dirty-Minded Manifesto for the Earth Mother in the Anthropocene*. Oxford: Oxford University Press.

Carrington, Damian. 2016. 'How the Domestic Chicken Rose to Define the Anthropocene', *The Guardian* 21 August 2016. https://www.theguardian.com/environment/2016/aug/31/domestic-chicken-anthropocene-humanity-influenced-epoch#:~:text=Global%20consumption%20of%20chicken%20expanded,60%20billion%20killed%20a%20year

Helle, Sophus. 2021. *Gilgamesh: A New Translation of the Ancient Epic*. New Haven: Yale University Press.
Parikka, Jussi. 2015. *The Anthrobscene*. Minneapolis: University of Minnesota Press.

**Graham Harvey** is emeritus professor of religious studies at The Open University, UK, and the series editor for *Religion and the Senses*. He has researched with Jews, Pagans and Indigenous peoples. Most of his recent work has engaged with 'the new animism'. He lives in Northumberland and has recently taken on an allotment in an effort to discover what 'retirement' means.

# Index

9 781800 504943